主编/张妍 白丹

我是商务英语达人

达人篇

内容提要

本书在《我是商务英语达人》(新手篇)的基础上,设置了若干与真实商务活动无差别的贸易环节和商务情景,并通过典型实用的对话,帮助学习者掌握主要商务活动的多种对话及交流策略,形成独立应对和处理各种商务环节的能力,以提升自身的商务英语口语技能,从而提升自身的职场能力。

图书在版编目(CIP)数据

我是商务英语达人.达人篇/张妍,白丹主编.—
南京:东南大学出版社,2015.8
 ISBN 978-7-5641-5735-7

Ⅰ.①我… Ⅱ.①张… ②白… Ⅲ.①商务-英语-口语 Ⅳ.①H319.9

我是商务英语达人.达人篇

主　　编	张妍 白丹	责任编辑	刘　坚
电　　话	(025)83793329/83790577(传真)	电子邮箱	liu-jian@seu.edu.cn

出版发行	东南大学出版社	出 版 人	江建中
地　　址	南京市四牌楼2号	邮　编	210096
销售电话	(025)83794561/83694174/83794121/83795801/83792174 83795802/57711295(传真)		
网　　址	http://www.seupress.com	电子邮箱	press@seupress.com

经　　销	全国各地新华书店	印　　刷	南京玉河印刷厂
开　　本	787mm×1092mm　1/16　印　张　14.75　字　数　290千字		
版　　次	2015年8月第1版		
印　　次	2015年8月第1次印刷		
书　　号	ISBN 978-7-5641-5735-7		
定　　价	35.00元		

* 未经许可,本书内文字不得以任何方式转载、演绎,违者必究。
* 本社图书若有印装质量问题,请直接与营销部联系。电话:025-83791830。

PREFACE

随着中国国际地位的不断提升，经济实力的持续增强以及"一带一路""亚投行"等国家级战略的实施，作为国际通用语言的英语的战略地位更加突出，尤其是对于从事国际商务活动的人士来说，在深谙国际商务知识的同时又能说一口流利的英语，是其驰骋职场的制胜法宝。

学好商务英语不仅仅是要勤奋，更重要的是能够通过真实的场景和案例，接触到地道的英语，学会英语国家人士的日常表达，鉴于此，本套书作者在分析了市场上现有多种商务英语类图书的优缺点的基础上，结合自己的工作经历，编写了本套书，即《我是商务英语达人》（新手篇）、《我是商务英语达人》（达人篇），以期通过丰富的场景下的经典案例，帮助学习者了解、熟悉并掌握各种商务环境下的英语表达，以提升其用英语进行商务交际的能力。

本书为《我是商务英语达人》（达人篇），共分为"贸易实务"和"应对及处理"两部分，每一部分又分为若干单元，内容主要涉及对外贸易商务工作的方方面面，将各个场景中的地道交流方式逐一进行了详细的介绍。具体的，每一单元又由"词汇宝典""经典句型""口语秘笈"等模块组成，依次形成从词到句、从句到篇章、循序渐进的结构，每一单元均涉及一个主题，全书学完便能够掌握涉及商务活动的中高级阶段的知识。

总之，学习者在学习完新手篇之后进入本书的学习，遵循本书的学习顺序，就一定能够成为"商务英语达人"，为其在职场实现人生的奋斗目标助一臂之力！

另外，王红、刘佳、赵志清、孙玉梅、田秋月、陈贵男等为本书的出版以及音频剪辑付出了大量的工作，谨致谢意！

编 者
2015 年 5 月

目录

第一部分 贸易实务

第一章 主要贸易环节

Unit 1　询盘与报盘　Inquiry and Offer 2
Unit 2　支付方式　Payment 12
Unit 3　质量与数量　Quality and Quantity 22
Unit 4　运输　Shipment 31
Unit 5　保险　Insurance 41
Unit 6　商品检验　Commodity Inspection 50

第二章 贸易和商业合作

Unit 1　商业代理　Business Agency 60
Unit 2　招标与投标　Tender 69
Unit 3　国际展卖　International Fairs 79
Unit 4　补偿贸易　Compensation Trade 88
Unit 5　技术转让与合作　Technology Transfer and Cooperation 97
Unit 6　合并与兼并　Merger and Acquisition 106
Unit 7　合作经营　Joint Venture 116
Unit 8　进出口许可证　Import and Export License 127
Unit 9　进口配额　Import Quota 135
Unit 10　通关和报关　Customs and Clearance 143

第一章 合同违约

Unit 1　品质违约　Quality Discrepancy 148
Unit 2　数量违约　Quantity Discrepancy 152
Unit 3　付款违约　Payment Discrepancy 156
Unit 4　交货期违约　Delivery Time Discrepancy 159

CONTENTS

第二章 解决争端
Unit 1 起因调查　Sorting out Problems..................164
Unit 2 应对策略　Handling Strategy..................168
Unit 3 解决办法　Finding Solutions..................173
Unit 4 应对不同的客户　Dealing with Different Clients..................176

第三章 应对索赔
Unit 1 提出索赔　Lodging Claims..................180
Unit 2 接受索赔　Accepting Claims..................184
Unit 3 拒绝索赔　Dismissing Claims..................188

第四章 保险理赔
Unit 1 要求理赔　Claiming for Settlement..................195
Unit 2 同意理赔　Promising the Settlement..................198
Unit 3 拒绝理赔　Refusing to Settle the Claim..................204

第五章 申请仲裁
Unit 1 仲裁事由　Reasons of Arbitration..................208
Unit 2 提请仲裁　Resorting to Arbitration..................211
Unit 3 受理仲裁　Processing of Arbitration..................215

第六章 法律诉讼
Unit 1 合同与协议　Contract and Agreement..................220
Unit 2 破产与债务　Bankruptcy and Liability..................223
Unit 3 消费者权益　Consumer Rights..................225
Unit 4 知识产权　Intellectual Property..................228

第二部分　应对及处理

1 贸易实务

第一章 主要贸易环节

Unit 1 询盘与报盘　Inquiry and Offer
Unit 2 支付方式　Payment
Unit 3 质量与数量　Quality and Quantity
Unit 4 运输　Shipment
Unit 5 保险　Insurance
Unit 6 商品检验　Commodity Inspection

询盘与报盘
Inquiry and Offer

几乎所有的生意往来、商业谈判都是从与对方约定会晤洽谈的时间与地点开始的。商业人士,尤其是西方的商业人士,他们的时间观念都非常强,生活节奏都比较快,日常时间都安排得很紧凑。因此,要洽商某些事宜,无论事情大小,一定要先与对方约好时间,以免给对方造成不便。大部分的预约见面都是当事双方通过电话联络确定的,也有当面进行约谈的。但是,无论采用哪种方式,都要确定彼此见面的时间和地点,以免失礼。本单元所介绍的日常高频句型以及对白,不仅适用于商业往来,还可以用于各种交际场合,职场人士如能灵活运用,必能为你的商业信誉和商业形象增光添彩。

词语宝典

inquire	询盘,询价,询购	payment terms	付款方式
inquiry	询盘	special orders	特殊订货
inquirer	询价者	favorable	优惠的
to inquire about	对……询价	price list	价目单
to make an inquiry	发出询盘,向……询价	to find a regular market	有销路
inquiry sheet	询价单	sales literature	销售说明书
quotations sheet	报价单	firm offer	实价,实盘
specific inquiry	具体询盘	non-firm offer	虚盘
sales conditions	销售条件	offer without engagement	虚盘
to make delivery	交货	offer sheet	报价单
to make prompt delivery	即期交货	the preference of one's offer	优先报盘
brochure	小册子	extend an offer	延长报盘
catalogue	商品目录	make a deal	成交
illustrated catalogue	附带图片的商品目录	to decline an offer	谢绝报盘

经典句型

询盘

- Your inquiry is too vague to enable us to reply.

你们的询盘不明确，我们无法做出答复。

- Heavy inquiries witness the quality of our products.
  大量询盘证明我们产品质量过硬。

- Here is the price list together with a booklet illustrating our products.
  这里有一份价目单和介绍我们产品的小册子。

- Inquiries for carpets are getting more numerous.
  对地毯的询盘日益增加。

- Inquiries are so large that we can only allot you 200 cases.
  询盘如此之多，我们只能分给你们 200 箱货。

- Please let us know your lowest possible prices for the relevant goods.
  请告知你们有关商品的最低价。

- If your prices are favorable, I can place the order right away.
  如果你们的价格优惠，我们可以马上订货。

- Would you accept delivery spread over a period of time?
  你方是否接受分批交货？

- Could you tell me which kind of payment terms you'll choose?
  能否告知你们将采用哪种付款方式？

- Will you please tell us the earliest possible date you can make shipment?
  能否告知我方最早船期吗？

报 盘

- We have the offer ready for you.
  我们已经为你准备好报盘了。

- Our offer was reasonable instead of wild speculations.
  我们的报价合理，而不是漫天要价。

- After a comparison, you'll see that our offer is more favorable than the quotations you can get elsewhere.
  比较之后你会发现，我们的报价比别处要便宜。

- This offer is competitive.
  此报盘很有竞争性。

- This offer is subject to your reply reaching us before June 30th.
  这份报价以你方的回复在 6 月 30 日前到达我方为准。

- All prices in the price lists are subject to our confirmation.

报价单中所有价格以我方确认为准。

- We want to make you a firm offer at this price.
  我们愿意以此价格为你报实盘。

- We have extended the offer as per your request.
  我们已按你方要求将报盘延期。

- This offer is subject to your reply reaching here before the end of this week.
  该报盘以你方答复本周末到达我地为有效。

- Would you like to renew your offer on the same terms and conditions?
  能否按同样条件恢复报盘?

还 盘

- We are sure no other buyers have bid higher than this price.
  我们肯定没有别的买主的出价高于此价。

- Would you like to make a counter-offer?
  您是否还个价?

- Your counter-offer is relatively modest.
  你们的还盘相对来说比较保守。

- Your offer is unacceptable unless the price is reduced by 5%.
  除非你们减价 5%,否则我们无法接受报盘。

- Your counter-offer is too low and groundless.
  你方还盘太低了,而且毫无根据。

- Since your counter-offer is unacceptable, we are sorry to return your order.
  由于你们的还盘我们难以接受,很抱歉只能退还订单。

- I'm sorry the gap between your counter-offer and our price is too wide.
  很抱歉你的还盘和我们的报价之间的差距太大了。

时尚对白

询实盘

A: Hi, John. Can you tell me the price of these goods?
B: Hi, Li. This is our latest price list. I'd like to know the quantity you require.
A: I think it depends greatly on your price. What's your lowest price?

A:你好,约翰。请报这批货物的价格。
B:你好,李先生,这是我们最新的报价单。你们想要多少?
A:我想这要看你们的价格。最低价是多少?

B:The price of this commodity is USD200 per piece.
A:Is this your CIF quotation?
B:No. FOB.
A:Are they firm offers?
B:Non-firm. They are subject to our final confirmation.
A:I wonder whether there are any changes in your prices.
B:Compared with that of last year, our price has changed somewhat. Now it is highly competitive.
A:When can I have your CIF firm offer?
B:Mm, I can give it to you tomorrow.
A:How long does your offer remain valid?
B:It remains open for 5 days.
A:OK, I'll phone you the day after tomorrow. See you then.
B:See you.

B：这种商品每件最低200美元。
A：是CIF价吗？
B：不，FOB价。
A：是实盘吗？
B：虚盘。以我方最终确认为准。
A：我想知道你所报的价格有没有变化。
B：同去年相比，价格多少有些改变。现在该商品相当有竞争力。
A：什么时候能收到你方的实盘？
B：嗯，明天能给你实盘。
A：有效期是多长时间？
B：5天。
A：好吧。我后天给你打电话。再见。
B：再见。

口语秘笈

"谈"是任务，而"听"则是一种能力，甚至可以说是一种天份。"会听"是任何一个成功的谈判员都必须具备的条件。在谈判中，我们要尽量鼓励对方多说，我们要向对方说："Yes"，"Please go on"，并提问题请对方回答，使对方多谈他们的情况，以达到尽量了解对方的目的。

 ## 要求更高的折扣

A:Thank you for your prompt offer. But after our investigation and comparison, it seems that your price is about 7 percent higher than those offered by your peers.
B:You'd better take quality into consideration. Our products are made of pure wool.
A:I appreciate your quality. But 7 percent is unacceptable to us anyway. We can't sacrifice too much for the high quality under the intense competition of the world market.

A：感谢你方的及时发盘。但是经过对比调查，我们发现你方报价比同行的要高出7%。
B：贵方最好将质量考虑进去。我们的商品可是纯羊毛的。
A：我很欣赏你们的产品质量，然而，我们无论如何也无法接受7%的差价。当今世界市场的激烈竞争迫使我们无法为高质量牺牲过多。
B：那样的话，如果你方能够把数量

B: In that case, if you adjust your quantity to 6,000, we'll consider allowing you a 1.5 percent discount.

A: 1.5 percent won't help. We believe 5 percent will do.

B: I'm sorry we can't give you 5 percent discount by all means. Considering you are a new customer, we'll exceptionally allow you a 2 percent cut which is the best we can do.

A: Well…does this price include seaworthy packing?

B: It is a general practice that outer packing is made for container transportation.

A: How long will this offer be available?

B: One week.

A: I'll contact our manager to see whether a 2 percent discount will do and give you the reply as soon as possible.

调整到 6,000 件，我方可以给你们 1.5% 的折扣。

A：1.5% 的折扣不行。我们认为 5% 的折扣才行。

B：很抱歉，无论如何我们也不能给你们 5% 的折扣。考虑到你是我们的新客户，我们破例给你 2% 的折扣，这是我们最大限度了。

A：嗯……这个价格包含海运包装的费用吗？

B：通常我们对商品进行外包装以适于集装箱运输。

A：报价有效期是多久？

B：一周。

A：我得联系一下经理看看 2% 的折扣是不是可以接受，并尽快答复你。

口语秘笈

发盘后，进口商常常会问："Can't you do better than that?" 对此发问，我们不要让步，而应反问："What is meant by better?" 或 "Better than what?" 这些问题可使进口商说明他们究竟在哪些方面不满意。例如，进口商会说："Your competitor is offering better terms." 这时，我们可继续发问，直到完全了解竞争对手的发盘。然后，我们可以向对方说明我们的发盘是不同的，实际上要比竞争对手的更好。

对 T 恤的询盘

A: I'm glad to have the opportunity of visiting your company. I hope we can do business together.

B: It's a great pleasure to meet you. I believe you have seen our exhibition in the showroom. What is it in particular you are interested in?

A: I'm interested in the cotton piece goods, such as T-shirts.

B: You'll not have any difficulty in the sales of these items, I'm sure.

A: No. There's a tendency in North America that more and more people like to buy cotton piece goods instead of

A：很高兴有机会参观你们的公司。希望有机会合作。

B：很高兴见到你。我相信你已经在展厅看过我们的商品了。有什么特别感兴趣的东西吗？

A：我对棉质产品非常感兴趣，比如 T 恤衫。

B：我相信销售这些产品绝不会遇到任何困难。

synthetic fabrics.

B: You are quite right.

A: Here is a list of my requirements. If the goods appear to be of good quality and the prices are reasonable, we expect to place regular orders for fairly large numbers.

B: Thanks for your inquiry. I can assure you of the best quality and lowest prices. Have a look at our latest catalogue.

A: If the price is right, we would be prepared to place a large order.

B: Please rest assured that our prices are the most competitive.

A：是的。在北美，现在越来越多的人喜欢棉制品而不是合成纤维。

B：确实如你所说。

A：这是我们的要求。如果价廉物美，我们会持续大量订购。

B：感谢你方的询盘。我方保证最优质量、最低价位。请看一下我们的最新目录。

A：如果价格合适 我们准备大批订购。

B：请放心 我们的价格最具有竞争力。

口语秘笈

出口商应用开放式的问题（即答复不是"是"或"不是"而需要特别解释的问题）来了解进口商的需求，因为这类问题可以使进口商自由畅谈他们的需求。例如："Can you tell me more about your company?"（您能让我再多了解您公司一下吗？）"What do you think of our proposal?"（关于我们的建议您觉得怎么样？）

对空调的询盘

A: The Hair Air Conditioners are the best selling lines. They are easy to handle and work with little noise.

B: I'm thinking about placing an order. I hope you could offer us your favorable terms.

A: I'm sure you'll find our prices most competitive. There is our offer sheet. All the prices on the list are without engagement. If your order is a sizable one, we could reconsider our prices.

B: Good. We plan to order thousands of them. Is it possible to deliver them in April?

A: I'm afraid we can't. Our factories are heavily backed up. It is very difficult for them to get the goods ready in April.

A：海尔空调是我们的畅销品牌，具有使用方便、噪音低的特点。

B：我正在考虑订购一批。希望你能报最低价格。

A：我保证我方的价格最具有竞争力。这是我们的报价单。单子上的所有价格都可议。如果你们大量订购的话，我们还可以重新商讨价格。

B：很好。我们打算订购几千套。四月份能发货吗？

A：恐怕不行。我们厂有很多积压的订单，很难在四月份将货备妥。

B:But we are in urgent need of the products, otherwise we'll miss the selling season. Can you get around the manufacturers for an early delivery?

A:All right. We'll get in touch with them to see what they can do for you and let you know tomorrow.

B:Thank you.

B：但是我们急需这批货，否则就会错过旺销季节。你能和生厂商商量一下尽早交货吗？

A：好吧，我联系一下看看他们能为你做什么，明天给你答复。

B：谢谢。

 展会咨询

A:Jenny, is it your first visit to the Fair?

B:No. It's the third time.

A:Is there anything you find changed here?

B:Yes, a great deal. The business scope has been broadened, and there are more businessmen than ever before.

A:Really indeed. Did you find anything interesting?

B:Oh, yes, especially your products.

A:I'm glad to hear that. What items are you particularly interested in?

B:Women's Blouses. They are fashionable. If they are of high quality and the prices are reasonable, we'll place a large order. Will you please quote us a price?

A:Of course. Please rest assured of our quality.

B:Good. When can I have your catalogue?

A:Tomorrow morning, OK?

B:All right.

A：珍妮，你是第一次来参加交易会吗？

B：不。这是第三次。

A：你发现这里有什么变化吗？

B：变化很大。经营范围比以前扩大了，参展人员比以前增多了。

A：确实如此。有没有发现感兴趣的商品？

B：有，尤其是你们的产品。

A：很高兴听你这样说。哪些商品引起了你的特别关注？

B：女式衬衫。很时尚。如果质量上乘，价格合理，我们会大量订购。报个价吧？

A：当然可以。对我们的产品质量，尽请放心。

B：好的。我什么时候能得到产品目录？

A：明天上午，好吗？

B：好的。

> **口语秘笈**
>
> 推销的秘诀在于如何活用问句，如"Do you want to see anything else?"（您想看看别的产品吗？）这类典型的发问，就是顺利展开推销的关键。更进一步地发问，就是把目的带入问句中，如"What about this one?"（这个怎样？）以套出顾客的想法。

 咨询交货期

A: I'm Brown from Sunrise Company. We met each other at the fair one week ago.

B: Ah, Mr. Brown, nice to see you here. What can I do for you?

A: I want to know whether we can place an order recently and when the delivery can be arranged at the earliest date.

B: It should be in August if your order is not excessively large.

A: Is the offer you gave to me at the fair a firm one?

B: Our offer is valid for two weeks. If you can tell us the exact quantity of the order, I will renew the offer and allow you a reduction on price.

A: Thanks. I am preparing the order sheet. It will be sent to you as soon as possible.

B: We are looking forward to it. Thanks for your inquiry.

A：我是金辉公司的布朗。我们一周前在博览会上见过面。

B：啊，是布朗先生，很高兴在这儿见到你。需要帮忙吗？

A：我想知道，近期是否能订到货以及贵方最早什么时间可以安排发货。

B：如果您的订单不是特别大的话应该在八月份就能发货。

A：上次您在博览会上给我的报价是实盘吗？

B：我们的报价两周内有效。如果您能告诉我具体的订单数量，我就可以给您更新报价了，并降低价格。

A：谢谢。我正在准备订单，将尽快发给您。

B：期待您的订单。感谢您的询盘。

 对棉质品的询盘

A: We're in the market for printed cotton piece goods. What can you offer?

B: We have pure silk fabrics, synthetic fabrics and mixed fabrics. As you know, silks are one of Chinese traditional exports. They are well received and enjoy high reputation for their superior quality and novel designs.

A：我们想购买印花布匹。贵公司在这方面能供应些什么？

B：我方经营纯丝制品、合成布料和混纺布料。如你所知，丝绸是中国传统出口产品之一。中国出口的丝绸因其质量上乘、设计新颖而蜚声海外，备受青睐。

A: Do you have any literature which I can take with me?

B: Yes, here are some catalogues and brochures.

A: May I have a price list with specifications?

B: Sure, here it is.

A: Thank you.

B: What about the commission? From European suppliers we usually get 5% commission for my import.

A: As a rule, we do not allow any commission. But if the order is large enough, we'll consider giving you 3% commission.

B: Good. Is your show room far from here? I want to see the exhibits on my own. First hand information is always more valuable than reading pamphlets.

A: No, it's only 15-minute ride. Let's go.

A：有说明书让我带回去看看吗？

B：有的，这是我们的一些目录和宣传册子。

A：能给我一份注有多种规格的报价单吗？

B：当然可以，给你。

A：谢谢。

B：那么佣金呢？我们一般能从欧洲供货商那里得到5%的佣金。

A：我方通常不给付佣金。但如果你方订购数量大，我方可以考虑给你3%的佣金。

B：好，你们的展厅离这里远吗？我想亲眼看看展品。掌握第一手资料远比读一些小册子有价值得多。

A：不远，只有15分钟的车程，咱们走吧。

口语秘笈

如果对对方的观点有条件地接受，可以用 "on the condition that..."（条件是……）这个句型，例如：We accept your proposal, on the condition that you order 20,000 units.（如果您订2万台，我们会接受您的建议。）。

延误发盘

A: Please accept my apologies for our delay in answering your inquiry.

B: That's all right. Unforeseen circumstances do occur, don't they?

A: You see, when we received your inquiry, the world market was suffering from financial crisis, which made it difficult for us to make a firm offer. Now the storm is more or less over, at least for the time being.

B: We understand your situation, but we're glad

A：请接受我方无法及时答复贵方询盘的深深歉意。

B：没关系。确实出现了难以预料的状况，不是吗？

A：你知道，收到你方询盘时，世界市场正处于金融危机的影响之下，这使得我方很难报出实盘。现在金融风暴差不多结束了，至少目前如此。

B：当然，我们能理解贵方的处境，

that you are better off now. I hope you would reconsider your price and bring it into line with the world market price.

A: Well, give me time then. I'll have to contact my head office.

B: That's fine. Please let us know as soon as you hear from them.

但很高兴看到贵方现在摆脱了困境。我希望贵方能重新考虑价格并使之与世界市场价格相一致。

A：好的，那么给我点儿时间，我必须同总部沟通。

B：好吧。收到答复请马上告知我方。

 文化点滴

在谈判中，双方都应该清楚：

1. why negotiate：谈判原因
2. whom to negotiate with：与谁谈判
3. what to negotiate：谈判内容
4. where to negotiate：谈判地点
5. when to negotiate：谈判时间
6. how to negotiate：谈判方式

不论谈判类型如何，谈判都具有以下共同特点：

1. Negotiation is at the heart of every transaction.
   谈判是交易的中心。
2. Negotiation can be a very trying process with confrontation and concession.
   谈判是一个既对立又要让步的过程。
3. Both parties share open information.
   双方要介绍各自的情况。
4. Both parties know that they have common and conflicting objectives.
   双方了解彼此的共同目标和差异。
5. Everything is negotiable.
   任何事情都是可以商量的。

支付方式 Payment

国际贸易支付方式是指国际间因商品交换而发生的、以货款为主要内容的债权债务的清算方式。不同的支付方式包含不同的支付时间、支付地点和支付方法。主要有：

1. 订货付现和装船前付现：前者是指买方须于合同签订或订货时，或其后指定的时间内，按约定的方式（一般是通过银行）将全部货款汇付给卖方。后者是指买方应在货物装船前若干天付清全部货款，作为卖方装船的条件。

2. 记账：记账又称专户记账。卖方将货物装运出口后，即将货运单据径寄买方，货款则借记买方帐户，然后按约定的期限，定期进行结算。

3. 托收：指债权人将金融单据或随附有关货运单据委托第三者收取款项或取得债务人对汇票的承兑的行为。

4. 信用证：在国际货物买卖中大量使用的商业跟单信用证，是银行应进口人的请求和指示，开给受益人并承诺在一定期限内，在受益人遵守信用证所有条件下，凭指定单据支付一定金额的书面凭证。

词语宝典

open account	赊账销售 / 先货后款	revocable L/C	可撤销信用证
documentary collection	跟单托收	irrevocable L/C	不可撤消信用证
documentary L/C	跟单信用证	D/P at sight	即期付款交单
negotiating bank	议付行	D/P after sight	远期付款交单
anticipatory L/C	预支信用证	cash in advance	预先付款 / 先款后货
back to back L/C	对背信用证	cash with order (C.W.O.)	随订单付现
reciprocal L/C	对开信用证	cash on delivery (C.O.D.)	交货付现
clean L/C	光票信用证	cash against payment	凭单付现，凭单付款
confirmed L/C	保兑信用证	clean payment	单纯支付
unconfirmed L/C	不保兑信用证	D/P:documents against payment	付款交单
deferred payment L/C	延期付款信用证	D/A: documents against acceptance	承兑交单
documentary L/C	跟单信用证		

经典句型

- The advising bank of an L/C should be our regular business bank in our own country.
  信用证通知行应是在我国境内同我方有稳固业务关系的银行。

- What's your reason for the refusal of payment?
  你们拒付的理由是什么？

- To push the sales of the new product, we'll consider accepting payment by D/P.
  为了推销新产品，我们将考虑接受付款交单方式。

- We require 100% value, irrevocable L/C in our favor with partial shipment.
  我们要求用不可撤销的、金额为全部货款的以我方为收益人的信用证，允许分批装运。

- This is the normal terms of payment in international payment.
  这是国际贸易中惯用的付款方式。

- We prefer to use letter of credit at sight.
  我们愿意用即期信用证付款。

- You are requested to protect our draft on presentation.
  你方应见票即付。

- Does the bill of exchange have to be endorsed?
  汇票必须背书吗？

- We've drawn a clean draft on the value of this sample shipment.
  我们已经开出光票向你方索取这批货的价款。

- The seller can't accept payment on deferred terms.
  卖方不能接受延期付款。

- We should confirm the good standing of your bank if the documentary credit is unconfirmed.
  如果信用证为非保兑，我们应确认你方银行的信誉状况。

- We never accept "Cash against Documents" on arrival of goods at destination.
  我们从不接受"货抵目的地付款交单"的方式付款。

- They draw on us by their documentary draft at sight on collection basis.
  他们将按托收方式向我方开出即期跟单汇票。

- As a special sign of encouragement, we'll consider accepting payment by D/P at this sales-purchasing stage.
  在此推销阶段，我们将考虑接受付款交单方式以资鼓励。

- An irrevocable L/C gives the exporter the additional protection of banker's guarantee.

  不可撤销信用证为出口商提供了银行担保。

- The wording of "confirmed" is necessary for the letter of credit.

  信用证上必须写明"保兑"字样。

- The bank in London is in a position to open letters of credit in RMB against the sales confirmation or contract.

  伦敦的银行可以凭销售确认书或合同开立人民币信用证。

- Which bank advises the beneficiary of the documentary credit?

  哪一家银行通知跟单信用证给受益人？

- Bank fees for documentary credits are much higher than those for documentary collections.

  跟单信用证的银行费用大大高于跟单托收的费用。

- The supplier has drawn a clean draft on us for the value of this shipment.

  供货商已经开出光票向我们索取这批货的货款了。

- The decline in prices might lead to refusal of payment.

  市场价格下跌会导致拒付。

- We refuse to pay until shipping documents for the goods reach us.

  没拿到货物装船单据之前，我们拒绝付款。

- If you fail to open the credit within the time limit, we shall have the right to terminate the contract.

  如果你们在时间期限内无法开立信用证，我们有权终止合同。

时尚对白

协商信用证和付款交单

A: Since we have settled down on the price, let's move on to the terms of payment.

B: All right. It is our general practice to accept payment by confirmed irrevocable L/C payable against shipping documents.

A: Well, could you make an exception to accept

A：我们已经解决了价格问题，现在讨论一下付款方式吧。

B：好的。我们通常接受保兑的不可撤销的见票即付的信用证支付方式。

A：哦。你方能否破例接受付款交单？

B：很抱歉，我们不能接受。只有经过

documents against payment?

B: I'm sorry we can't accept that. Only when we have done business for a certain period of time, we could think over that. But now, L/C is a must.

A: To be frank with you, the opening of L/C would increase our cost on imports. We have to pay a deposit, which will tie up our money and increase our importing cost.

B: I understand. But why not consult with your bank to see if they will reduce the deposit to the minimum.

A: When should the L/C be established?

B: The deadline is July 7th.

A：坦白地说，开立信用证会增加我们的进口成本。向银行申请开立信用证，我们必须支付押金，这就会束缚我方的资金并使进口成本增加。

B：我明白。但是为什么不同银行进行协商看看是否能将抵押金降到最低。

A：什么时候开立信用证？

B：7月7日是最后期限。

一段时间的业务往来后，我们才能考虑接受付款交单。眼下必须使用信用证。

> **达人点拨**
> 我国企业使用 L/C 的比例高达 85%，但坏账率超过 5%，有的甚至达到 30%（国际平均水平为 1%）。可见，采用托收和赊销等商业信用方式是国际货款支付方式的发展趋势。我国的外贸企业应认清这一趋势，不要因为从表面上看 D/P 付款方式风险大而不敢做这笔交易，从而丧失了商机。

展品费用支付

A: There is a fair to be held in Xinghai Exhibition Centre next week. We want to import some products for exhibition, after which the goods would be shipped out of China. What kind of payment shall we make?

B: What are the imported goods?

A: Printers and some printing paper.

B: Printing paper is a consuming product. Under temporary import and export regulations, it's not allowed to be imported. The other products can be imported by paying a certain sum of money as deposit. You needn't pay customs duties for the goods. Other payments depend on actual happenings.

A: I see.

B: Does your company have the authority to engage in

A：下周星海会展中心有一个博览会。我们想进口一些商品用于展览。展出之后再运出中国。我们需要支付哪些款项？

B：你们进口的是什么产品？

A：打印机和打印纸。

B：打印纸属于消耗品。按现行的进出口条件不允许进口。其他产品可以在交保证金的前提下进口。不用付关税。其他款项按实际情况支付。

A：明白了。

B：你们公司有进出口经营权吗？

import and export business?
A: Not presently, but we are applying for the qualifications.
B: So, now you have to entrust the authorized company to deal with your importation.
A: OK. How long will it take us to get our cargo?
B: On showing complete formalities, you can get them very soon.
A: Many thanks.
B: Sure thing.

A：目前还没有。不过，我们正在申请该资格。
B：那你现在应委托一家有进出口经营权的公司办理进口。
A：好。我们多长时间可以拿到货？
B：手续齐全的话，很快就能拿到。
A：多谢。
B：不必客气。

 灵活支付方式

A: Do you accept payment by documentary L/C?
B: I'm sorry to say it is difficult for us to do so. You know this is only a small sample order. We are unwilling to pay for high costs of documentary credit.
A: Yes, I understand. But although the degree of risk is not high due to the small quantity ordered, we still want to make sure that we can get payment on time.
B: Are there any other flexible ways?
A: How about payment in advance?
B: In this way, we pay you prior to your shipment of the goods ordered, still leaving us at great risks.
A: Well, are you willing to pay some portion in advance? Say, 50% by prepayment and 50% by deferred payment?
B: Thank you for the concessions you have made. Could you make sure that the goods will be delivered before June 30th so that we can catch up with the selling season?
A: In this case, you'd better make the prepayment as soon as possible.
B: That'll be fine.

A：你方是否接受跟单信用证的付款方式？
B：很抱歉我方很难接受信用证的付款方式。这次不过是一笔小的试订单。我方不愿意支付高额的跟单信用证费用。
A：是的，我明白。尽管订购数量不大，风险较小，我们依然想确保能够准时收到货款。
B：有没有什么变通的付款方式？
A：预付货款如何？
B：这种方式使我方面临巨大的危险，因为在你方装运货物前我们就要支付货款。
A：你们愿不愿意提前支付一部分货款？比方说，50% 预付，50% 延期支付？
B：谢谢你们的让步。你方能否确保 6 月 30 日前交货以便我方能赶上旺销季节？
A：这样的话，你方最好尽快支付预付款。
B：好的。

> **口语秘笈**
>
> 如今分期付款很流行，所以要学会说"You can buy them by installment."还要会解释："You pay a down-payment of five hundred dollars, and then, within a year, one hundred for each and every month."（可以先付订金500元，然后在一年内，每月付100元。）

讨论分期付款

A: Apparently, it is practical to make our payment for the complete set by installments, because the order includes not only your equipment, but also your service of installation, trial run and staff training.

B: Sure. What is your opinion on the installment payment?

A: We think it is fair that we make a down-payment on the delivery of the equipment. And then we will pay off the rest in three months according to the progress of the project.

B: We may agree with your proposal. So the down-payment actually is the equipment that you purchase.

A: We would like to pay it by L/C.

B: Sure. But you must open L/C at sight one month before the shipment is made.

A: No problem.

A：显然，分期支付整套设备的货款是可行的。因为订单中不仅包括了你的设备还包括安装服务、试运行和员工培训。

B：当然。对于分期付款你们有什么看法？

A：我觉得交货付首付是很合理的。剩余款项根据项目进展情况于三个月内付清。

B：我们同意你方的提议。这样的话，首付款实际上是你方所购买的设备的价值。

A：我们希望用信用证支付。

B：当然，但是你方必须于装运前一个月开出信用证。

A：没问题。

承兑交单和远期付款交单

A: Let's talk about the payment terms for this deal.

B: OK. As the buyer, we hope to pay by D/A so that we can have time to raise the funds and resell the merchandise.

A: Well, from the seller's point of view, we think D/A will put us at great risks since the banks

A：我们现在谈谈这笔交易的付款方式吧。

B：好的。作为买方我们希望通过承兑交单付款，这样我们就会有时间筹措资金和转卖商品。

A：从卖方的角度说，我们认为承兑

involved do not guarantee payment. What about payment terms of D/P? We may have higher degree of security and protection.

B: That's reasonable. But we prefer D/P after sight as it has features of both D/A and D/P.

A: Yes, this term leaves you sufficient time to raise funds to make payment. At the same time, our security will also be guaranteed, since the title to our shipment will not be handed over to you until your payment has been made.

B: Absolutely right. So we've reached an agreement on the payment term of D/P after sight, right? Then, what is your expected due date of the draft?

A: Do you agree the time draft will fall due on August 19th this year?

B: Agreed.

交单会将我方置于极大危险之中，因为有关银行不担保付款。付款交单如何？我方可以获得较大程度的安全和保护。

B：比较合理。不过我方更喜欢远期付款交单的方式。这种方式兼具承兑交单和付款交单两种支付方式的特征。

A：是的。这种方式使得你方有足够的时间筹措资金以支付货款。同时我们的安全也得到了保证，因为货权只有在支付后才能转移至你方手中。

B：确实是这样。这样的话我们就远期交单付款方式取得了一致，对吧？那么，您希望汇票的到期日是哪天？

A：今年8月19日到期怎样？

B：好。

 支付货币

A: The terms of payment are described in our proposal. I hope you pay for your import according to the terms specified in our proposal.

B: So we have to pay in Deutsche Mark, right?

A: Yes, we propose to price the commodities in terms of Deutsche Mark.

B: Why confined to D.M.? As a British importer, we certainly prefer to Pound Sterling, if you don't mind.

A: I'm afraid I can't accept it. As everybody knows, in the past few years, the Pound Sterling, like the Dollar, has depreciated many times. It's a lesson worthy of remembering, isn't it?

B: Well, I understand your position. Though the

A：我方的报价书中对付款条件有说明，我希望你们按照我方报价书中的条件支付进口货物货款。

B：那么我们必须用德国马克支付，对吧？

A：是的，我方建议用德国马克给商品计价。

B：为什么仅限于马克呢？作为英国的进口商人，如果你方不介意的话，我们当然倾向于使用英镑。

A：恐怕我方无法接受英镑支付。众所周知，过去几年中，英镑同美元一样贬值了多次，这是应该记住的教训，对吧？

B：是的，我理解贵方处境。虽然货币

currency crisis is over, I agree to your payment if you insist.

A: Very well, thank you for your cooperation.

危机已过，但如果你方坚持的话，我方同意用马克支付。

A：太好了，感谢贵方的合作。

口语秘笈

分期付款与收取其他货款相比除手续稍微复杂一点外，并没有多大不同，前提是"May I have some money as a deposit?"（您可以付部分订金吗？）。

 咨询信用证详细信息

A: Ms. Wang, when do we have to open the L/C if we want the goods to be shipped in October?

B: Usually, a month before the time you want the goods to be delivered, your L/C should reach us …

A: You mean in September?

B: Yes, exactly.

A: Why such a long time be needed?

B: You know, we should get the goods ready, make out the documents and book the shipping space. All this takes time. You can't expect us to make a delivery in less than one month.

A: Then I'll arrange for the L/C to be opened as soon as I get home.

B: All right, thank you.

A: Ms. Wang, how about the validity of our L/C? Can we set the shipment date and validity date on the same date?

B: Usually the validity date of the L/C should be fixed two weeks after the shipment date. Thus we may have enough time for negotiation.

A: I see. Now I want to know what documents we will have.

B: As general practice, we provide a full set of shipping

A：王女士，如果我方希望十月份能将货物装运的话应该什么时候开立信用证？

B：通常是发货前的一个月。你方信用证应该……

A：你的意思是九月份？

B：是的，完全正确。

A：为什么需要提前这么长时间？

B：你要知道，我们要备货、制单和预订舱位。所有这些都需要时间。我们无法在不到一个月的时间内交货。

A：那样的话，我一到家就安排开立信用证。

B：好的，谢谢。

A：王小姐，还有信用证的有效期问题。我们能不能把装运日期和信用证的到期日定为一天？

B：通常信用证的到期日应该在装运后的两周内确定，这样我们就会有充足的时间进行协商。

A：我明白了。我想知道我们都将拿到哪些单据。

documents such as the bill of lading, the invoice, the insurance policy, the certificate of origin and the certificate of inspection. We can also provide other documents on request.

A:OK. I'll take it down.

B：通常，我方提供全套的运输单据，如提单、发票、保险单、原产国证明和检验证书。应要求我方也能提供其他单据。

A：好的，我记下来。

 ## 消除双方误会

A:I want to tell you that the time of payment for this transaction is already due, but up to now, we have not received your letter of credit or payment notification whatsoever from you. Can we have your explanation?

B:Yes. We have not opened the L/C, though it is due time to do so. The reason is that, so far, we've not received any notification of shipment of goods on your side. As stated in the contract, for each transaction, the relevant letter of credit can be opened when there is notification of shipment.

A:But we have already made notification to your offices at the port of loading.

B:Is that so?

A:Yes, we've sent you a fax three days ago.

B:I'm sorry, Mr. Zhao. Could you hang on a moment and I'll ask my office about it?

(Several minutes later…)

B:I'm very sorry, Mr. Zhao. My secretary forgot to tell me about it when I returned from a business trip.

A:Would you please effect the payment immediately?

B:Sure. We'll advise our bank to open the L/C at once and to make this payment through telegraphic transfer.

A:OK.

A：这笔业务的付款期已经到了，但直到现在，我们还没收到你们的信用证或其他来自你方的付款通知。能解释一下原因吗？

B：是的，虽然付款时间到了，但我们还没开信用证。原因是到现在为止我们还没收到来自你方的装船通知。根据约定，每笔业务只有在收到装船通知后才能开立相关的信用证。

A：但我们已经通知你们在装卸港的办事处了。

B：是这样的吗？

A：是的，我们在三天前就已经给你发了一份传真。

B：很抱歉，赵先生。你请先等一下，我问问我们的办事处。

（几分钟后……）

B：实在很抱歉，赵先生。出差回来，我的秘书忘了告诉我这件事。

A：你能马上支付货款吗？

B：当然，我会让银行马上开立信用证，通过电汇支付账款。

A：好的。

> **口语秘笈**
>
> 在商务往来中，给对方以承诺通常是我们交流的一种方法。承诺会增强彼此的信任感和责任感，可以说"I give you my word that the payment will be made not later than the end of June."（我保证六月底前支付货款。）等类似表达。

文化点滴

谈判双方有一共同之处：即从交易中获得利润并最大限度地减少风险。

1. When choosing which means of payment is to be used in international trade, the buyer and the seller should be clear about the fact that the risks and costs are often not balanced for both parties.

   当选择何种国际贸易结算方式，买卖双方都应该清楚一点，风险和成本通常对双方并非均等。

2. In new trading relationships, it always makes sense to start on more conservative terms such as L/C and, after experience and greater familiarity, proceed to deal on more liberal terms.

   在新的贸易关系下，先使用较为保守的支付方式，如信用证，然后随着经验的积累和相互熟悉度的加深，再采用较为自由的方式。

3. In negotiation of payment terms, one party should try best to know as much as possible about all the issues and concerns of the other party and to show a degree of trust.

   在支付方式的谈判过程中，一方应该尽量了解对方关注的问题并表示一定的诚意。

4. International transaction often requires a compromise on the part of the seller and the buyer that leads to relative security of payment terms for both sides.

   国际交易通常需要买卖双方的妥协，以达成对双方都相对安全的支付方式。

UNIT 3 质量与数量 Quality and Quantity

商品的品质

商品的品质是指商品的内在素质和外观形态的综合。前者包括商品的物理性能、机械性能、化学成分和生物特性等自然属性，后者包括商品的外形、色泽、款式或透明度等。表示商品品质既可以实物表示，亦可用文字说明。

商品的数量

商品的数量是指以一定的度量衡单位表示商品的重量、数量、长度、面积、体积、容积等。国际上常用的度量衡制度有公制、英制、美制和国际单位制。

词语宝典

choice quality	精选的质量	sales by description	凭说明书买卖
color sample	色彩样品	sales by sample	凭样品买卖
counter sample	对等样品	standard quality	标准质量
common quality	一般质量	actual tare	实际皮重
duplicate sample	复样	gross for net	以毛作净
Fair Average Quality (F.A.Q.)	良好平均品质	gross weight	毛重
fair quality	尚好的质量	quantity production	大批生产
fine quality	优质	quantity buying	大量购买，定额购买
popular quality	大众化的质量	quantity delivered	供给量，交付数量
prime quality	第一流的质量		

经典句型

- As long as the quality is good, it doesn't matter if the price is a little bit higher.
  只要能保证质量，售价高点儿无所谓。

- Nothing wrong will happen so long as the quality of your article is good.
  只要商品质量可靠，就不会发生差错。

- There is no qualitative difference between the two.

两者在质量上无差异。

- Prices are based on their quality.
  价格按质量的好坏而定。

- If you find the quality of the products unsatisfactory, we're prepared to accept return of the goods within a week.
  如果贵方对产品质量不满意,我们将在一周内接受退货。

- The new product possesses very vivid designs and beautiful colors.
  新产品设计新颖,色泽鲜艳。

- We devote ourselves to improving the quality of our products and production effectively.
  我们致力于改进产品质量,提高生产率。

- You should have received the outturn samples of the inferior quality goods.
  你们应该已经收到了质量低劣产品的到货抽样。

- We find the quality unsuitable for our market.
  产品质量不适合我们的市场。

- Our cotton goods are of unsurpassed quality and appearance.
  我们的产品在质量和外形上无可比拟。

- Our brand name itself proves that our goods are superior.
  我们的品牌本身就证明我们的商品是优质的。

- It is always our practice to supply high quality goods at reasonable prices.
  我们的一贯做法是以合理的价格供应高质量的商品。

- Goods are sold as per the sales sample, not the quality of any previous supplies.
  销售产品是以货样为标准,而不是凭过去任何一批货的质量。

- Your quantity is too small. If it runs into 1,000 sets or more, we can give you better terms.
  你们的订货量太少了,如果在 1,000 套或以上,我们可以给你更优惠的条款。

- We hope you give us a discount for such a big quantity.
  我们希望贵公司能给我们这么大的订单一个折扣。

- We need to make sure if there is any quantity limitation for the import of coal from China.
  我们需要弄清楚从中国进口煤是否有数量限制。

- This is the maximum quantity our productivity allows at present.
  这是目前我们的生产能力所能提供的最大数量了。

- This year we want to enlarge our order with an extra 5,000 bottles.
  今年我们打算扩大订量,增加 5,000 瓶。

时尚对白

修改样本

A: Hello, Lucy. This is Chen.

B: Hi, Miss Chen. How do you like our samples?

A: Our clients think your samples are almost acceptable. However, there are still some points that need to be improved.

B: Is that so? What is that?

A: They sent me some photocopies to show you the difference. Here you are. The copies were marked with notes.

B: Well, it is unbelievable. Perhaps it is a problem of workmanship. We have a lot of things to do in order to meet the standard you require.

A: I think so. Our client is waiting for the revised samples to fix the specification in the contract.

B: All right then. We will inform you as soon as possible when the sample is ready.

A：露西，你好。我姓陈。
B：嗨，陈小姐。你觉得我方的样品如何？
A：我方客户觉得你方样品基本可以接受。然而仍然有几点需要改善。
B：是吗？什么方面？
A：他们寄给我一些影印本以使你方能找出区别，给你。影印本上做了记号。
B：啊，真是难以置信。可能是工艺的问题。为了达到你方的要求，我们做了很多努力。
A：我看得出来。我方客户正等着修订的样本以确定合同中的规格。
B：那好吧。样本备妥后我会尽快通知你。

口语秘笈

"It's of good quality and sold for low price."（价廉物美。）这句流行用语可谓中外皆宜。

货品可供数量

A: What cute designs they are! They must sell well in our country. I'd like to order these two with the amount as follows: New Material Dolls No.1 quantity 50,000, Synthetic Fiber Dolls No.2 quantity 20,000.

A：好可爱的设计啊！在我们国家一定会畅销。我选两种：新材料洋娃娃1号50,000只，化纤洋娃娃2号20,000只。

B: I'm sorry to tell you that the demand for the New Material Dolls No. 1 is so great that we can only supply you with 30,000 pieces. It is said that synthetic fiber dolls are popular with American people. Why don't you order more?

A: 30,000 New Material Dolls No.1 are far from enough. Can you supply us with another 10,000? As to the synthetic fiber dolls, the price is pretty high.

B: We'll try our best to meet your demand for the additional 10,000 of New Material Dolls No.1. What's more, the prevailing price of synthetic fiber dolls on the international market has gone up recently, and the price we offer is the lowest.

A: Thank you. We'll increase the size of the order for Synthetic Fiber Dolls No.2 by 20,000 and leave the others as they are.

B：新材料洋娃娃1号的需求很大，我们只能供应30,000只。据说美国人喜欢化纤洋娃娃，你怎么不多订一些呢？

A：新材料洋娃娃1号30,000只太少了，你能再加10,000只吗？至于化纤洋娃娃，我觉得价格太高了。

B：我方尽力满足你方要求。再供应你们新材料洋娃娃1号10,000只。还有，国际市场上的化纤洋娃娃的价格已经普遍上涨了，我们的报价是最低的。

A：谢谢你。化纤洋娃娃2号我方再追加20,000只，其他保持不变。

口语秘笈

商务谈判中，要想方设法留住客户。从对话中看出客户不够满意，可以尝试从另一侧面突出商品的优点。如："Why don't you look at it this way? It's more expensive, but much better value for money?"（为什么不这么看呢？它是贵了一点儿，但它物有所值啊。）"You're right to be cautious, but owing to the limited supply available at present, we suggest you act quickly."（谨慎当然不错，但是目前可供数量有限，建议您及早采取行动。）。

新产品特性介绍

A: Let me show you around.

B: Thank you. Which one is new? We'd like to know more about new products.

A: **There they are. No. 35 and No. 36 are the latest** designs. They are not only beautiful and bright but also more durable than others.

B: Could you explain why they feel so different from

A：让我带你四处转转。

B：谢谢。哪一个是新的？我想知道更多的关于新产品的信息。

A：在那儿。35和36号是最新款，不仅美观亮丽而且比其他型号更经久耐用。

B：能解释一下为什么它们摸上去跟

others?

A: Of course. First, the raw material is selected carefully and used as yarn after a special process. You know, for fabrics, the yarn is very important. The special process can enhance their toughness and luster.

B: Then how about the weave?

A: The yarn is twisted and woven tightly in the new products.

B: But generally, if the yarn is woven too tightly, the fabrics will become shiny which wear very quickly.

A: You are right. That's quite a common phenomenon. But our fabrics will be an exception which can retain its luster without becoming shiny.

B: The special process makes that possible. Well, I am deeply impressed by the display. I think we can talk about the contract now.

其他的商品这么不一样吗？

A：当然可以。首先，用经特殊工序精挑细选的原材料作纱线。你知道，对于纺织品来说，纱线的选择十分重要。特殊工序可以增强韧性和光泽度。

B：织法怎样？

A：纱线经过捻揉，牢牢地织入新产品中。

B：但是通常情况下，如果纱线织得过紧，织物就会发亮而很快磨损。

A：你说的很对。那是太正常的情况了。然而我们的织物是个例外，它可以保持光泽而不发亮。

B：是特殊工序使这种现象成为可能。你们的展品给我留下了深刻的印象。我想我们可以谈合同了。

口语秘笈

展示商品可以说"Please take a look at this."或"That one, madam?"（那个好吗，女士？）。配合产品加以说明时，则用"As you can see, ..."（正如您所见，……）。

推销口香糖

A: Our new chewing gum will soon be put on the market.

B: What is the price?

A: $2 per pack.

B: God, a little too expensive.

A: But it offers two pieces for free.

B: Well, that sounds reasonable.

A: The gum has four different flavors: lemon, mint, strawberry and watermelon.

A：我们的新款口香糖要上市了。

B：价格怎样？

A：一包两美元。

B：天哪，有点儿贵吧？

A：每包还免费赠送两片呢。

B：还算合理。

A：新款一共四种口味：柠檬、薄荷、草莓和西瓜味。

B:Interesting! I think children will be glad to taste it.
A:That's what we expect.
B:What are its advantages over our previous products?
A:It's smoother and perfumes your breath.
B:When will it be launched?
A:If everything goes well, it will be on the market in the coming March.

口语秘笈

没有顾客指定要购买的物品时，千万不要到此为止，必须迅速反应："Sorry, we haven't got that. Do you prefer Salem?"（抱歉，我们没有那个。您喜欢用 Salem 来代替吗？）这种持续维持积极销售的态度，才是制胜的不二法宝。

调整数量

A:Good morning. Nice to see you in Dalian.
B:Nice to see you, too.
A:I'm sorry to say that I'm here on my own to tell you about the quantity of our order.
B:Anything wrong? As stipulated in the contract, we'll supply you with 3,500 cases of oranges, right?
A:Yes, that's true. However, at our end the supply has exceeded demand for what we have ordered.
B:Well, how will the quantity be changed?
A:We want to change the quantity to 2,000 cases.
B:You mean the rest of 1,500 cases will be deleted? Are you kidding? I'm afraid this big change is unacceptable. Personally, I feel you are compelled to make this decision in a particular situation. But I am not sure if my company can accept it without taking it as a breach of the contract.
A:We are really sorry for that. But I think since you have such a wide distributing channel, it will be no

difficulty for you to sell them to other buyers. We promise to place a repeat order of 1,500 cases very soon.

B: I must consult with the manager to see what we can do. But one thing is for sure. The oranges can't be sold to you at the price we agreed to as you reduce the quantity.

A: Yeah. It seems that we have nothing to do but accept.

A: 么广的销售渠道，将它们卖给其他买方是不会有困难的。我方承诺会尽快再订购 1,500 箱柑橘的。

B: 我必须和经理商量看看怎样处理。但是有一件事是确定的，因为你方更改数量，柑橘不能按照所商定的价格卖给你。

A: 好。看上去我们别无他法只能接受了。

口语秘笈

在与外商，尤其是欧美国家的商人谈判时，如果有不同意见，最好坦白地提出来而不要拐弯抹角。比如，表示无法赞同对方的意见时，可以说"I don't think that's a good idea."（我不认为那是个好主意。）或者"Frankly, I can't agree with your proposal."（坦白地讲，我无法同意您的提案。）。

讨论计量单位

A: The quantity of merchandise to be shipped by the seller should always be stated.

B: Sure. There is a possibility of misunderstanding here, as with the price, if such terms as hundredweight or ton are used.

A: How does one avoid a dispute over the fulfillment of a contract if the exporter uses metric tons in his calculation and the importer uses long tons?

B: Well, the exporter should state clearly in the contract whether the weight can be gross, metric, or net ton, or even better, 2,000 pounds or 2,240 pounds per ton.

A: In many cases, it is difficult to ship the exact number of units as per the contract.

B: Yes, but sometimes there is an allowable tolerance and the percentage usually varies from three to five percent.

A: 我知道，卖方必须写明所装载的货品数量。

B: 当然，因为如果使用"英担"或"吨"这类名词，在此就有可能发生诸如价格方面的误解。

A: 如果出口商使用"公吨"来计算，而进口商使用"长吨"，那么在履行合约时如何避免发生争端呢？

B: 这个嘛，出口商必须在合约上清楚写明，重量单位是用"重吨"、"公吨"，或是"净吨"。最好是标明每吨为 2,000 磅，或每吨 2,240 磅。

A: 多数情况下，很难丝毫不差地依照合约装运。

B: 是的，但有时候有一种公差，通常在 3% 至 5% 之间。

按买方样品买卖

A: Do you want to see some of our samples?
B: Right. Thank you. Oh, what a beautiful display of garments!
A: Our garments have been sold in over 80 countries and regions for their novelty.
B: That's great. The majority of your exports are shirts, trousers, work clothes and pajamas, right?
A: Yes, we have been doing this for years. Now our export garments also include sports suits such as ski suits, hunting suits, etc.
B: Your elaborate workmanship is something we appreciate most.
A: We are quite proud of our craftsmanship.
B: Mm. The material is superb.
A: It's comfortable too. We can also produce garments designed after the fashions of different markets or according to the buyer's samples.
B: Really? That sounds good. Could the garments be made especially for our market, I mean, according to the samples given?
A: Of course. We can arrange production to meet national characteristics and habitual tastes of different countries.
B: Do you have any pamphlets for my reference?
A: Here you are. Go over it and you'll definitely find some attractive designs.
B: Thank you very much.

A：想看看我们的样品吗？
B：好的，谢谢。哦，多美的服装啊！
A：我们的服装因样式新颖而行销80多个国家和地区。
B：太厉害了！你们的出口产品主要是衬衫、裤子、工作服和睡衣，对吗？
A：是的，我们一直经营这些产品。现在我们出口的服装还包括运动套装，如滑雪衫、狩猎装等。
B：我们最欣赏你们精细的做工。
A：我们也为自己的工艺感到自豪。
B：嗯，这面料不错。
A：而且穿上也很舒服。另外，我们还可以按不同市场的流行款式或客户来样制作不同款式的服装。
B：是吗？太好了。你们可以为我们市场特殊定做吗？我的意思是按我方提供的样品定做。
A：当然可以。我们可以根据不同国家的国情和风俗习惯来安排生产。
B：有没有商品宣传册让我看看呢？
A：给您。翻翻看，肯定会发现一些非常精美的设计。
B：非常感谢。

花生数量咨询

A: I'd like to buy groundnuts of good merchantable quality.

A：我想购买品质上好的花生仁。
B：我公司供应的货物品质良好。我

B: The goods we supply are of fair average quality. Our brand name itself proves that our goods are superior.

A: We demand that the maximum moisture should not exceed 13% and the oil content should be 45% at its minimum.

B: I think our products will satisfy your requirements. Here is our catalogue.

A: Thank you. Does the catalogue form an integral part of the contract?

B: Yes, the quality is as the catalogue we've provided.

A: That's great indeed.

们的品牌本身证明我们的货物质量是上乘的。

A：我公司要求含水量最高不得超过13%，含油量最低不少于45%。

B：我想我们的产品会满足贵公司的要求。这是我们公司的产品目录。

A：谢谢。该目录是合同的一个组成部分吗？

B：是的，品质与目录中所述一致。

A：真是太好了。

文化点滴

在选择合适的产品进行销售时，卖方掌握以下几点十分重要：

1．Know your product line.
熟悉你经营的产品系列。
2．Work well with local companies.
处理好与当地公司的关系。
3．Make certain that the management of the company you are dealing with is flexible about packaging, design, and such.
确保你代理产品的生产企业能够灵活处理类似包装、设计等方面的问题。
4．Constantly improving the quality and steadfastly maintaining high quality standard has become a powerful means to secure big shares in the competitive export markets.
在竞争激烈的出口市场中，要想确保占有较大的市场份额，只有不断改进质量并坚持高质量标准。
5．Appropriate products to appropriate quality and price levels.
使产品对应适当的质量和价格层次。
6．It is very important for the exporter to maintain the agreed specification.
出口商必须保证产品符合预订的规格。

运输 Shipment

在国际货贸运输中,涉及的运输方式很多,有海洋运输、铁路运输、航空运输、河流运输、邮政运输、公路运输、管道运输、大陆桥运输以及由各种运输方式组合的国际多式联运等,其中海洋运输是最主要的运输方式,其优点在于价格低、运量大、航程远。

出口商通过货运代理安排货物的进出口事项。他们能提供包括收货、安排船期、包装、准备各种单证(含提单)、购买保险、发送商业发票、替客户向船公司付款等服务。货运代理还负责向进口商方的货运代理发出通知,通知对方货物已发送。进口商方的货运代理然后通知进口商有关信息,并负责把货物运往进口商手中或安排仓储。许多国家进口商的货运代理同时兼做报关代理,处理报关手续,并把货物送达进口商手中。

词语宝典

unloading/discharging	卸货	shipping documents	运输单据
tariff	运费表	bill of lading	海运提单
cargo freight	运费	airway bill	航空运单
cargo space	货舱	combined transport	多式联运单据
combined transportation	联运	commercial invoice	商业发票
direct vessel	直达船只	customs invoice	海关发票
initial shipment	第一批货	deliver	发货
load off	卸货	to effect shipment	交货,装运
loading charge	装船费	to take delivery of the goods	提货
loading list	装运单	advance shipment	提前装运
customs declaration	海关申报单	delay shipment	延期装运
mate's receipt	大副收据	speed up shipment	加速装运
punctual shipment	按时装运	transshipment prohibited	不允许转运
shipping advice	装运通知	transshipment entry	转运报单
shipping documents	装运单据	transshipment manifest	转运仓单
shipping instruction	装运指示单	additional charge /fee	附加费
time of delivery	装运期,装运时间	transportation cost	运输成本

customs formalities	海关手续	mode of transportation	运输方式
estimated time of departure (ETD)	预计离开时间		

经典句型

- We don't think it is proper to transport the goods by railway.
  我们认为此货不适合铁路运输。

- When the goods have been loaded, you can get the B/L signed by the master of the vessel.
  货装上船后，你可以得到由船长签字的提单。

- As our factory is located in a costal city, we expect to have the cars sent by sea.
  由于我们的工厂坐落在沿海城市，我们期望将这些汽车通过海运来运输。

- Your prompt reply will speed up the shipment.
  你们的及时答复将会加速装船。

- The trouble was that the vessel did not call at your port.
  问题是该船不在你们的港口停靠。

- Can our order of 1,000 accordions be shipped as soon as possible?
  我们订的 1,000 台手风琴能尽快装运吗？

- We are sorry to inform that we can't advance the time of delivery.
  我们非常抱歉地通知您，我们不能将交货期提前。

- We can ship the goods duly, but your L/C must reach us in time.
  我方可以及时交货，但你方的信用证要按时到达我方。

- I'm sorry that we are unable to give you a definite date of shipment until now.
  很抱歉，现在我们还无法告诉您确切的装船日期。

- We are so happy to hear that the order is ready for shipment.
  听到货物已经备好待运了我们很高兴。

- Since the order is urgently in demand, we have to ask you to speed up shipment.
  由于我们急需订单所订货物，请你们加快装船速度。

- Please get the goods ready for shipment at an early date and ship them without delay.
  请尽快备货，并按时发货。

- Since there is no direct vessel, we have to arrange combined transportion by rail and by sea.
  既然没有直达船，我公司只能安排海陆联运了。

- The facilities for shipping goods in Southeast Asian countries have changed a lot.

东南亚国家货物的装运条件已大大改善了。

- As soon as shipping space is booked, we shall advise you of the name of the ship.
  一旦定好了仓位，我公司会将货轮的名称通知你方。

- It is to inform that the shipment has arrived in good condition.
  特此告知，运到之货物情况良好。

- There are more sailings at Shanghai, so we have chosen it as the loading port.
  因为上海的船次多，我们把这里定为装运港。

- Clients are willing to choose big ports as the loading ports.
  客户希望选择较大的港口作为装运港。

- We have had a brief talk about the loading port.
  我们已经就装运港问题简短地谈过了。

- We can deliver that from stock to meet your requirement.
  我们可以从库中调货以满足你方要求。

- We insist that Dalian is the proper loading port.
  我们坚持大连是适合的装运港。

时尚对白

季节性产品的运输

A: When do you think is possible to effect the shipment?
B: By the mid June, I think.
A: Could you possibly make your delivery date no later than May? You see, June is the right season for the goods. We can't miss the selling season.
B: It is understood. To meet your demand, we can manage to advance the shipment by one month. But we can only deliver 50% of the goods.
A: The goods we ordered are seasonal goods. So it will be better to ship them all at once.
B: I'm sorry. 50% is the best we can do, because there won't be enough spacing for the goods.
A: Still, I don't want to give up trying. A timely

A：你认为什么时候能发货？
B：六月中旬吧。
A：能不能不晚于五月份交货？你知道，六月正是该产品的旺销季节。我们不能错过销售旺季。
B：可以理解。为了满足你方的要求，我们设法将装运期提前一个月，但是只能交付一半的货。
A：我们定的货是季节性产品，所以最好能一次性交付。
B：很抱歉，因为仓储空间也不足，50%已经是最大限度了。
A：我还是不想放弃努力。你知道及时

delivery means a lot to us, you know.

B: All right, we will contact our producer and shipping company and see what they can do.

A: Thank you for your cooperation. We will be waiting for your reply.

交货对我方意义重大。

B：好吧，我方会联系制造商和船运公司看看他们能不能有办法。

A：感谢你们的合作。敬候佳音。

 集装箱运输

A: How about the delivery of goods?

B: Your goods will be first shipped to H.K. in a container ship, and then transshipped to Los Angeles, of course, in another container ship.

A: Container ship?

B: Yes. Containerization is faster, safer and more convenient. It can also save a lot of wrapping and the cost of freight.

A: What if my cargo is less than a container load?

B: Then the cargo will be held according to ports of discharge and nature of cargo at the CFS until there will be a full container load for shipment.

A: Then it will take time, won't it? And I am worried about…

B: Don't worry. It wouldn't take much time. We will pay more attention to that, and you are guaranteed to get the goods on time.

A: How do you know when my goods will be ready to leave your country?

B: We keep in touch with the shipping company all the time. We have close business relations with them.

A: Are the containers temperature-controlled?

B: Yes. They are also watertight and airtight to protect goods from being damaged by heat, water or dampness. The containers can be opened at both ends, so that loading and unloading can be made at the same time.

A：我想谈谈所订货物的运输问题。

B：货物先由集装箱船运往香港，在香港转船运往洛杉矶。

A：集装箱船？

B：是的。集装箱运输更快、更安全、更便利，还可以省下一笔包装费和运输费。

A：如果我的货不满一整箱怎么办？

B：集装箱码头将会根据货物的卸货港和货物的类别进行拼箱。

A：这需要时间吧，我担心……

B：别担心。不需要太多的时间的。我们会密切关注，一定会确保你方准时收到货物。

A：我们如何知道货物已经发运了呢？

B：我公司会与船运公司一直保持联系。我们有着密切的业务往来。

A：集装箱是恒温的吗？

B：对，同时集装箱还防水、密封，货物不会受热、受潮。集装箱两端都能打开，所以能同时装卸货。

催促交货

A: If we place an order now, when can you ship the goods?
B: I am afraid the earliest should be in October. We've already had a lot of orders at hand. Nothing can be fulfilled beyond the production schedule.
A: Is there any possibility for you to arrange a prompt shipment before October? I am afraid our stock doesn't allow us to wait too long.
B: Well, as this is our first transaction, I wish we can make a deal. We will try our best to advance the shipment before October. Perhaps some other orders will be cancelled. We'll keep you informed.
A: Let me put it in this way. We concluded the deal on an FOB basis. Even if you deliver the goods at the beginning of October, we need to spend about two weeks to go through Customs. If you can do us a favor to manage a delivery two or three weeks earlier, everything will be fine and we will be able to make it.
B: The best we can do is to effect shipment at the end of September.
A: I think I have got your promise on the shipment at the end of September. That's very kind of you. I'm looking forward to receiving your advance of shipment as early as possible.
B: OK. You take my words. But your L/C should be opened early before September.
A: I promise.

A：如果我们现在订货，什么时候能够装运？
B：恐怕最早也得十月份。目前我们手上已有大量订单，我们不可能完成超过生产计划的订单。
A：有可能十月前交货吗？我们的库存恐怕撑不了太久。
B：那么，既然这是我们第一次做生意，希望能成交。我们会尽最大努力在十月前交货。其余的一些订单可能会取消。我想你方明白这点。
A：这么说吧。我们按FOB价成交。尽管你方于十月初交货，我方还需要两星期办理通关。如果你方能帮忙提前两到三星期交货，一切会很顺畅。
B：我们只能做到九月底发货。
A：我想我们已经得到你方九月底交货的承诺。太谢谢了。期待尽早收到你方的装运通知。
B：好。我们决不食言。但是你方信用证必须早于九月开出。
A：我保证。

口语秘笈

在哪里装货、在哪里卸货，这个问题可要讨论清楚。不然运费的多少是小事，不能及时到货可就是大事了，所以"A timely delivery means a lot to us."（及时交货对我们来说关系可大了。）应时常挂在嘴边。

空运药品

A: Now instead of sea transportation, we are going to arrange the railroad transportation for the medicine.
B: But won't it still take weeks from here to the last destination? Our end users want them to arrive in a few days.
A: So what you mean is to ship the medicine by air freight?
B: Yes, that's what I want.
A: But it's difficult to book the shipping space with the Civil Aviation Administration of China within such a short time.
B: I know you have difficulties and I hate to bring you any extra trouble. But our goods are really something that must meet a dyer need. So I insist on their being transported through airway.
A: If you insist, so I'll try my best to meet your demand.
B: Thank you very much.

A：我们不打算海运，准备通过铁路来运送你们的药品。
B：可是从这里到目的地，火车不得走几个星期吗？我们的客户希望几天内就能拿到货。
A：那么你的意思是空运这批药品？
B：对，我正是这个意思。
A：可是时间这么短，我们很难在中国民航订到舱位。
B：我们知道你们有困难，我也不想给你们添麻烦，可是我们订的药品确实是急需之物品，因此我还是坚持空运。
A：如果你坚持，我将尽力满足你的要求。
B：非常感谢。

海陆联运

A: I propose multi-model combined transport by rail and sea. The goods can be carried first by rail from Beijing to Tianjin and then by sea from Tianjin to Hamburg.
B: The combined transport may cause a delay in shipment or even lose the goods completely. Besides, the formalities are too complicated.
A: The facilities for shipping goods to European countries have changed a lot in the last few years. Lately, we have been able to transship European-bound cargoes from rail to ship at Tianjin without mishaps. As to formalities, we'll handle them at our end.

A：我提议采用铁路运输和海上运输相结合的联运方式。先通过火车将货物运到天津，然后通过海运从天津运往汉堡。
B：联运可能会误船期，也可能导致货物完全丢失，而且手续也太复杂了。
A：近几年，出口到欧洲国家的货物的运输条件已经得到了大大改善。在天津转船到欧洲，从未发生过任何麻烦。至于手续问题，由我

B: Well, in that case, we have to pay extra transportation charges.

A: No, all transshipment charges will be included in the CIF price. Besides, it is more simple and cheaper for both of us to arrange multi-model combined transport.

B: All right. But we'll not pay until we get the shipping documents for the transshipment of the goods from Tianjin.

A: Certainly, we'll also telephone you the vessel's name, departure time from Tianjin and the number of the B/L as soon as we can.

方负责。

B：那么，转运我们得多付运费吧？

A：不是的，转运的费用已经包含在 CIF 价里面了。这样的联运对彼此都好。

B：好吧，但是见不到天津的货轮单据，我们不能付款。

A：当然。我们会尽快电话告知你们船名，天津起航日和提单号。

口语秘笈

持有不同意见时要明确表示，不应模棱两可。如："I'm totally against the proposal of making transshipment at Hong Kong."（我完全反对在香港转船的建议。）。

转船注意事项

A: Is it necessary for us to ask the exporter to ship on a vessel sailing directly to the port of discharge?

B: You know, transshipment adds to the risk of damage and breakage and also delays arrival.

A: What are the factors we should pay attention to if transshipment is necessary?

B: There are two important factors. The first thing is that we should arrange with the shipping company so that we can decide on a good carrier.

A: As many clean bills of lading state, the steamship company's liability for the goods terminates upon discharge from its vessels. Is that what you mean?

B: Yes, and second, we should instruct our shipper to ship the goods to the nearest inland point,

A：我们是否有必要请求出口商用船运货直抵卸货港？

B：你知道，转船容易增加损毁和破裂的风险，而且会延误到货期。

A：如果必须转船的话，我们得注意什么要点呢？

B：有两项重要因素。第一，我方安排船运公司，由此我们可以选定一个满意的承运人。

A：如清洁提单所述，船运公司对货物负有的责任待货物卸载完毕便予以解除。你是这个意思吧？

B：是的。第二，我方指令托运人将货物运至最近的内陆地点而不是将

instead of transshipping the goods to the port of shipment.

A: I see.

| 货转运至装运港。 |
| A：我明白了。 |

口语秘笈

提单是最重要的运输单据，谈判中明确区别不同种类的提单有重要意义。类似表达应牢记于心："The bill of lading should be marked as 'freight prepaid'."（提单上应该注明"运费预付"字样。）。

限期交货和分批装运

A: Now that we have reached an agreement on the packing, we can go to the next problem—hipment. What's your opinion?

B: That's good. Would you tell me when and how you ship the goods?

A: We usually ship the goods by regular liners.

B: For this lot, could you consider prompt shipment? It is badly needed by our users.

A: No, I'm afraid it's difficult for us to do so because we can't get all the goods from our manufacturers soon.

B: Are there any flexible ways?

A: In order to make it easier for us to get the goods ready for shipment, we hope that partial shipment will be allowed.

B: Would you please deliver them all at one time? We are ordering for the festival, or we will miss the selling season.

A: Sorry, we can't ship them all at the same time because it so happens that there is no direct steamer from here to your port in these two months. I was informed by our shipping department yesterday that liner space for America up to the end of next month has been fully booked up. I'm afraid we can do nothing about it.

A：既然我们已经就包装问题达成了一致，接下来我们谈谈运输问题吧。您意下如何？

B：好。能说说你们打算什么时候、如何装运吗？

A：我们通常使用班轮运输货物。

B：对于这批货，你方能否考虑即期装运？我们的客户急等着这批货呢。

A：不行。恐怕很难即期发货，因为我方无法短期内从厂商那拿到所有的货。

B：有什么变通的方式吗？

A：为了更方便我方备货待运，我们希望能够允许分批装运。

B：你方能否一次性交付？我们是为了赶上这个节日订的货，否则就会错过销售旺季。

A：很抱歉。未来两个月没有直达船驶往你方港口，我方无法一次性交货。昨天我接到公司运输部的通知，直到下个月末，发往美国的班轮舱位已全部订满。我们也无能为力。

> **口语秘笈**
>
> 贸易中，出于礼貌，往往避免正面拒绝对方。因此，有不同意见时一定要注意表达方式上的委婉。可以说"We're not prepared to accept your proposal at this time."（我们这一次不准备接受你们的建议。）有时，还要讲明拒绝的理由，如"To be quite honest, we don't believe this product will sell very well in China."（说老实话，我们不相信这种产品在中国会卖得好。）。

数量货差和装运通知

A: Do you allow any quantity difference when the goods are loaded on board the ship?

B: Yes, there may be some difference, but it can't exceed 5% of the quantity stipulated.

A: How do we calculate the difference?

B: We'll calculate it according to the price provided in the contract at a later time.

A: The seller should bear all the costs of transportation, right?

B: Under CIF price terms, the seller is responsible for cost, insurance and freight, including any customs duties on export, as well as any service charges on goods to be exported.

A: As stipulated in the contract, I will inform you of the shipping instruction by fax within 20 days before shipment.

B: And we will send you the shipping information by cable after shipment, telling you the name of ship, expected delays, loading capacity, contract number and the shipping agents.

A: I'm very glad that we both agree upon the terms of shipment and packing.

A：你方是否允许装船时出现数量上的差异？

B：允许。可能会出现数量上的不一致，但不能超过规定数量的5%。

A：怎样计算数量差呢？

B：我们会在晚一些的时候依据合同规定的价格进行计算。

A：卖方承担运费，对吧？

B：按照CIF价格术语，卖方承担成本费、保险费和运费，其中包括出口关税和出口货物的其他服务性费用。

A：依据合同，我应该在货物装运前的20天内通过传真向你方发出装船指示。

B：装运后我方通过电报给你方发出装船通知，告知船名、预期延误期、装载容积、合同编号和运输代理商。

A：很高兴我们在运输和包装问题上达成了一致。

文化点滴

在谈判中买卖双方必须就装运时间、装运港和目的港、转船和分批装运等问题加以商定。

1. time of delivery：交货时间

   If the goods can be supplied from stock, the seller may adopt prompt delivery. Under L/C, the seller should connect the time of shipment with the opening of the L/C.

   如果是现货供应，卖方可接受"即期装运"条款。如果是信用证付款，卖方可将装运时间与信用证的开证时间结合起来。

2. port of shipment and port of destination：装运港和目的港

   Generally speaking, the port of shipment is suggested by the seller and agreed upon by the buyer.

   一般来说，装运港由卖方提出，并经买方同意后确定。

3. partial shipment and transshipment：分批装运和转运

   When large quantities are involved and ships are difficult to be chartered, the seller will propose partial shipment or transshipment.

   如果成交数量大、租船困难时，卖方应争取允许分批装运和转船。

4. shipping advice：转船通知

   The seller should immediately advise the buyer that the loading of the goods has been completed.

   一旦货物完成装运后，卖方应立即通知买方。

保险
Insurance

　　对外运输货物保险是以对外贸易货物运输过程中的各种货物作为保险标的的保险。外贸货物的运送有海运、陆运、空运以及通过邮政送递等多种途径。对外贸易运输货物保险的种类以及保险标的的运输工具种类相应分为四类：海洋运输货物保险、陆上运输货物保险、航空运输货物保险、邮包保险。有时一批货物的运输全过程使用两种或两种以上的运输工具，这时，往往以货运全过程中主要的运输工具来确定投保何种保险种类。

　　海洋运输货物保险的主要险别有：

（1）平安险（Free from Particular Average，简称 FPA）；

（2）水渍险（With Particular Average，简称 WPA）；

（3）一切险（All Risks）。

　　办理货运保险的一般程序是：确定投保的金额，填写投保单，支付保险费，取得保险单，提出索赔手续。

词语宝典

cargo insurance	运输险	insurance coverage	保险范围
average	海损	insurance premium	保险费
fine print	细则	insurance proceeds	保险收入
insurance applicant	投保人	insurance underwriter	保险承包人
the insured	被保险人	insurance amount	保险金额
insurance broker	保险经济人	insurance value	保险价值
insurance clause	保险条款	cover note	承保单
insurance company	保险公司	underwriter	保险业者
insurance conditions	保险条件		

经典句型

- If you cover an All Risks, it means you have every sort of hazard covered.
  如果你买了一份一切险，那就是说你保了所有的险种。

- Not every breakage is a particular average.
  并不是所有的破碎险都属于单独海损。

- Total loss implies the goods are lost or become worthless.
  全损是指货物都损失或变得毫无价值。

- Generally, the term "all marine risks" is liable to be misunderstood and its use should be avoided in L/C.
  一般情况下，"一切海洋运输货物险"容易被误解，应该避免在信用证中使用。

- The underwriters are responsible for any claim within the scope of cover.
  保险公司负责赔偿在保险责任范围内的索赔。

- If a W.P.A. policy does not cover small losses, it usually states that the percentage over which the loss is covered.
  如果水渍险保险并不承保小额损失，它一般都说明承保损失的百分比。

- After the goods get loaded on board, they will go to have them insured.
  装船后，他们给货物投保。

- Do the risks cover those as required or stipulated?
  投保险别与要求或规定的是否相符？

- What's the duration of the insurance?
  保险的有效期是多久？

- Are the number and other details on the insurance documents consistent with the other shipping documents presented?
  保险单据上的件数和其他细节是否与提交的其他货运单据一致？

- According to co-insurance clauses, the insured person must pay usually 20 percent of the total expenses covered.
  根据共同保险条款，保险人通常必须付全部费用的20%。

- Insurance broker can quote rates for all types of cargo and risks.
  保险经纪人会开出承保各类货物的各种险别的费用。

- We have covered the goods against F.P.A. for the amount of $ 30,000 with PICC.
  我们已向中国人民保险公司为货物投保平安险，金额为3万美元。

- Please cover insurance on this shipment against W.P.A. for the amount of USD 25,000 with the PICC.
  请向中国人民保险公司为这批货物投保金额为25,000美元的水渍险。

- Please cover the goods for 110% of the invoice value against all risks.

请按发票金额的 110% 为货物投保一切险。

- Please cover this lot (shipment) for 45,000 Euros.
  请为这批货物投保金额为 4.5 万欧元的保险。

- We usually cover the goods against W.P.A. and War Risk.
  我们将按一般惯例投保水渍险和战争险。

- It is our usual practice to cover against F.P.A. and T.P.N.D. on CIF basis.
  在 CIF 条件下,我方一般只投保平安险加偷盗险。

- We suggest that you cover the insurance with PICC.
  我方建议你方向中国人民保险公司投保。

- We'll accept your request for insurance to be covered up to the inland city but the extra premium is borne by you.
  我们接受你们的要求,将保险延伸到内陆城市,但额外的保费要由你们支付。

- Insurance rates vary with different types of cargo and risk.
  保险费率根据货物种类和险别的不同而不同。

- I am sorry but the loss in question is beyond the coverage granted by us.
  很抱歉,但是这个损失不在我方承保的范围内。

- Among these kinds of risks, you can choose the proper one suiting your consignment.
  在这些险别中,你可以选择适合你货物的险别进行投保。

时尚对白

咨询复杂的共同海损条件

A: How do you do, Mr. Yang?
B: How do you do, Mr. Smith? What can I do for you?
A: Yes, I've made a careful study of your new Ocean Marine Cargo Clauses and found something I don't quite understand. Will you be so kind as to explain them to me?
B: With pleasure. What is it?
A: It is concerning Total Loss. Does it mean goods must be totally lost or irretrievably lost?
B: Under the Total Loss Condition, we shall be

A:您好,杨先生。

B:您好,史密斯先生。需要帮忙吗?

A:是的。我仔细研究了一下新的海洋货物条款,有些新的内容不太明白。您能帮我解释一下吗?

B:很高兴能够帮上忙。什么问题啊?

A:是关于全部海损的。全部海损的意思是不是要求货物已全部缺失或已造成无可挽回的损失?

liable to pay the claims when the insured goods are totally destroyed or the assured is deprived of the possession of the insured foods.

A: What should be done if there are total losses that due to a natural calamity which is not specified in the Clause?

B: Well, sometimes, this kind of loss does occur due to pouring rain without any blast for instance. It seems a bit complicated as the scope of natural calamities is limited to heavy weather, lightning for example and claims may be dealt with according to the local practice.

A: What evidence would be acceptable to you to demonstrate heavy weather? Would a Master's Protest be sufficient?

B: In general, the captain's Sea Protest will be considered as a sufficient evidence of heavy weather.

A: Thank you very much for your detailed explanations.

B: Don't mention it.

B：根据全部海损条款，当被保货物全部损坏或投保人被剥夺了被保货物的所有权，我们负责赔偿。

A：由非约定的自然灾害所造成的全部损失该如何处理？

B：嗯，有时候确实会发生这样的损失，比如没有风的倾盆大雨。这有点儿复杂，因为自然灾害的范畴局限于恶劣天气，如闪电，这样的索赔按当地惯例处理。

A：恶劣天气需要出具什么样的证据？大副收据够不够？

B：通常，船长的海难声明被当做有利的恶劣天气证明。

A：感谢您的详尽解释。

B：不用客气。

口语秘笈

话题转换要自然、流畅。"What shall we discuss next? I suggest we have a word about insurance."（我们接下来讨论什么呢？我建议谈谈保险问题。）提醒对方注意的同时，引出自己的话题。

介绍中国人民保险公司

A: Well, could you tell me more about PICC?

B: You mean?

A: Some basic information like the major categories of risks that PICC covers.

B: Usually we use sea transportation for our goods. PICC provides three basic categories of risks: F.P.A., W.P.A. and All Risks. The insurance can

A：您能多讲一讲中国人民保险公司的情况吗？

B：您是指什么？

A：一些基本信息比如中国人民保险公司承保的主要险种目录？

B：通常我们的货物从海路运输。中国人民保险公司提供三个主要险种：

cover the whole way of transit.

A: And what shall I do if an insurance claim happens?

B: When you buy the insurance, your insurance policy will designate a claim settlement agent to you. To make a claim, you apply for an inspection from your agent firstly. Then you can submit your formal claim to PICC with all required documents including insurance policy, bills of lading, invoice, and packing list. Don't forget your list of claim.

A: Thank you. I will know more about PICC as we develop our business in China.

A：如果出险我该做什么？

B：当你买保险时，你的保险单会指定一家投诉处理机构。投诉时，你先向这家机构申请检查。然后你能向中国人民保险公司提交正式投诉，同时附上所有必要的文件，包括保险单、提货单、发票和装箱单。别忘了你的投诉单。

A：谢谢。随着我们在中国业务的发展我将会深入了解中国人民保险公司。

单独海损不赔的平安险，单独海损赔付的水渍险和全险。保险能给货物全程保险。

 如何填写保单

A: What do we need to pay particular attention to in presenting the insurance document?

B: Firstly, you must make sure the insurance document indicates the cover is effective from the date of loading or from taking the goods by the carrier.

A: Secondly?

B: The information in the insurance document concerning mode of transport and transport route must be consistent with the documentary credit.

A: OK. What else do we need to ensure?

B: The insurance document must specify coverage for either CIF or CIP value of the shipment, or at least 110% of the gross amount of the invoice.

A: What about the currency of the insurance document?

B: You must make sure that the currency of the insurance document must be in consistency with

A：在提交保险单方面我们需要注意什么问题？

B：首先，您必须确保保险单据表明保险是从商品装船之日或承运人接管商品之日起生效。

A：第二呢？

B：保险单据上有关运输方式和运输路线的信息必须和跟单信用证完全一致。

A：好的。我们还需要确保别的什么？

B：保险单据必须规定保险金额至少是该批货物的 CIF 或 CIP 价，或发票总金额的 110%。

A：保险单据的计价货币怎样？

B：您必须确保保险单据的货币和信用证的完全一样。也就是说，它们

the credit. Namely, they should be the same currency so as to eliminate exchange rate risks.

A: Finally, should the insurance document be endorsed?

B: Of course, it must be properly endorsed as it is required to do so in the credit.

A: Thanks a lot.

B: You are welcome.

A: 应该是同一种货币，以便减少汇率风险。

A: 最后，保险单需要背书吗？

B: 当然，必须按照信用证的要求适当地背书。

A: 多谢。

B: 不用谢。

 讨论保险金额

A: I'm sorry I have to mention this again. After a second thought I think we'd better have the insurance of the goods covered at 130% of the invoice value. Do you think that can be done?

B: I think so, but please note that our insurance coverage is at 110% of the invoice value only, therefore, the premium for the difference between 130% and 110% should be on your account.

A: I see. Then, how about your covering All risks and War Risk at 130% of the invoice value with the PICC?

B: I'll do that. You can rest assured that we will have the goods insured as soon as they are shipped.

A: 很抱歉我又提起这事。经过仔细考虑之后，我认为最好将这批货按发票金额的130%来投保。你觉得可以吗？

B: 可以。但请注意，我们的保险范围只是发票金额的110%。因此，如果要求更高的险别，130%到110%之间的保险费差额将由你方负担。

A: 我明白。那么请按发票金额的130%向中国人民保险公司投保综合险和战争险。

B: 我会照办的。一旦货物发出，我会立即投保，这点请尽管放心。

 保险单和保险凭证

A: Should the insurance document be issued as a policy or a certificate?

B: An insurance certificate should be issued as it is clearly stipulated in the L/C.

A: In case an insurance policy is presented, what will banks do with it?

B: Banks are entitled to refuse to honor the presented documents.

A: 保险单据应该签发为保险单还是保险凭证？

B: 应该签发为保险证，因为这是信用证上明确规定的。

A: 在这种情况下，万一提交的是保险单，银行将如何处置？

B: 银行有权拒绝承兑提示的单据。

A: Since these two types of insurance documents have the same legal force, why do banks refuse their payment?

B: Because UCP600 specifies that banks will not honor documents presented to them if these documents are not in conformity with the terms and conditions of an L/C on their surface.

A: That is to say, we must be very careful in preparing such a document.

B: You are absolutely right. In addition, to be safer, we also need to ensure the insurance document to be insured and signed by an underwriter, not by a broker.

A: All right. We will be very cautious in the preparation of the insurance document.

A：既然两种保险单据具有同等法律效力，银行为何会拒付？

B：因为信用证统一条例600规定，如果单据表面上与信用证条款不相符，银行将拒付出具的单据。

A：也就是说，制作这样的单据必须非常仔细。

B：完全正确。此外，为了更加安全，我们还需要确保保险单据是由承运人而不是由经纪人签发签字的。

A：好的。我们会十分谨慎地制单的。

 ## 介绍三种基本险

A: What's the difference between F.P.A. and W.P.A.?

B: W.P.A. covers you against partial loss in all cases, while an F.P.A. policy only covers you against total loss in the case of minor perils such as damage by sea water, though it covers you against partial loss in the case of major perils such as sinking, collision and fire.

A: We were insured for All Risks because I think with All Risks, we are covered for everything.

B: Not quite so, it is true that "All Risks" is of the broadest coverage, but it does not really cover all risks. For instance, the "All Risks" clause excludes coverage against damage caused by war, strikes, riots…

A: Thank you very much for explaining the insurance clauses. Well, with whom do you say can I claim for losses through rough handling in transit or during unloading? Insurance company?

B: As I see it, the insurance company may well turn

A：平安险和水渍险有什么区别？

B：水渍险在任何情况下都包含部分损失，平安险只有在发生较小的风险，如因海水侵蚀受损这类危险时，才包赔全部损失，而在发生较大的例如沉船、碰撞以及失火的危险时只赔付部分损失。

A：我们只投保了一切险，因为我认为一切险有利于抵御所有的风险。

B：并不完全是这样。虽然一切险是投保范围最广的险别，它却并不保障所有的风险。比如，战争、罢工及民变等造成的损失就不在一切险的承保围内。

A：十分感谢您为我做的保险条款的解释。运输或卸货过程中由于粗鲁搬运造成的损失，您认为我应向谁索赔呢？保险公司吗？

B：在我看来，保险公司完全可以拒绝

down to pay for the damage thus caused.
A: Why?
B: Obviously, because it is the shipping company that caused the damage. The responsibility should rest with them, don't you think so?
A: Well, thank you very much for all the information.
B: It's my pleasure.

赔偿由此造成的损失。
A：为什么呢？
B：很明显，损坏是由船运公司造成的，责任当然应由船运公司承担，您说呢？
A：非常感谢您为我们提供的这些信息。
B：不客气。

达人点拨

投保时应注意的问题主要有：根据货物的性质和包装，选择适当的投保险别；根据具体情况，加适当的附加险；确定保险金额；支付保险费；取得保险单或保险凭证；注重保险索赔。

为易碎品投保

A: I have a batch of porcelain ware to be shipped to New Zealand. What risks should be covered?
B: Here is a broad range of coverage against all kinds of risks for sea transportation, such as F.P.A., W.P.A., All Risks and Extraneous Risks.
A: Which one will you recommend me to take?
B: In view of the special features of your consignment, I advise you to take W.P.A. and additional coverage against Risk of Breakage.
A: Sounds reasonable. What about the insurance premium?
B: The premium is to be calculated in this way. First find out the premium rate for porcelain, which is 0.3%. Secondly, consider what risks are covered. What you've covered is W.P.A. plus Risk of Breakage. So the total premium is…
A: Good. Thank you for your assistance.

A：我有一批瓷器要运往新西兰。应该投保什么险？
B：这是一系列海运险种。平安险、水渍险、一切险和附加险。
A：你建议我保哪个呢？
B：考虑到你方货物的特殊性，我建议你投保水渍险和附加险中的破裂险。
A：很有道理。保险费怎样计算？
B：保险费是这样算的。首先找出瓷器对应的保险费率，0.3%。其次，考虑投保的险别。你投保的是水渍险和破碎险，因此总的保险费是……
A：好的，谢谢你的帮助。

口语秘笈

对于你不知道，或不知道怎么回答的话，一律用"It's hard to explain now. Could we have a discussion later?"（现在很难说清楚，我们一会儿再讨论吧？）另外多踢皮球，介绍你的同事来帮你解围"I will introduce you my peer who is in charge of it."（负责该项事务的同事将来为您解答。）。

投保一切险

A: Now, let's discuss what type of risk we need to cover. B: OK. If we are required to choose from F.P.A., W.P.A. and All Risks, we hope to cover All Risks. Do you agree with us? A: Yes, we do. But we think it is better to cover All Risks plus War Risks, Strikes and Riots. B: Why so? A: The reason is that the so-called "All Risks" doesn't include coverage against war, strikes, riots, etc. B: I see. But won't it mean there will be more premium? A: Yes, of course. However, it is worthwhile to do so. B: You are correct.	A：现在，我们讨论一下我们需要投保哪种险别吧？ B：好的。如果我方从平安险、水渍险和一切险中选择的话，我们希望投保一切险。你说呢？ A：是的，我同意。不过，我们认为最好投保一切险加上战争、罢工和暴乱险。 B：为什么呢？ A：这是因为所谓的"一切险"是并不包括战争、罢工、暴乱等险种。 B：我明白了。不过，这不就意味着我们应该支付更多的保费吗？ A：当然。不过，这样做是值得的。 B：你说得对。

 文化点滴

保险谈判技巧

1．在保险谈判中，双方必须清楚合同中接受什么样的价格条件。
2．在谈判过程中，双方必须牢记清楚、准确地指明在国际结算中需要哪一种具体的保险单据。
3．在谈判中，双方还须确保所投保的金额是充分的，而且投保的计价货币是正确的。

投保时应注意的问题主要有：
1) 根据货物的性质和包装，选择适当的投保险别；
2) 根据具体情况，加保适当的附加险；
3) 确定保险金额；
4) 支付保险费；
5) 取得保险单或保险凭证；
6) 注重保险索赔。

49

商品检验
Commodity Inspection

商品检验是国际贸易发展的产物。它随着国际贸易的发展成为商品买卖的一个重要环节，同时也是买卖合同中不可缺少的一项内容。商品检验体现着不同国家对进出口商品实施的品质管制。这种管制在出口商品生产、销售和进口商品按既定条件采购等方面发挥积极作用。

我国进出口商品检验工作主要有四个环节：

（1）接受报验；（2）抽样；（3）检验；（4）签发证书。

商品检验类型主要有：包装检验、品质检验、卫生检验、安全性能检验。

词语宝典

inspect	检验	inspection certificate	检验证书
inspection	检验	notary public	公证行
to inspect A for B	检查 A 中是否有 B	inspector of tax	税务稽查员
inspector	检验员	inspection of commodity	商品检验

经典句型

- The certificates of quality and weight issued by the bureau shall be final and binding upon both parties.
  由该局签发的品质和重量证书将是终局性的，对双方都具有约束力。

- Shall we take up the question of inspection today?
  今天咱们讨论商品检验问题吧。

- The inspection of commodity is no easy job.
  商检工作不是那么简单。

- Mr. Black is talking with the Chinese importer about inspecting the goods.
  布莱克先生与中方进口商就商品检验问题进行洽谈。

- You should engage a surveyor.
  你们应该联系公证员。

- It is complicated to get goods inspected and reinspected.
  货物检验和被检验很复杂。

- As an integral part of the contract, the inspection of goods has its special importance.
  作为合同里的一个组成部分，商品检验具有其特殊的重要性。

- The certificate will be issued by Entry-Exit Inspection and Quarantine Bureau of the People's Republic of China or by any of its branches.
  检验证明书将由中国出入境检验检疫局或其分支机构出具。

- And as you may know, CCIB enjoys a great popularity in the world for its impartiality.
  你知道，中国商检局的公正全球闻名。

- By the way, don't forget to have a duplicate sample sealed after the inspection.
  另外，不要忘记检验以后封存一份复样。

- We should inspect this batch of porcelain ware to see if there is any breakage.
  我们要检查一下这批瓷器是否有破损的。

- The exporters have the right to inspect the export goods before delivery to the shipping line.
  出口商在向船运公司托运前有权检验商品。

- Where do you wish to reinspect the goods?
  你希望在哪里复验商品？

- We have subjected the goods to strict inspection before shipment.
  货物装运之前必须经过严格检验。

- The inspection should be completed within a month after the arrival of the goods.
  商品检验工作在到货后一个月内完成。

- Usually, the inspection at the destination should be taken as final.
  通常来讲，目的港的检验被认为是终局的。

- How should we define the inspection rights?
  商检的权利怎样加以明确呢？

- I'm worried that there might be some disputes over the results of inspection.
  我担心商检的结果会产生争议。

- Clauses on quality and inspection must be defined before the contract is signed and concluded.
  合同敲定和签订前必须明确质量和检验条款。

- We'll accept the goods only if the results from the two inspections are identical

with each other.
如果双方的检测结果一致，我们就收货。

- Inspection shall be made by sampling.
  应该根据抽样来进行检验。

- China Import and Export Commodity Inspection Bureau is taken as one of the best surveyors.
  中国进出口商品检验局被认为是最好的公证行之一。

时尚对白

检验与复检

A: Let's discuss the matter of inspection in detail.
B: Good.
A: We'd like to have the cargo inspected at the port of destination.
B: We won't object to it, but you have to choose a reliable organization.
A: That can be arranged.
B: The inspection shall be done within one month after the arrival of the goods. Otherwise, we'll consider the goods as accepted.
A: We agree.
B: If you have any discrepancies after the reinspection, please inform us within two weeks.
A: We'll see to it. Do you also agree to reinspect at the CFS? You know it is very difficult to have the equipment inspected at the port.
B: All right.

A：我们详细谈谈检验的问题吧。
B：好。
A：我们想在目的港检验商品。
B：我方不反对，但必须选择可信赖的机构。
A：可以。
B：而且检验必须在到货一个月内进行，否则我方将认为货物已被接受。
A：我方同意。
B：复检之后如有任何不一致的地方，请在两周内通知我方。
A：我们会注意的。你们是否也同意在集装箱货场进行复检？你知道，很难在目的港检验设备。
B：没问题。

由商品检验局进行检验

A: We want the goods to be inspected at the port

A：我方希望在目的港对货物进行检验。

of destination.

B: We agree, but the goods must be inspected by an inspection organization acceptable to us.

A: I think the China Commodity Inspection Bureau is acceptable to you.

B: Yes, we respect it.

A: We want to draw your attention to the fact that the certificates of quality and weight issued by the bureau shall be final and binding upon both parties.

B: I see. What we want to emphasize is that the method used in the inspection shall be the same as stipulated in the contract.

A: You can rest assured of that.

B: And don't forget to have a duplicate sample sealed after the inspection.

B：同意，但我们要求必须是由我方认可的检验机关进行检验。

A：我相信中国商品检验局是可以接受的吧。

B：是的，我们很相信该局。

A：请注意该局所签发的重量和质量检验证书是终局性的，且对我们双方都有约束力。

B：我明白。我们所强调的是检验方法必须与合同规定的一致。

A：尽请放心。

B：不要忘了检验之后留存复样。

 抱怨粗鲁搬运

A: Hi, Miss Cheng. How is the shipment?

B: Nice to hear your voice, Brown. The consignment is here already. But we found some problems.

A: What's wrong? We had executed the stipulations of the contract strictly.

B: Take it easy, Mr. Brown. It is not your problem. Upon arrival, some bottles were found broken. We engaged the Dalian Commodity Inspection Bureau as the surveyor. Their inspection certificate states that the fruit juice inside is inedible.

A: How could that be?

B: The shipping company is determined as guilty for their careless loading and unloading. Since we made the deal on the basis of FOB, we are negotiating with the shipping company and expecting their reply.

A: Well, I am sorry to hear that. If there is anything we can do, just let us know.

A：陈小姐，你好。货物怎么样？

B：很高兴听到你的声音，布朗。货物已经到了。但我们发现一些问题。

A：出了什么问题？我们严格地执行了合同中的条款。

B：不用着急，布朗先生。不是你们的问题。到货时发现有些瓶子碎了。我们请大连商检局做了检验。检验证书表明瓶中的果汁不宜食用。

A：怎么会发生这样的事情？

B：船运公司应该为其粗鲁的装卸负责任。由于我们是按FOB价成交的，我们正在和船运公司协商并等待他们的答复。

A：很遗憾听到这样的事情发生。如果有什么我们能帮上忙的，请尽管开口。

要求法文版的检验证书

A: In addition to the certificate you mentioned, could we have another one showing the goods to be free from radioactive contamination? You see, some of our clients are very sensitive about this.
B: Your request is understandable. Well, I'll get in touch with the Inspection Bureau and see what they have to say.
A: That would be very kind of you. And we'd like to have a copy of each of the certificate in French.
B: As a rule, our certificates are made out in Chinese and English.
A: Oh, I see. A copy in English would do as well. And the certificate will be signed by the commissioner of your Bureau, am I right?
B: Our certificates are made valid through the official seal and personal chop of the commissioner.
A: I see. Thank you for your explanation.
B: Don't mention it.

A：除了您刚才提到的那个证明外，能不能再出具一张证明货物没有受到放射线污染的证书？您知道，我们的一些客户对这一点很敏感。
B：您的要求可以理解。好吧，我联系一下商检局，看看他们有什么意见。
A：非常感谢。而且我们希望每一张证书都能有个法文版。
B：通常我们的证书都是用中英文开复的。
A：哦，我懂了。英文版本也可以。证书应由商检局局长签字吧？
B：检验证书以加盖公章和局长私人章为有效。
A：我明白了。谢谢。
B：别客气。

 调整检验条款

A: Well, I'd like to modify the inspection clause first.
B: Why?
A: I am sorry to tell you that most of the chicken sent last time failed to reach the standard you have promised. Therefore, we hope the quality shall be determined by inspection organization and the certificate thus issued shall be taken as final in the coming year.
B: But we concluded the business following our usual practice last time.
A: Yes. But I am afraid the quality certificate issued by your inspection bureau is not fully trustworthy.

A：我们想更先改检验条款。
B：为什么？
A：很抱歉地告诉你们，上次大部分鸡肉不符合你们承诺的标准。因此，我们希望明年由我方的检验机构来检验，其签发的质量证书是终局的。
B：但是我们上次是按照惯例成交的。
A：是的，但是我们认为你们检验机

B:Do you have any evidence to prove it?
A:Well, we have the impression that the chicken was not up to our standards after our inspection, which has led to our loss.
B:If you don't have any evidence, I think we cannot accept your demand for modifying the inspection clause.
A:We will show you the relevant evidence in a few days.
B:Well, wait for your news.

构颁发的质量证书不能完全信赖。

B：你有什么证据？

A：我们还记得，检验完货物后，鸡肉的不达标给我们造成了损失。

B：如果你方没有任何证据，我方无法接受你们更改检验条款的要求。

A：过几天我们会寄给你相关证据。

B：那我们等你们的信儿。

口语秘笈

在商务谈判中，有些时候不能给对方一个确切的答案，但是又不能一口否定，那么要使谈判有回旋的余地就得回避明确的答复。"I'm afraid I can't give you a definite reply now."（恐怕我现在无法给你一个明确的答复。）或 "We are still a little unsure about the prospect, though."（不过，我们对于前景还是有点儿不能确定。）。

以装船质量、数量、重量为准

A:There's still one minor point to be cleared up.
B:Yes?
A:Yesterday you remarked that you sell on shipped quality, quantity and weight.
B:So we did. The goods will be inspected by the China Commodity Inspection Bureau, who will then issue a certificate of quality and a certificate of weight. These will be taken as final and binding.
A:But how about shortweight or disqualification?
B:I assure you that is not going to happen. Our goods must be up to the standards before the Commodity Inspection Bureau releases them.
A:I know your products have a good reputation. But what if there is shortweight or disqualification?

A：还有一个小问题需要澄清。

B：什么？

A：你昨天说你方收货以装船质量、数量和重量为准，对吧？

B：是的。货物由中国商品检验局进行检验，出具质量和重量检验证书。这些证书是终局的并对双方都有约束力。

A：但如果出现短重或质量不合格怎么办？

B：我方保证不会出现这种情况。我们的货物只有达到了出口标准，商检局才能放行。

A：我方知道贵方商品信誉良好，但万一出现短重或质量不达标怎

B:In that case I don't think the responsibility should rest with us. The goods must be spoiled or the weight gets short during transit. A claim would then be lodged with the insurance company.

A:I see.

B：那样的话，我方不承担责任。货物可能在运输途中发生破损或缺失，应向保险公司索赔。

A：我明白了。

 讨论检验条款

A:There is another point we have to discuss and clear up. That's inspection. How will the clause of inspection be stipulated in the contract?

B:The goods will be inspected by the Dalian Commodity Inspection Bureau at the port of departure. And the Certificate of Quality and Quantity shall be issued.

A:Do you mean that you sell on shipped quality and quantity?

B:Yes.

A:But I'm worried about the disqualification or short-weight on arrival.

B:Please rest assured. Our goods must be up to export standards before the certificates are released. You know, the Dalian Commodity Inspection Bureau enjoys high reputation all over the world.

A:I never doubted it. Yet we have the right to reinspect the goods at the port of discharge.

B:Of course. But the reinspection should be made within 7 days upon arrival and if any discrepancies are found, you may lodge claims with us within 30 days. This is international practice.

A:I wish that would not occur.

B:Nor do I.

A:Well, I'm clear now. Thank you so much for being patient with me.

B:Don't mention it.

A：还有一点我们需要讨论并明确。那就是检验事宜。我们在合同中怎么规定检验条款？

B：该货物在离岸港由大连商检局检验并出具品质证明和数量证明。

A：你是说按照装运时的品质和数量出口？

B：对。

A：但我担心货物到达时出现品质不合格或短量。

B：放心吧。在检验证书出具之前，我们的货物必须符合出口标准。你知道，大连商检局在世界上享有盛誉。

A：这一点我从不怀疑。但我们有权在卸货港复检。

B：当然。但复检应在7天内进行。如有异议，你们可以在30天内向我方提出索赔。这是国际惯例。

A：我不希望发生这样的事。

B：我也不希望。

A：现在清楚了。谢谢你这么有耐心。

B：别客气。

如何进行复检

A: As for inspection, our practice has proved to be quite reasonable and has been accepted by our customers.
B: Yes, I think so. But when should the reinspection be made?
A: For this item, it's international practice that the reinspection should be made within 10 days upon the arrival and if any discrepancy is found, claims must be raised within 30 days. However, claims which fall within the responsibility of the shipping company and underwriters shall not be entertained.
B: When the reinspection is made, can we appoint any authentic surveyor without your approval?
A: In order to carry out the contract smoothly and avoid any unnecessary disputes, it's best to name the inspection agency which shall be approved by both sides and be stipulated in the contract.
B: What if the results from the two inspections do not coincide with each other?
A: We'll have a seminar of specialists and surveyors from both sides to clarify which is correct.
B: After this conference, I suppose we can resolve the differences through friendly consultation, instead of submitting the case for arbitration.
A: I hope so.

A：关于检验，我们的做法非常合理并为广大客户所接受。
B：是的，我也这样认为。但是复检应该在什么时候进行呢？
A：这种商品，国际惯例是在货物到达目的地后十天内进行复验。如果发现与合同不符则应在30天内提出索赔。然而，不受理对运输公司或承运人的索赔。
B：复验时，我方能否不经贵方同意指派可信赖的检验员？
A：为了顺利履行合同和避免发生不必要的争议，最好指定双方认可的检验机构并在合同中加以规定。
B：万一两次检验的结果不符怎办？
A：我们会成立一个研究小组，由双方选定专家和检验员，明确哪一方的检验结果是正确的。
B：会后，我想我们能够通过友好协商的形式解决分歧，而不至于提交到仲裁。
A：希望如此。

口语秘笈

任何一个冲突或误解的产生，都有潜在原因。为什么你的老客户这次不向你的公司订货？为什么对方不能达到你的要求？这种情况发生时，要立刻积极地探索原因，向对方探询"What seems to be the trouble？"（有什么困难吗？）或问一句"Is there something that needs our attention？"（有什么需要我们注意的吗？）都能表示你对事情的关切。知道问题的症结，才有办法进行沟通。

文化点滴

为保证品质条款得到执行，如果出口商是一家中国企业，则出口商应争取采用下列形式的检验条款：

1. 双方同意以装运港中国进出口商品公司所签发的品质检验证书作为最后依据，并对双方具有约束力。（It is mutually agreed that the Certificate of Quality issued by the China Import and Export Commodity Inspection Company at the port of shipment shall be regarded as final and binding upon both parties.）

2. 双方同意以装运港中国进出口商品公司所签发的品质检验证书作为交货依据，并对双方具有约束力。（It is mutually agreed that the Certificate of Quality issued by the China Import and Export Commodity Inspection Company at the port of shipment shall be taken as the basis of delivery and binding upon both parties.）

贸易实务

第二章 贸易和商业合作

Unit 1 商业代理　Business Agency
Unit 2 招标与投标　Tender
Unit 3 国际展卖　International Fairs
Unit 4 补偿贸易　Compensation Trade
Unit 5 技术转让与合作　Technology Transfer and Cooperation
Unit 6 合并与兼并　Merger and Acquisition
Unit 7 合作经营　Joint Venture
Unit 8 进出口许可证　Import and Export License
Unit 9 进口配额　Import Quota
Unit 10 通关与报关　Customs and Clearance

UNIT 1 商业代理 Business Agency

在国际贸易中,除了贸易双方直接进行业务洽谈并达成交易外,也可以根据需要选择可靠的客户建立代理关系。常见的代理是由卖方或出口方委托代理人寻找买方或进口方并开拓国外市场。委托代理人的一个重要原因是出口方可以利用代理商熟悉目标市场的特点帮助自己建立并巩固扩大出口市场。

贸易代理双方签订代理协议后,委托人即出口方授权给代理人,而后者代表前者与第三方签订合同。委托人以佣金的形式支付给代理人酬金。

常见的代理形式有三种:

独家代理:代理人经委托人的授权在特定区域和特定时期内享有独家代理销售某项协议商品的专营权。如果委托人在该区域与第三方进行直接交易,要按照协议比例给付代理人其交易额的部分作为补偿。

一般代理:代理人在特定区域只是接受委托人的委托代为销售商品,收取佣金,不享有独家代理的专营权利。

总代理:总代理被委托人授予更为广泛的权限,可以代表委托人推销商品,签订合同,还可以从事一些非商业性活动,而由委托人承担法律责任。

词语宝典

business agency	商业代理	agency territory	代理区域
exclusive agency	独家代理	agency duration	代理期限
sole agency	独家代理	currency of the agreement	合同生效期间
ordinary agency	普通代理	agency agreement	代理协议
general agency	总代理	distribution channels	分销渠道
principal	委托人	sales promotion	促销
commission	佣金	dispute settlement	争端解决

经典句型

- We would like to appoint you as our sole representative in your territory.
  我们打算请您作为我公司在贵方所在区域的独家代理。

- Can I represent a larger area?
  我代理的区域可以更大一些吗?

- Now the key issue: commission. What's your offer on that?
  现在的关键问题是佣金。您所提供的数额是多少？

- You must promise not to promote the products of our rivals that are of competitive nature.
  希望您能承诺不会推销我们竞争对手的给我方带来竞争压力的产品。

- I agree to devote my best efforts to promoting the sales of your products.
  我会不遗余力地推销贵公司的产品。

- The agreement is to run for a trial period of one year.
  该代理协议试行期为一年。

- Now do you have any arrangement about dispute settlement?
  在争端解决方面您有什么安排？

- In the case of any dispute, an arbitrator shall be appointed. That shall be in conformity with general practice.
  我们可以通过聘请一个仲裁机构来解决可能出现的争端，这符合惯例。

- Well, I believe we have discussed everything and have spelt out all the obligations and provisions.
  好了，我想我们已经讨论完了所有问题，并已详细理清了双方的责任和条款的内容。

- I suppose we can start drafting the agency agreement now.
  我想现在我们可以起草代理协议了吧。

- Party A and Party B have mutually agreed that Party A appoints Party B to act as its sales agent to sell the commodity mentioned below under the terms and conditions specified as follows.
  A、B双方已达成协议，A方委托B方为其销售代理商，按下列条件代理销售下列商品。

- Upon the expiration of the agreement and Party B's fulfillment of the total turnover mentioned in Article 1, Party A shall pay to Party B 10% commission on the basis of the aggregated amount of the invoice value against the shipments effects and relevant payment received.
  本合同期满之日，若B方已完成条款一中规定的数额，A方应按照已收到货款的全部发票的累计金额付给B方10%的佣金。

- Party B shall have the obligation to forward once every three months to Party A detailed reports on current market conditions and of consumers' comments.
  B方每三个月向A方提供一份有关市场情况和消费者意见的详细报告。

- Party B shall bear all expenses for advertising and publicity within the aforementioned territory in the duration of this agreement.
  B方在本协议有效期内，负担在协议区域内的一切广告和宣传费用。

- This agreement, when duly signed by the parties concerned, shall be enforced for one year as from January 16, 2009 to January 16, 2010.
  该协议经双方签字后生效，有效期从2009年1月16日至2010年1月16日。

- Party A shall not supply the contracted commodity to any other buyers in the above-mentioned territory.
  A方在上述的销售区域内不得对其他买主提供本协议中所规定的货物。

- For any transactions between the governments of both parties, Party A shall have right to handle such direct dealings.
  若双方政府间达成协议，A方有权进行直接贸易，而不受本协议的约束。

- Direct inquiries, if any, shall be referred to Party B.
  若有询价，应交给B方洽办。

时尚对白

力争独家代理权

A: First of all, I would like to thank you for your invitation extended to me to visit your beautiful country. I hope my visit will promote a friendship between us.

B: We have been looking forward to your visit. And it is always more convenient to discuss things face to face.

A: I would like to tell you that our clients are very interested in the toys you produce. But as far as I know, you also sell your products to some other American importers. And this tends to complicate my business. As an experienced businessman in selling toys, I have a mind to sign a sole agency agreement with you on this item for 3 years. What do you think about it?

B: We appreciate your good intention and efforts

A：首先感谢您邀请我拜访您美丽的国家，希望此次访问会增进我们双方的友谊。

B：我们一直期待着您的到访，能面对面地讨论也更方便。

A：想告诉您的是我们的客户对你们生产的玩具非常感兴趣。但是据我所知，你们的产品也销售给其他美国进口商，这会使我们的生意变得复杂了。作为一个在玩具销售方面有经验的经销商，我有意和您针对此产品签订三年期的独家代理协议，您认为怎么样？

B：非常感谢您在推销我方产品方面的好意和努力，但是据我方所知，

in pushing our products. But as far as we know, although there is a large demand in your market, the total amount of your order there is moderate. Unless you increase your turnover we can hardly appoint you as our sole agent.

A: That's what I'm going to talk about.

尽管该产品在您那里拥有庞大的市场需求，你们的订单总量都不大。除非你方增加销售额度，否则我们很难任命你方为我们的独家代理商。

A：这正是我要谈到的话题。

 争执独家代理条件

A: My proposal is this: I sell annually your toy cars 50,000 sets within the area of the whole New York market. We expect a 5% commission.

B: Don't you think this annual turnover is rather conservative for a sole agent? We propose a sole agency agreement for our toy cars for a duration of 3 years; 60,000 to be sold in the first year, 70,000 in the second year, and 80,000 in the third year, commission 5%.

A: You certainly drive a hard bargain.

B: We both understand the popularity of our toys in your market. And with the sole agency in your hands, there will be no competition and you will certainly control the market. I'm sure you will fulfill the agreement without much difficulty.

A: Well, if you put it this way, I have no objection. When shall we sign the contract?

B: Tomorrow morning.

A：我方建议：每年在纽约市场代理销售你们的玩具车50,000辆，我们期望获得5%的佣金。

B：作为独家代理您不认为这个年销售额度太保守吗？我们建议您作为我方的独家代理期限为三年，代理销售玩具车，第一年销售60,000台，第二年70,000台，第三年80,000台，佣金是5%。

A：您真是会讨价啊。

B：我们双方都知道我们的玩具在你们市场十分畅销。一旦拿到独家代理权就没有竞争对手，而你们将控制整个市场。我们相信你们履行这份代理协议不会有难度。

A：好吧，既然您这么讲，我没有异议了。我们什么时候签合同？

B：明天上午。

 讨论独家代理的权利和义务

A: We would like to appoint you as our sole agent in your territory, including Shanghai and the surrounding area. Your primary function will

A：我方有意任命你方为我方在你方销售区域的独家代理，包括上海市和周边地区。你方主要的任务是获

be to secure orders and promote sales. You should also report to us the market development periodically. In return you are paid a commission for your services.

B: Do I handle the goods myself?

A: You can leave the delivery and export procedures to us, but you must be in charge of importing formalities, such as customs clearing, storage and forwarding to the final buyers.

B: Do I have the freedom of setting the prices and selecting the models?

A: You have the freedom to set the prices, of course, but you should show concern for both the ready-selling models and the more difficult ones.

B: Do you want me to carry on sales promotion activities? If so, what support can I get from you?

A: You carry our samples and catalogues. You should be responsible for sales promotion, advertising and relative activities, not on your own but together with us. That means we supply the agent free of charge with materials and samples for publicity. And we will pay for any advertisement when it has been authorized by us.

取订单和开展促销活动，并定期向我们报告市场进展情况。我们支付给您佣金作为回报。

B：我方自己处理货物的相关事宜吗？

A：关于运输和出口手续交给我方处理，但是你们要负责进口手续，比如像通关、库存、发货给最终买家等。

B：我方是否有定价、选择样本的自由？

A：您有定价的自由，你们应兼顾畅销的和不太畅销的型号。

B：您希望我方开展促销活动，对吧？如果是这样，我们能从您那里获得什么样的支持？

A：你方从我们这里拿取样本和产品目录。你方，不是独自而是和我们一起负责促销、广告和相关的活动。这就意味着我方提供给代理商免费的样本和材料以供产品的推广。而且如果是我方授权的广告，我方将支付广告费用。

达人点拨

在双方协商代理权问题时，未来代理方应该明确这样的问题："Do I have the freedom of setting the prices and selecting the models?"（我方是否有定价和筛选样品的自由？）或是如果委托人需要代理人做产品促销，要明确在促销活动中的相关费用支配，常见的表达是："We provide the agent free of charge with materials and samples for publicity. And we will pay for any advertisement when it has been authorized by us."（我方免费提供宣传资料和样品。如果是我方授权的广告，我方支付广告费用。）。

定夺佣金和各种支出

A: Now regarding commission, what's your suggestion?

B: We pay you a commission 5% of the FOB value of all orders for our products during your duration as our sole representative, whether or not the

A：现在，关于佣金，您有何建议？

B：在你方担任我们独家代理期间，无论代理产品为你方直接销售与否，我们都按照订单的 FOB 价的 5% 支付给您作为佣金。但是佣金

orders are sent directly to you. But such commission is only payable when the goods have been paid for by customers and the payments are to be made quarterly.

A: I accept the commission, but you must pay me for any expenses involved in visiting your company at your request.

B: That's a reasonable requirement. But you must promise not to promote or sell the products of other companies of a competitive nature.

A: I agree to spare no effort to promote the sales of your products.

B: Another point, you have to pay for all traveling, office stationary, postage and administrative expenses.

A: Yes, of course.

B: Well, I think we can start drafting the agency agreement.

A：我接受该佣金，但是应你方邀请来访的开支应由你方负责吧。

B：这个要求合情合理。但是您要承诺不要促销或代销对我公司造成竞争力的其他公司的产品。

A：我们承诺会不遗余力地促进你方产品的销售。

B：另外，关于出差、办公用品、邮寄和行政管理方面的费用由你方自己支付。

A：那是当然。

B：那么，我想我们可以起草代理协议啦。

达人点拨

在代理协议中最重要的一项就是规定代理商的"commission"（佣金）啦。在佣金计算的比例和支付条件方面要尽可能地详细。比如，所参考的销售额是按照 FOB 价或是 CIF 价。佣金怎么支付呢，是在客户已经付清货款之后还是之前，付款周期多久？所以，掌握这样的对白很重要："Commission is only payable when the goods have been paid for by customers and the payments are to be made quarterly."（只有客户支付货款之后方可支付佣金，并按照季度结算。）。

如何续签独家代理权

A: I'm pleased to meet you again, Mr Green.

B: Pleased to see you too, Mr. Smith. I've come here again to renew our sole agency agreement for another 2 years.

A: You have done very well in fulfilling the agreement. And we appreciate your efforts

A：很高兴再次和您见面，格林先生。

B：我也是，史密斯先生。我再次来这儿的目的是要和您续签两年独家代理协议。

A：你方在履行协议方面做得很好。我们非常感谢您在促销我方的椅子

in pushing the sales of our chairs. You are experienced in this line.

B: Thank you.

A: But I think annual turnover of 30,000 chairs for a sole agent is rather conservative. What about an annual sale of 40,000 chairs for the new agreement?

B: No, no. That's too big a number to be acceptable. Let's put it at 35,000. And we'll strive for more, of course.

A: All right, let's fix it as 35,000 chairs then. But we would like to emphasize it again. As our sole agent, you will neither handle the same or similar products of other companies nor export the goods to the territories outside your responsibility.

B: No, certainly not. That is a reasonable restriction.

A: Another thing is that every six months we would like to receive from you a detailed report on current market conditions and the customers' comments on our products.

B: Yes, we have prepared one and I have brought it here. I'll put it forward at the meeting tomorrow.

A: Good, that's all then.

方面做的种种努力。在这方面你方的确很有经验。

B：谢谢。

A：但是我们认为作为一个独家代理，每年30,000把椅子的销售额度太过保守。在新的协议中把销售额度改为40,000您觉得如何？

B：不行。这个数额太大我们无法接受，定在35,000吧，当然我们会争取尽量多的订单。

A：好吧，那就定在35,000，但是我们想再次强调，作为独家代理，你方不能代理其他公司生产的和我们相同或类似的商品，也不可以在你方代理区域权限外出口该产品。

B：不会,当然不会。这个限制合情合理。

A：另外，我们想每隔半年收到一份来自你方的详细的市场情况报告和客户的产品使用意见反馈。

B：好。我们已经准备了一份，我随身带来了。在明天的会议上我会展示给您看。

A：很好。那就这样吧。

达人点拨

作为商品的委托人或是卖方，在签订独家代理协议时一定要反复强调您的"sole agent"（独家代理人）不能同时兼任其他同类商品的代理工作。其常见表达是："As our sole agent, your will neither handle the same or similar products of other companies."（作为我们的独家代理人，你方不可以代理其他公司的相同或类似产品。）有时，独家代理出于利益的驱动会跨越所管辖的区域行使非法代理，所以有必要提醒对方"Exporting the goods to the territory outside your responsibility is not acceptable."（我方不能接受在你代理的指定区域外出口该产品。）。

独家代理和普通代理的区别

A: Well, Mr. Smith, I'm still not clear about the

A：是这样，史密斯先生，关于独家代

difference you have mentioned between an exclusive agency and an ordinary agency. So, could you put it one more time?

B: Sure. No problem. Exclusive agency is also called sole agency, and it is an exclusive right granted by the principal to the agent. A sole agent is responsible for selling the stated commodities within the specific region and time.

A: Then, what about the seller or principal who sells the commodity himself? Would it affect possible interest of the assigned agent?

B: The exclusive agent, under the agreement, as long as he fulfills the agent agreement within the negotiated period and area, shall be paid commissions in proportion with the total sales, even if some of the goods are handled directly by the principal on his own.

A: That sounds reasonable. But where is the advantage as a sole agent over an ordinary agent?

B: Ordinary agency or agency, compared with the exclusive agency mentioned above, doesn't enjoy the exclusive business right. Under this agreement, the principal or the seller can choose one or more agents within the specified period and region. And the commissions claimed by the agent are only based on the sales he has dealt with on behalf of the principal. There is nothing to do with the direct commodity trading is done by the principal.

A: I see. Thank you so much for your help, Mr. Smith. Your explanation has really enlightened me.

 独家代理协议条款

A: To be honest, this is the first time we handle business agency. As an experienced agent, what would you suggest in our agent agreement?

B: First of all, it should identify the entrusted commodities, including name, specification, size, quantity, and the more detailed, the better.

A: OK. Then what about the next item?

B: The next part should confirm territory and time limit entrusted to me, your agent. Especially the market under my charge. You know, we have seen several disputes between agents and principals due to misunderstanding on business regions.

A: Thank you for your kind warning. I think the next item should come to obligations and rights involved in the agency. Is it right?

B: You said it. And don't forget the most important part, commissions paid to the agent. These are the basic elements to be covered in a sole agency agreement.

建议吧。

B：首先，协议里应该确定被委托的商品，包括名称、技术规格、尺寸、数量等，越详细越好。

A：好的，然后呢？

B：然后就是您的代理人确认代理的区域和期限，尤其是我所管辖的市场。您也知道，在商务领域里因为代理人和委托人之间的误解经常会发生争执。

A：谢谢您善意的提醒。下一项应该规定双方的权利和义务了吧？

B：没错。别忘了最重要的是，付给代理商的佣金条款。这些就是一份独家代理协议里包含的基本条款啦。

 ## 文化点滴

如何与日本商人打交道

1．在日本做生意，名片起着重要的作用，是建立信用的关键所在。请在背面将名片的内容翻译成日语。
2．在日本文化中，保留"面子"和一个人的荣誉以及社会地位有密切联系。如果一个人丢了颜面，哪怕是无意中造成的，都会对商务谈判产生灾难性的破坏。
3．和日本商人打交道时最好使用委婉用语。如果有必要传达或是协商一个负面信息，请通过中间人，比如将您介绍给该公司的那个人。
4．如果想和日本人做生意，要充分考虑到他们的声誉和尊严。
5．要特别尊重年长的日本商业伙伴，在日本文化中年龄和级别拥有同样的地位。
6．最佳策略是在会谈开始的最初15分钟后再讨论商务问题。
7．级别最高的人可能是在座当中最沉默的。当他们在尽量用心倾听的时候，有时会把眼合上，做睡觉状。
8．经常把"对不起"挂在嘴边上是礼貌的行为。比如，日本人会因为任何一点儿个人的疏忽而道歉。
9．日本人会遵守口头协议，可以通过点头或是一个浅浅的鞠躬来表达协议生成，而不是通过握手。
10．合同是可以谈判修订的，在日本商业规则中，一份合同不是最终的协议。

UNIT 2 招标与投标 Tender

招标和投标是一项交易的两个方面。招标是指卖方按事先通过媒体公布的通知或交易条件，公开邀请买方发盘的行为；而投标则是买方根据招标条件应邀发盘。

同其他贸易方式相比，招标属于在给定时间和地点一次性报价成交的贸易方式，双方无须进行反复磋商。

国际上常用的招标方式主要有：（1）公开招标，即整个招标活动处于公开监督之下；（2）选择性招标，又称邀请招标，即招标人根据自己的业务关系和情报资料对客商进行邀请，通过资格审查后，再由他们进行投标。

招标流程一般分为三个阶段：招标阶段、投标阶段、开标签约阶段。

词语宝典

source of funds	资金来源	cash deposit	现金投标保证金
eligible bidders	投标人资格	letter of guarantee	保证函
bidding documents	招标文件	submission of bids	标件交付
language of bid	标件语言	bid opening and evaluation	开标与评估
bid form	标单	award of contract	决标
bid prices	标价	award criteria	决标标准
bid currencies	标价货币	notification of award	中标通知
bid security	投标保证金		

经典句型

- I heard that your company is prepared to call a bid for off-shore oil exploration in the Bohai Sea.
  我听说贵公司准备就开发渤海石油进行投标。

- We shall tender for the erection of that building.
  我们将为那座大楼的兴建进行投标。

- We do not think buyer will bid a higher price.
  我们认为买方不会出比这更高的标价。

- When do you intend to open the tender?
  你们打算什么时候开标？

- The time period for the bidders to submit their bids is set temporarily.
  投标人的投标期限是暂定的。

- Before submitting the tender, we need to know all the details about the conditions for the bid.
  在投标前我们需要了解该招标条件的所有细节。

- Could you tell me something about your conditions for a bid?
  能告诉我你们的招标条件吗？

- We shall be pleased to tender for the whole project on a turnkey basis. We have the finance and know-how.
  我方愿意对整个项目进行全包全揽性的投标。我们有资金和技术。

- Just to remind you of the details of what I said earlier: we have companies in the Group, which manufacture many silicon-based products.
  只是想提醒您我之前讲话的细节：我们集团下属许多公司负责生产硅产品。

- Should the bidders make a cash deposit?
  投标人应该用现金支付保证金吗？

- Bidders need to hand in a cash deposit or a letter of guarantee from a commercial bank.
  投标人需要提交投标保证金或商业银行出具的投标保证函。

- The Purchaser prefers that certain Goods and ancillary services should be provided by the Supplier, and has accepted a bid by the Supplier for the provision of those Goods and services in the sum of USD 100,000,000 (One hundred thousand US dollars).
  买方希望供应方提供相应的货物和配套的服务，并接受了供应方的投标，提供上述货物和服务，合同总价为一亿美元。

- The Goods supplied under this contract should conform to the standards mentioned in the Technical Specifications and to the authoritative standard appropriate to the Goods' country of origin.
  本合同所供货物，必须符合技术说明中规定的标准，并适合货物的原产国制定的强制性标准。

- Within 30 days after the Supplier's receipt of notification of award of the contract, the Supplier shall furnish performance security to the Purchaser in the amount of 10% of the Contract Price.
  在供方收到中标通知后30天内，供方需向买方支付履约保证金，金额为合同金额的10%。

时尚对白

咨询投标相关信息

A: It is a great pleasure for us to have you for a visit since you are taking office in Beijing. So far, cooperation between our two corporations has been satisfactory. Of course, it will be further promoted in the future, I hope.

B: Quite right. Since China has pursued market economy, our trade performance is more flexible than before. What's more, I am very interested in the new development in China. I have heard that your company is prepared to call for a bid for a telecommunication engineering construction project in Northwest China, is that true?

A: Yes, it is time to make arrangement now for invitation to be sent out. You are well informed.

B: When do you intend to start the invitation to tender?

A: We expect to send the tender invitation sometime next week.

B: What kind of equipment would you like to buy?

A: The item we would like to buy is the advanced electronic signal submitter.

B: Have you confirmed the time set for the bidders to submit their bids?

A: The time period for bidding is temporarily set from 10th January to the end of the month.

B: To whom will the bid be sent?

A: You may send it to the International Tendering Department, China National Telecommunication Engineering Corporation, Dongcheng District, Beijing, China 100013.

A：您在北京上任后能来我公司进行访问，对此我们深感荣幸。到目前为止，我们双方的合作是愉快的，当然我希望在未来双方会有进一步合作。

B：您说得很对。自从中国推行市场经济，我们的贸易方式比以前更灵活了。而且，我非常有兴趣在中国取得新的进展。我听说贵公司打算进行招标，在中国的西北部搞电信工程建设，是真的吗？

A：是的，我们现在正打算发出招标邀请，您的消息好灵通啊。

B：您打算在什么时候开始发出招标邀请呢？

A：我们希望能在下周的某个时间发出招标邀请。

B：你们打算购买什么样的设备呢？

A：我方意欲购买技术先进的电子信号发射器。

B：已经确定了投标人的投标日期了吗？

A：暂时定在1月10日到1月31日。

B：标书应该寄给谁呢？

A：您可以按照这个地址投寄标书：中国国家电信工程公司国际招标部，中国北京东城区，邮编100013。

是否提交投标保证金

A: I've got another question. Do the bidders have to make a bid security?

B: Yes, certainly. According to the international practice, bidders need to hand in a cash deposit or a letter of guarantee from a commercial bank. If one fails to win the award, the cash deposit or the letter of guarantee shall be returned to the bidder within one week after the decision on award is declared.

A: When do you expect to open the tender, and where?

B: The 1st of March, in Beijing.

A: Is tender-opening done in public?

B: Yes, tender-opening is done publicly this time, all the bidders shall be invited to join us to supervise the opening.

A: May I know something more about the conditions for the tender?

B: Invitation shall be sent out next month, in which you can find all the details.

A: Our company is very interested in this bidding, and we will make every effort to win the award.

B: I understand how you feel. If the conditions of your tender are fully suitable for our requirement, we will accept your tender.

A: Thank you very much. Let's keep in touch with each other now and in the future.

A：我还有一个问题。投标人要递交投标保证金吗？

B：是的，当然。根据国际惯例，投标人要递交现金保证金或出自商业银行的保函。如果未能中标，所上交的现金或保函会在公布中标结果一周内退还给投标人。

A：贵公司想在何时、何地开标呢？

B：三月一日，在北京。

A：是公开开标吗？

B：是的，这一次是公开开标，所有投标人都将被邀请和我们一起来监督开标过程。

A：关于招标条件我可以知道点儿更多的内容吗？

B：投标邀请书将在下个月寄出，里面包含所有的细节。

A：我们公司对参与此次投标非常有兴趣，并将竭尽全力争取中标。

B：我很理解您的心情。如果你方的投标方案完全满足我方的要求，我们会接受您的投标。

A：非常感谢。希望我们双方现在和将来都能保持密切联系。

达人点拨

在 "bidding"（招投标）过程中，有些术语必须要清楚，比如 "bidding inviter"（招标方）； "bidder or tender"（投标方）。同时大部分的投标人要随 "bidding documents"（投标文件）一起附上 "bidding security"（投标保证金），可以是 "cash deposit"（现金）形式的，也可以是 "a letter of guarantee"（银行签发的保函）。当然，如果投标人 "fail to win the award"（没能中标），保证金会在一周之内退还。

讨论选择性投标

A: Perhaps you know that we are going to erect two large office buildings in Xi'an, either the first or the second half of this year.

B: But you haven't submitted any preliminary tenders, have you?

A: Not yet, but we gather from your last letter that you intended to get bids from us.

B: Yes, there are some doubts about the materials of the construction. However we have decided to go ahead with the most advanced environment friendly material and design.

A: I see. Then would you like us to draw up general plans and specifications?

B: Yes, and for the purpose of bidding, you can quote for a project featured with green nature, ranging from the construction material to the design as whole, taking into account of the power and water efficiency. One more thing, the project should also be of humanistic atmosphere.

A: Fine. Now what about the price? Can you indicate what budget you are preparing to allocate for the project?

B: I can tell you that we are willing to go up to 5,000,000 US dollars for each building, but the terms of payment must be considered together with the price.

A: Well, we can proceed on the basis of the amount you accept. Shall we submit our tender to your Shanghai office?

B: Yes, either directly or through your representative in Shanghai. Who is your representative in Shanghai now? You have a new man there, I

A：或许您已经知道了，我们打算在西安建造两座办公大楼，不是今年上半年就是下半年。

B：但是你方还没有递交任何初步的投标文件，对吧？

A：还没有，但是从你方最近的一次信件中我们获知你方想选我们为投标人。

B：是的，我们在建造材料方面有些疑虑。但是我方已经决定采用最先进的环保材料和设计。

A：我明白了。您是希望我方起草大体的规划和技术规范吗？

B：是的，为了能够中标，你方的报价应着眼于绿色环保，无论是建筑材质还是整体设计，还应考虑到节电节水。还有，该方案应该具有人性化的氛围。

A：好的。价格方面呢？您能否提示一下你方预计方案的预算？

B：可以告诉您的是我方对每幢大楼的预算是500万美元，但是付款方式要和价格一起考虑。

A：好的，我们会在你方能接受的价位下进行，投标书要递到上海分公司吗？

B：是的，可以直接投递，也可以经由你方在上海的代表。现在你们上海分部的代表是谁，我听说你们换了一个新人。

believe.

A: Yes, Mr. Johnson. He took his office last month and will be there for two years.

B: Is that so? I'll call him when I am back in Shanghai.

A: Sure. That'll be convenient.

A: 是的，约翰逊先生，他上个月上任的，将在那里任职两年。

B: 是这样？回到上海后我会给他打电话。

A: 很好，这样会方便些。

 展示投标人的实力

A: May I make it clear: Our company will do everything we can to help fulfill your project. And we shall be pleased to tender for the whole project on turnkey basis. We have the finance and know-how.

B: Thank you for your interest and cooperation in this very project. We will consider either turnkey or package bids. But please give us a quick summary of what's involved in your turnkey bid.

A: Well, just a summary of what we can deliver: We have a company in our group in Seattle, mainly in charge of solar energy development and relative product design and manufacture. Of course, we also have a company that can guarantee a huge market for our energy efficient products.

B: Can you make it more detailed, say your production capability?

A: Please look at this figure. Now the optimum production of solar cells in our processing units is around eighteen thousand per annum, which makes the most economical use of the new process. The capital cost of the factory would be enormous. Then you have got enough import source to handle such a big output.

B: The manufacturing competence and capability

A: 我可以明确地表示，我公司会尽全力协助贵公司的招标方案。我方很愿意对整个项目进行整体投标，我方有财力和技术。

B: 感谢您对这个方案的兴趣和合作。我方会考虑是实行部分或是全部工程招标。但是能否简单归纳一下您的全部工程投标方案？

A: 好的，那么就简述一下我们能够提供的条件：我们集团在西雅图的分公司主要负责太阳能开发和相关产品的设计和生产。当然，我们还有个分公司为我们的节能产品提供强大的市场。

B: 您能说得更详细些吗？说说你们的生产能力？

A: 请看这张图表，目前我们加工车间的太阳能电池的最优化生产能力是每年18,000个，这是对新生产流程的最经济的利用。工作所耗资金成本可观，你们也会有足够的进口资源来满足产量。

B: 你公司的生产能力的确很吸引人。还

are really attractive. One more point, how about the customers' comments on your cells?

A: We have manufactured solar cells and relative products for ages. They are now accounting for nearly two thirds of the Southeast market, which is more than enough to verify we have a great number of loyal customers.

B: It is indeed very inspiring.

有一点，客户对你们电池的反映如何？

A：我们生产太阳能电池和相关产品已有多年了，而且我们的产品几乎占据整个东南地区市场的三分之二，这足以证明我们拥有大批的忠实顾客。

B：这的确令人振奋。

达人点拨

为了中标，展示投标人的实力是非常重要而必要的，所以在双方的商务会谈中常会遇到这样的表达，"We shall be pleased to tender for the whole project or turnkey basis. We have the finance and know-how."（我方愿意对整个项目进行全包全揽性的投标。我们有资金和技术。）为了表明投标方的实力，他们会"tender for the whole project"（投标整个方案），或者是"tender on turnkey basis"（交钥匙工程），并且具备足够的"finance and know-how"（财力和技术）。

展现投标方的独特性

A: And I must tell you that our system has many advantages over our competitors. You see, we produce square solar cells rather than round ones. Here are some samples. Please take a look.

B: You developed the square cell yourself?

A: Yes. We developed it in our own research laboratories. If our bid is successful, we will try the new model in the project.

B: What is the advantage of a square cell, rather than a round one?

A: Round cells have gaps. Square cells can be laid side by side. So we get the same output of electricity from a smaller panel. And if you have smaller panels, you can cut down costs on other materials. And of course, since the panels are smaller and lighter, they're cheaper to transport.

A：而且我要告诉您我公司的产品和其他竞争者的相比具有许多优势。您看，我们生产的是方形太阳能电池，而不是圆形。这里有一些样品，请看。

B：你们自己开发的方形电池吗？

A：是的，我们在自己的实验室开发的该产品。如果我们投标成功，我们将在这个方案中尝试使用这个新型号。

B：方形电池和圆形电池相比，有什么优点呢？

A：圆形电池之间有空隙，而方形电池之间可以紧密摆放。所以提供同样的电量我们电池板小，而小型的电池板会节省其他材质。当然，电池板越小越轻，在运输上也更节省成本。

B:That sounds interesting.

A:And while other companies can only make bids for various parts of the project, our group can make a turnkey bid for the whole project. In a word, as I have mentioned above, we are big enough to play a leading role in your tender. There are not any other groups that big.

B:That's right, there are not. But there will be.

A:Well, I know you are extremely busy. I won't take up any more of your time.

B:Well, it was very good of you to call us, and I hope you enjoy your stay here.

B：听起来很有趣。

A：其他公司只能投标给各个不同的部分 我们公司可以为整个工程投标。一句话，正如我之前提到的，我们公司规模很大不会比其他投标公司差，还没有其他公司拥有如此大的规模。

B：是的，现在还没有，但是将来可能会有的。

A：好吧，我知道您很忙，不占用您更多的时间啦。

B：是呀，很高兴您能来拜访我们，希望您此行愉快。

 ## 投标贸易与其他贸易形式的不同之处

A:Good morning, Ma'am. I have come here to your consultancy in order to make it clear how different the tender is from other trading terms. As you know, as a new business, we are so eager to get familiar with diversified international business collaborations. But sometimes I am still wondering why some enterprises advertise on bidding announcements instead of looking for partners privately?

B:Sure, no problem. Tender is also a kind of trading characterized with a one-time offer and dealing, and the parties concerned do not need to negotiate back and forth. But traditional trading collaborations are focused on frequent and long-time contact and discussions before they come to a deal.

A:I see. So what items are normally covered in a bidding document, I mean, in addition to

A：早上好，女士。我来您的咨询公司是想请问投标贸易和其他贸易的不同之处。您也知道，作为一个新公司，我们很想了解国际贸易的多样化。时常从媒体上看到某些公司刊登投标公告，他们为什么不私下寻求贸易伙伴？

B：愿意为您效劳。投标也是一种贸易形式，其特点是一次性交易，双方无需来回地谈判。但是传统的贸易合作的特点是在达成交易之前要经过反复的、长期的联系和商讨。

A：我明白了。那么在一份投标文件里通常情况下我们应该准备哪些内容，我的意思是除了技术规范之外？

technique specifications?

B: The bidding process is featured by the competitions of bidders who may offer different terms, prices and warranties for the sake of reaching the bidding contract. In that case, the most important factor in a bidding submission is the price you could offer.

A: Since the offer is so crucial, can I ask for what the price bidding inviter could afford beforehand?

B: That is impossible, for an open bidding, which is a business activity under the open inspection, and the bidding announcement is usually made publicly by means of newspapers, magazines, TV or any other media. The exposure of any element determining success before opening day is unfair and illegal.

A: All right. The last point, when does a company prefer tender to other trading terms?

B: Most enterprises choose tender to import a large amount of commodity, such as construction materials, transportation tools, military goods, and chartering projects. As far as I know, it is not necessary for companies to adopt this trading if their business is not big and complicated enough.

A: OK, your explanations are really helpful to me. Thanks a lot.

B：投标过程的一个特点就是投标人之间的竞争，他们为了能中标可能提供不同的条件、价格和担保。在这种情况下，最重要的是投标书里的价格。

A：既然报价这么重要，我能不能事先问问招标人能接受的价位？

B：如果是公开招标，这是不可以的。公开招标是在公开监督下进行的，招标文件也是通过报纸、杂志、电视或其他媒体公开进行。在开标日前暴露任何决定性的内容都是不公平的、违法的。

A：那就算了。最后一个问题，什么时候一个公司采用招标的形式而不是其他的贸易形式？

B：大多数企业，在进口大量的商品时会考虑投标形式，比如建筑材料、交通工具、军用物资，或是承包项目等。据我所知，如果业务的规模不是很大或是复杂化，没必要采取这种贸易形式。

A：知道了。您的解释对我真的很有帮助。太感谢了。

 文化点滴

如何与韩国商人打交道

私人交往经常比商业伙伴关系更具有优势，所以交往很重要，因为韩国人容易对他们不认识的人持不信任态度。

韩国人不愿意直接说"不"，而他们通过齿间吸入空气的姿态就是表达了"不"。他们表达"可能"的时候也是掩饰着一个否定的回答。

对一个肯定的回答不要从字面上去理解。比如，一个"是的"可能被用来掩盖一个非承诺性的回应，就好像"我会考虑考虑"或许是一个直接的"不"。

韩国是一个崇尚集体主义的民族，所以凡事注重的是集体而不是个人。

三角形在这个文化中具有负面的内涵，所以在使用图示材料或可视性工具时应该避免这个图形。

韩国人通常先签署一个合同大纲，之后再讨论细节问题。对一些韩国人来讲，一份合同就是一个大纲，甚至还不如双方的人际关系重要。

在书写人名的时候禁止使用红色墨水，否则意味着那个人已经去世。

谈判过程的语调可能会非常激烈，同时伴有情感的爆发。您可能发现您的韩国伙伴很快就表达生气或是沮丧。

不要在韩国人面前吸烟或是戴太阳镜。

您和您的同事如果在介绍时没有带名片，可能会很"丢脸"。您的商务名片上要强调您的职务。

国际展卖
International Fairs

同其他贸易方式不同，展卖是将出口商品的展览和销售结合起来，边展边销。这种贸易形式有利于宣传出口商品，扩大商品的影响力，招揽潜在买主；有利于扩大销售地区和范围；有利于开展市场调研，听取消费者意见，改进产品性能，增强出口竞争力。

常见的国际博览会可分为两种形式：综合性国际博览会，又称"水平型博览会"，即各种商品均可以参加展览并洽谈交易的博览会；专业性博览会，又称"垂直型博览会"，即仅限于某类特定商品参加展销的博览会。

展卖方式比较适合于与该展卖商品有密切客户关系或代理关系的市场。其较多地应用于开辟新领域、新市场，尤其适用于一些地理上与展卖商品生产国距离遥远的地区。

词语宝典

consignment	寄售	the objective of the fair	展会的目标
consignor	寄售人	sponsorship	主办权
consignee	代售人	exhibit	展品
general international fairs	综合性国际博览会	exhibitor	参展商
horizontal fairs	水平型博览会	protocol for the fair	展会议定书
vertical fairs	垂直型博览会	exhibition booth	展间或展区
venue and time	展会时间和地点		

经典句型

- We think China would be the best candidate to host the next International Trade Fair.
  我们认为中国是举办下一届国际博览会的最佳候选国。

- The purpose of our current visit here is to hold consultations with you on the proposed trade fair to be held in Guangzhou in 2017.
  我们此次来访的目的就是要和贵方商榷一下 2017 年即将在广州举办的国际博览会。

- Can we deal with the details first before we come up with a protocol confirming the implementation of the plans for organizing the event?
  在我们确认此项计划实施方案前,是否该商讨一下相关的细节问题?

- Let's decide on the official name of the event, which is the Asia-Pacific International Trade Fair, isn't it right?
  让我们确定一下该交易会的正式名称,是叫做"亚太国际博览会",没错吧?

- The objective of the upcoming fair should be to promote economic cooperation, trade expansion and technology communication.
  即将举办的这届博览会的目的是促进经济合作、贸易发展和技术交流。

- With regards to sponsorship, the fair is to be jointly sponsored by SECAP and BBTP, and Beijing will be the host city.
  关于发起人,本次博览会是由SECAP和BBTP联合发起举办的,北京是主办城市。

- Exhibits may be sold during the fair and can be delivered after the closing day.
  展品在展会期间可以销售,在展会结束日后可以发货。

- Exhibitors will have the option of renting either a turnkey exhibit booth, or an empty exhibit space for the exhibitor to design and build his own booth.
  展商有权租用已备好的展间,或租用某处空白展区自行设计和搭建展区。

- The consignee must try to sell the consignments at the best possible price after obtaining the approval of the consignor as to price, terms, etc.
  代售人在征得寄售人关于价格、条款等的同意后,必须尽力以最好价格出售寄售商品。

- The consignee shall collect the shipping documents including B/L from the consignor's bank against Trust Receipt duly signed by the consignee.
  代售人以签字的信托收据从寄售人银行换取包括提单在内的装运单据。

- And the venue and time. The fair is tentatively proposed to take place in Beijing during the fourth quarter of 2017, lasting about two to three weeks.
  现在我们讨论一下展会的地点和时间。博览会暂定于2017年的第四季度在北京举行,历时约两到三周。

- The next item is the objective of the event. Our opinion is that the upcoming fair is to promote trade and investment opportunities for member countries and strengthen regional economic cooperation.
  下一项是该展会的目的。我们的想法是即将举行的这次博览会旨在促进成员国的贸易和投资机会,强化地区经济合作。

- During the fair, technical exchange meetings, business talks and national day programs can also be arranged.
  在展会期间,还可以安排技术交流会议、商务洽谈和国庆活动等。

时尚对白

讨论主办国际展卖的主要议题

A: China's economy has maintained its strong growth momentum. The successful reform and opening-up efforts have paved the way for China's steady and healthy development and made China a magnetite for international traders and investors. Therefore, we think China would be the best candidate to host the next International Trader Fair. The purpose of our current visit to Bejing is to hold consultations with you on the proposed trade fair to be held in Beijing in 2017.

B: Thank you very much for the kind words about our country. Can we deal with the relevant details before we come up with the final protocol or agreement confirming the implementation of the plans for the event?

A: Yes. That is what we would like to do too.

B: Now, the first thing. Let us decide on the official name of event, which is the Asia-Pacific International Trade Fair, isn't it right?

A: Correct. And the venue and time. The fair is tentatively proposed to be held in Beijing during the first quarter of 2017, lasting about two weeks. I think we have exchanged the information previously between us during our correspondence.

B: That's agreed to. The next item is the objective of the event. The aim of the upcoming fair should be to promote economic cooperation, trade expansion and technology communication among member countries and organizations.

A：中国经济一直保持着强劲的增长势头。成功的改革和开放实践已经为中国稳定健康的发展铺平了道路，使中国成为一块引力巨大的磁石，吸引着外商和外国投资者。因此，我们认为中国是主办下届国际展卖会的最佳候选国。我们此次北京之行的目的就是要和贵方商榷我们提议的于2017年在北京举办展卖会的事宜。

B：非常感谢您对中国的赞美之词。我们在确定此项计划最终的实施方案前，是否该商讨相应的细节？

A：是的，这也正是我们的目的。

B：现在让我们先来确定此次活动的正式名称，是"亚太国际展卖会"，对吧？

A：是的。活动的地点和时间：该展会暂定在北京举行，历时约两周，在2017年的第一季度内举行。我想之前在双方的往来信函中我们已经交换了意见了。

B：我们已经就此达成一致意见。下一个议题是活动的目的。这次展会的目的就是促进各个成员国和组织之间的经济合作、贸易发展和技术交流。

第一部分 贸易实务

达人点拨

在"international fairs"(国际展卖)的谈判当中,双方经常会围绕着主办地、展会主题、主要活动等进行协商,所以下面的"lines"(表达)会助您一臂之力。"And as of the venue. The Fair is tentatively proposed to be held in Beijing."(提到地点,该展会暂时定在北京举办。)或者是"The aim of the upcoming fair should be to promote economic cooperation, trade expansion and technology communication among member countries and organizations."(本次展会的目的是促进成员国和组织之间的经济合作、发展贸易和技术交流。)

协商展会的主要活动

A: Our opinion is that the theme focuses on how to optimize new technology and skilled manpower to contribute further to the dynamic development of the member countries and regions in the new circumstance.

B: That sounds great. May we set the sub-theme as helping participants to share advanced management and marketing strategies. With regard to sponsorships, the Fair is to be jointly sponsored by Asia-pacific Economic Cooperation Council and the Beijing Bureau of Trading Promoting. Beijing will be the host city.

A: And the participating countries and regions will mainly be from Asia and the Pacific Regions. Countries from other areas are also invited if necessary. The issuance of the invitation will be taken care of by BBTP's Organization Committee.

B: Sure. Exhibits may be sold during the fair and can be delivered after the closing day. Exhibitors have the freedom to rent either a turnkey exhibit booth, or an empty exhibit space for themselves to design and build.

A: We propose that in addition to the display of products and services, a series of technical exchange meetings, business talks and other seminars with related topics should also be

A: 我们的想法是主题可以集中在如何优化新技术和行业背景浓厚的人力资源,以便进一步为新环境下的成员国和地区的动态发展贡献力量。

B: 听起来不错。我们可以把副主题定位为让与会者共享先进的管理水平和营销策略。关于发起人,该展会由亚太经济合作理事会和北京贸易促进局共同举办,北京是主办城市。

A: 参展国家和地区主要来自亚洲和太平洋地区。如果有必要还可以邀请其他国家和地区的组织。邀请函的发送由北京贸易促进局的组织委员会负责。

B: 当然。展品可以在展会期间出售,但要等到闭会之后发货。租赁一个装修好的展间,还是租赁一个空白展区自行设计和搭建,参展商有选择的自由。

A: 我们建议除了展示产品和服务之外,应该举行一系列的技术交流会、商业洽谈和其他相关话题的座谈会。

arranged.

B: Now let's move on to the last item: Steering Committee. To promote the work of the fair and to coordinate the overall work, the Steering Committee should also consist of the representatives of SECAP and BBTP.

A: I think we have covered all the major points to be discussed. Now it is time to put them down on paper, in the form of protocol or agreement.

B：现在让我们进入最后一个议题：运作委员会。为了促进展会顺利进行和协调整体工作，该委员会应该由SECAP和BBTD双方的代表组成。

A：我想我们已经讨论完所有的主要问题，现在应该形成文字，以议定书或是协议的形式皆可。

达人点拨

在展会的组织工作中，通常有展会的"sponsor"（发起人）和"host"（主办者）。双方可以是一个组织，也可以不是，所以要区分这两个术语。同时，为了确保展会的顺利进行，还会成立一个"steering committee"（运作委员会），以确保展会的顺利召开和进行。

国际展卖的主要特点

A: Excuse me, Professor Wang, the international fair you have mentioned last week is a new business concept for me, do you mind if I ask you some questions about it?

B: Certainly. What do you want to know?

A: Is it truely new business collaboration between businessmen? I mean, I'm so familiar with agency, and compensation, but there is not so much information on that in my textbook.

B: No, actually it is as old as human civilization. Local open-air fairs or markets are the original version of international fairs. International fairs, as one of the historical trading transactions, take advantage of international exhibitions or trading fairs as its trading platform with the purpose to sell displayed commodities or services.

A: I see, with the improved technology and communication and transportation, trading fair

A：打扰了，王教授，您上周讲的国际展卖对我而言是一个全新的商务概念，我向您请教几个问题，您不介意吧？

B：当然没问题。你想问什么问题？

A：国际展卖是全新的外贸合作方式吗？我是说，我熟悉的外贸形式有代理、补偿贸易，但是教材上关于国际展卖没有详细的介绍。

B：不是，其实展卖是和人类文明的历史一样古老。那些露天市场就是国际展卖的最初形式。国际展卖，作为一种古老的贸易形式，利用国际展览或是贸易集市等作为交易平台，目的是推销展示的商品或服务。

A：我明白了。随着技术、通讯和交

has become more internationalized, featured with larger-scale and variety. Am I right?

B: Absolutely. And this transaction is the combination of displaying, promoting and selling.

A: Then, what are the advantages of selling at the international fair instead of a local market?

B: Compared with other transactions, international fairs play a positive role in promoting advertising and searching potential purchasers, establishing and expanding sales territories.

A: That is really a great idea to put together advertisement and selling process. Thank you, Professor Wang.

B: You are welcome.

通的完善，交易会越来越国际化，其特点是规模更大、更多样化，是吗？

B：完全正确。这种交易就是展览、推广和销售的结合。

A：那么，不在当地市场，而是选择在国际展览会上进行销售有什么优势呢？

B：和其他贸易形式相比，国际展卖在广告宣传、寻求潜在买家、建立和扩展销售市场等方面起着积极的作用。

A：这个想法真不错，能把广告和销售结合在一起进行。谢谢您，王教授。

B：不客气。

 国际展卖类型

A: We are so excited to attend this year's International Fair hosted by your organization. That's bound to be a great opportunity to expand our global market. But I also notice that in the participant companies you have listed, there are some other firms that are not in line with our business. Isn't it a fair of mobile phone businesses?

B: Well, actually this upcoming fair hosted by us is a general international fair, or a horizontal fair. It means all kinds of commodities are shown to be sold at the fair. And there is not strict stipulation in terms of business scope.

A: Do you mean it is with a full product catalogue and on a large scale?

B: Sure. And based on business practice, this kind of international fair lasts longer than other fairs.

A: I see. Then you have also sponsored fairs displaying and selling one single type of commodity, right?

B: Of course. That is called specialized international fair,

A：加由能参加由贵组织主办的国际展卖我们真的很高兴。这对于扩展我方的国际市场一定是个绝佳的机会。但是我注意到在您列出的参展商的名单里，有的公司和我们的业务不一致，这难道不是移动电话业务的展卖会吗？

B：是这样。我方主办的这次展卖会是综合性的国际展卖会，也叫"水平型"展卖会，意思是在展会上各种产品都可以展示和出售，在经营范围上没有严格的规定。

A：您的意思是这个展会含括所有的产品范围，规模盛大？

B：当然。根据商业惯例，这种国际展卖持续的时间也比其他的展卖会长久。

A：我知道了。那么您也主办过只展销一种产品的展卖会，是吧？

B：当然。那种叫做专业性的国际展

or vertical fair. And most of the companies invited to the fair are required to be connected with stipulated lines. But the scale is small with shorter duration.

A: I got it. Since you put it this way, I prefer horizontal fairs. It should offer more chances to get acquainted with firms dealing with various lines. And I cannot wait to sharing business experiences with them.

B: Well, it is hard to decide which one is better for your business. That depends on what a participant wants from the fair and other considerations.

卖会，也叫做"垂直型"展卖会。受邀参加展会的公司要和规定的展会业务相关。但是这种展会规模小、时间短。

A：是这样啊。既然您这么说，那我更偏爱"水平型"展会。这种展会可以提供给我们更多的机会熟悉不同行业的公司。我真是等不及要和他们交流经营经验呢。

B：其实，很难说哪一种对你的公司更好。这取决于参展商参展的目的和其他方面的考虑。

达人点拨

在国际展卖中，常见的有"vertical"（垂直型）和"horizontal"（水平型）两种，而垂直型展卖"small scaled and short term"（规模小会期短），通常限制在一个专业领域；相比之下，综合性展卖会或水平展卖，各种产品都可以展出和出售，没有在经营范围上给予严格的界定。

为什么选择国际展卖

A: As far as I know, there is an increasing trend to sponsor and attend international fairs. So why not our company get prepared for this kind of promotion activity, which is also a wonderful chance to sell our products abroad?

B: It is indeed a great trading method. But to my knowledge, the corporations who particularly favor it usually have loyal customers and experienced agents in the target markets.

A: Do you mean if a company is short of fixed foreign customers and established overseas market, it is not advised to participate in international fairs?

B: No, that is not my point. What I want to say is that there are also a large number of enterprises

A：据我所知，主办和参加国际展卖越来越成为一种趋势。那为什么我们公司不准备一下也参加这种促销活动，也可以有机会在国外销售我们的产品啊。

B：这的确是一种不错的贸易手段。但据我所知，钟情于展卖的公司都在目标市场有忠实的客户并拥有有经验的代理商。

A：您的意思是一个公司如果缺乏固定的国外客户和有经验的海外代理，最好不要参加国际展卖吗？

B：不，不是那个意思。我想说的是

attending it in order to explore new trading territories. Especially when their products and services are far away in geography from their potential markets, they would give priority to international fairs.

A: OK. As I understand it, we should make each effort to develop and promote our brand at home before we make enough preparation to participate in international fairs. Anyway, it is obviously a shortcut to expand and publicize our commodity to foreign market.

也有大量的公司参展是为了开拓新的贸易领域。特别是当他们的产品和服务在地域上远离他们的目标市场时，一般会采取国际展卖的方式。

A：好吧。那么我们应该竭尽全力先开发和推广我们的国内市场，做好足够的准备再参加国际展卖。不论怎样，这显然是一条可以把产品推向国际市场的捷径。

 寄售和展卖

A: Excuse me, Professor Green, can I take up some of your time? I am still confused about the international fairs you talked about in class.

B: Sure, no problem. What is puzzling you?

A: Well, we learnt consignment last week, but I find out there are so many similarities between International fair and consignment. You see, under both transactions, the firms concerned send out the goods to overseas markets, and try their best to sell them to make profits.

B: How smart you are! You are right, they do share some common points. But basically they can be distinguished from each other in many aspects. Under consignment, the consignor or exporter sends the commodities in advance based on trust. And there is a signed agreement between consignees and consignors. And the consignee is paid by means of commission.

A: Do you mean there is no such agreement under international fair transaction?

B: That depends. Anyway the purpose of internatio-

A：格林教授，能占用您几分钟时间吗？您今天在课堂上讲的国际展卖，我还是不太明白。

B：没问题。你哪里不明白？

A：是这样。我们上周学过了寄售，但是我发现在寄售和国际展卖之间有太多的相似处。您看，在两种贸易模式下，都是由相关人员把商品发送到国外市场，并竭尽全力把商品卖掉获取利润。

B：你真是聪明啊。你说的对。它们的确有共同点。但是基本来说他们在许多方面是有区别的。在寄售项目下，寄售人或出口商在信托的基础上把货物提前运出。双方，即寄售人和委托人是要签订协议的，而寄售人通过获取佣金的方式获得报酬。

A：您的意思是在国际展卖方式下双方没有协议吗？

B：那得依情形而定。无论怎样国际展

nal fair is promotion and advertisement, while consignment is aimed to make profits by selling goods. So to some extent, we can say international fair is under consignment. Is my explanation clear to you?

A: Yes, your further interpretation is really helpful to my understanding. Thanks a lot.

卖的目的是促销和宣传，而寄售的目的是通过销售获取利润。因此从某种程度讲，我们可以说国际展卖是属于寄售项目下的。我的解释清楚吗？

A：是的，您这进一步的解释让我明白多了。太谢谢了。

 文化点滴

如何与印度商人打交道

1. 在印度一切都要讨价还价，所以在确定一个靠谱的价格前要和来自不同领域的多家公司进行沟通。
2. 印度人倾向于联想式的思维模式。印度商人通常受过高等教育，该国文化对有大学学历的人才十分尊重。
3. 在印度，外部信息和全新的观念只有在不和主体宗教信仰发生冲突时才会被接受。
4. 在印度，种姓制度具有很强的影响力。在印度的商业文化中，对真理的理解是受个人情感支配的，对宗教的信仰也十分普遍。
5. 在印度，大部分商业都是家族式的，所以最终的决定总是在家长手中。
6. 雇佣一个知道如何和印度复杂的官僚体制打交道，如何得到有签字和盖章的批文的人通常很有帮助。
7. "不"的直接表达在印度是非常刺耳的，含蓄性的回答更容易被接受。比如，如果您不得不拒绝一个邀请，更礼貌的回答是"我尽量去"而不是"我不能去"。
8. 在印度文化中，在正式商务会谈之前的闲聊是非常必要的。
9. 当有人送上甜点时，按照传统是第一次拒绝，但是第二次或第三次要接受，而拒绝饮料会被当做是一种侮辱。
10. 在印度，好客之道是做生意的本质部分。

补偿贸易
Compensation Trade

补偿贸易通常是由缔约一方以赊销方式向对方提供机械设备和技术等,同时承诺向对方购买一定数量或金额的商品,也就是在信贷的基础上,用产品或双方协议的商品偿还货款的一种贸易方式。这里的产品可以是直接产品,即用进口的机械设备直接生产出来的产品,或者是间接产品,即与进口设备或生产线无关的产品。

在磋商补偿贸易的过程中,设备进口方应对进口设备的技术性能、先进性和适用性有明确的规定。作为设备的出口方,在合同中对有关信贷的条件,补偿产品的名称、金额、补偿时间、数量和质量等都应有明确的说明。

词语宝典

reimburse	偿还	labor compensation	劳务补偿
offset	抵偿	material processing	来料加工
payback	返销	purchase arrangement	购买协议
compensation trade	补偿贸易	sales arrangement	销售协议
direct compensation	直接补偿	contract fulfillment	合同履行
indirect compensation	间接补偿	installment	分期付款
counter trade	互购	foreign exchange	外汇
parallel trade	平行贸易,即互购	sliding price	按照物价涨落而定的价格
product buyback	产品回购	production capacity	生产能力
resultant product	直接产品	current price	现行价格

经典句型

- Since we are short of foreign exchange, compensation trade is considered favorable.
  由于我们缺乏外汇,补偿贸易是一种可以优先考虑的贸易方式。
- Seller shall deliver the goods to Buyer within thirty days from the commencement of production.
  卖方应该在生产日起30天内将货物发送给买方。

- Since we are short of foreign exchange, the option might be to undertake compensation trade.
  由于我们缺少外汇，补偿贸易是可供选择的做法。
- You can supply us with the canning equipment and we'll pay for the machines with canned food produced by the machines.
  贵方可以提供给我们罐装设备，我们用贵方所提供的设备生产的罐头食品来抵付购买设备的货款。
- It certainly sounds very promising. Thus we could get around the hard currency problem.
  这个主意听起来不错，可以绕过硬通货的问题。
- We've never done such trade before, but we agree to do compensation trade on the basis of mutual benefit.
  我们从来没有做过这类贸易，但是我们同意双方在互利的基础上进行补偿贸易。
- We are well placed to meet your requirement for wool.
  我们完全有条件满足你们对羊毛的需求。
- The stipulations in your L/C are not in accordance with the contract.
  你方信用证的规定与合同不一致。
- They feel sure that you will fulfill your promise.
  他们确信你方将履行诺言。
- Party B has machines and equipment, which are now used in Party B's manufacturing of steel wire rope, and is willing to sell to Party A the machines and equipment.
  B方拥有用于生产钢丝绳的设备并愿意出售给A方该设备。
- Party B agrees to buy the products, steel wire rope, made by Party A using the machines and equipment Party B supplies, in compensation of the price of the machines and equipment.
  B方同意购买A方使用B方提供的设备生产的钢丝绳，以作为对购买该设备的价格补偿。
- The price of the machines and equipment shall be compensated with the products, the steel wire rope, manufactured by Party A using the machines and equipment. The payment of the total prices shall be effected three times equally in three successive years.
  合同项目下购买的机器设备以A方使用该设备所生产的钢丝绳产品作为价格补偿。支付总额在连续三年期间分三次等额支付。
- Party B guarantees that the machines and equipment are unused, sophisticated and of best quality, and that the machines and equipment are capable of manufacturing the steel

wire rope with agreed specifications.

B方要确保该合同项目下的机器设备是全新的、先进的、高质量的，而该设备具有生产符合双方协议规格的钢丝绳的能力。

- All necessary parts and materials supplied by Party A are as per the list attached hereto.

所有A方提供的必需的零配件和原料均应按照随附的清单办理。

时尚对白

直接补偿贸易谈判

A: Glad to meet you. The purpose of inviting you to come here is to discuss purchase of canning machines.

B: Good, our canning machines are very advanced in technology and high efficient, isn't it right?

A: Yes, your equipment is a bit better than others'. But your price is skyrocketing, and much higher than our payment ability. You know because we are short of foreign exchange, it is difficult for us to buy the canning machine of your company this year. Furthermore, the same machines of other brands are not that bad.

B: If so, we can consider the possibility of undertaking compensation trade?

A: Why not? We'd be happy to negotiate with you for such a deal. Which do you prefer, buy-back or counter-purchase?

B: I guess the buy-back is easier. Since we do often import a lot of canned food from abroad, you can pay for the canning machine with the canned food produced by them.

A: That sounds promising. Do you wish to have total compensation trade or partial one?

B: It depends on your production capability. In other words, the more you can produce in a given

A：很高兴见到您，此次邀请您来的目的是讨论购买罐装设备的事宜。

B：很好。我们的罐装设备技术先进而且效率高，是吧？

A：是的，您的设备比其他公司的好一些，但是价格太高了，远远超出了我们的支付能力。您知道由于外汇短缺，我们很难在今年购买你们公司的设备。而且，其他品牌的设备也还不错。

B：既然这样，我们可以考虑一下补偿贸易的可能。

A：可以啊，很高兴与您就此事进行协商。您是倾向于返销还是回购模式的补偿贸易？

B：我想返销更容易一些。既然我们经常进口大量的罐装食品，你方可以通过提供由我们设备生产的罐装食品来抵付货款。

A：听起来很好。您是想接受完全补偿还是部分补偿贸易？

B：这取决于你们的生产能力。换言之，你们在规定时间内生产的产品越

period, the sooner you pay for the machine.
A: As for us, it is better to do total compensation trade.
B: It's quite alright for us. Total compensation trade may be good for both of us.

多，你们就会在更短的时间内付清货款。
A：至于我方，最好是完全补偿贸易。
B：我方也认可。完全补偿贸易对双方都有益。

达人点拨

在补偿贸易谈判中一定要和对方敲定是"buy-back"（返销）还是"counter-purchase"（回购）。返销比较简单，即通过用进口的设备生产的商品出售给设备出口方来抵销所欠的设备进口货款，而回购是通过销售其他商品来补偿所欠的设备进口货款。同时，要学会这样的常用句型"Do you wish to have total compensation trade or partial one?"（你方是希望接受完全补偿还是部分补偿？）。

补偿贸易支付细节

A: If I calculated this right, it will take about two years to complete the payment. How do you like it?
B: May I say that your estimation is not 100% correct. Compensation trade is, in a way, a kind of loan where you need to pay the interest on the loan every year.
A: In that case, I'm afraid the payment cannot be completed within two years.
B: You are right. Will three years be long enough?
A: I think so. That's settled. We'll complete the payment within three years from the commencement of the production. May I remind you of your responsibilities for technical assistance, the performance of the machines and finally a smooth and successful start-up.
B: Certainly we shall fulfill our obligations. Meanwhile, we hope you meet our requirements on the quantity, quality, packing and the time of shipment for all the canned food you deliver to us.
A: We will certainly comply fully with the contract

A：如果我算得没错，大概需要两年时间付清货款，您认为怎样？
B：我想您的估计不完全正确。补偿贸易，在某种程度上，也是一种贷款方式，您需要每年支付贷款利息。
A：那样的话，恐怕不能在两年内付清货款了。
B：没错。三年期限可以吗？
A：可以。就这么定了。我方从生产之日起三年内付清所有货款。同时想提醒您有责任提供技术协助，设备的运行调试以确保最终平稳成功的启动。
B：当然，我们会履行义务的。同时，我们希望你方所发的罐装食品能满足我们对质量、数量、包装和发运时间的要求。
A：我们当然会完全遵从合同条款。

terms.

B: Good. Would you please get the draft contract ready as soon as possible?

A: Yes, we will.

B：好的，您可以尽快准备好合同草案吗？

A：是的，我们会的。

协商间接补偿贸易

A: I had a discussion with the technicians of our corporation. They showed great interest in your sewing machine, and thought it is at the international level of sewing technology, and it could solve our long-standing problems in garment industries.

B: I think so. After you import them, you can quickly balance the foreign currency spent on imported equipment and technology with the foreign currency earned from exporting products.

A: Do you mean the machine can be quickly installed and put into operation? Our aim is to raise the annual output from 4 million pieces now to 6 million pieces in the near future.

B: You may rest assured. And we provide you with easy-worn-out spare parts and components free of charge.

A: Good. But if the equipment fails to give normal operation, you are to repair them at your cost, aren't you?

B: Yes.

A: What about counter-sale products? We are sure you have close cooperation in selling the products.

B: Well, we agree in principle to use other products to offset the value of our equipment and technology.

A: That is in accordance with business practice. And the products we provide will be especially

A：我和我们公司的技术人员讨论过了，他们对你方的缝纫机非常感兴趣，认为是达到了缝纫设备的国际水准，并能解决长期困扰我们的制衣业问题。

B：是这样的。一旦进口我们的设备，您可以迅速通过出口平衡在设备和技术引进方面的外汇支出。

A：您是说该设备能迅速安装并投入使用吗？我们的目标是在不久的将来，从现在的年产量400万件提高到600万件。

B：您完全可以放心。我们还免费提供易损零部件。

A：太好了。如果设备不能正常运行，你方会付费维修，是吧？

B：是的。

A：那么关于回购商品呢？我们相信你方在销售该产品方面有密切的客户关系。

B：是的，原则上我们同意使用其他商品来补偿我们的设备和技术价值。

A：这样也符合贸易惯例。我们提供

manufactured according to your specific requirements, which are not in line with our domestic market.

的商品会严格按照你方的技术要求。而且这些产品的技术规范和我们的国内需求也不一致。

 ## 间接补偿支付方式

B: Very well then. Can we now come up to the way the prices of compensation are fixed?

A: For equipment, we shall use a sliding price.

B: That is a good idea.

A: The counter-sale product shall be determined according to the prevailing world market prices at the time of each shipment.

B: That's what I am going to say. Then what is your proposal as regards the payment for the equipment and products?

A: What do you think of sight L/C for counter-sale products and deferred terms for equipment?

B: That is what I am thinking. I think we should prepare a memo containing what we have covered just now before we move on to more detailed terms. Is that OK?

A: OK. I am glad to have such an opportunity to exchange our views on compensation trade.

B：很好。现在我们可以谈谈补偿价格的确定？

A：对于设备，我们采纳实时价格。

B：好极了。

A：回购的商品由每次发货时的市场价格决定。

B：这也正是我想说的。那么您认为该如何支付设备和商品的货款呢？

A：您认为对产品采用即期信用证支付，而设备采用延期支付，可以吗？

B：这正合我意。我认为我们应该准备一个备忘录记录下我们刚才讨论的内容，然后再进入细节问题，您看呢？

A：好的，很高兴有机会就补偿贸易和您交换意见。

达人点拨

在实施间接补偿贸易的过程中，双方一定要协商好补偿商品或设备的支付方式和条款，否则很容易引起纠纷。常见的表达有"counter-sale product shall be determined according to the prevailing world market prices at the time of each shipment, and payable based on the sight L/C."（回购的商品由每次发货时的市场价格决定并按照即期信用证方式支付。）或者是"We provide you with easy-worn-out spare parts and components free of charge."（我方免费提供易损零配件。）。

补偿贸易的可行性

A: To give some ideas of what our clients in Tokyo require concerning the embroidered belts, I've brought a sample with me. Here it is.

B: It seems the stitches are especially neat and fine. But I'm afraid our manufacturers cannot produce such attractive needlework, unless they use machines from Japan.

A: You said it. I am sure this problem can be easily solved with the new type of machine. I have realized this and obtained the catalogues for you from our Japanese supplier.

B: It is very smart of you to do so. But as you know installing new equipment will be a huge investment for our manufacturers. May I suggest that we combine the two trades under compensation arrangement?

A: Well, your suggestion sounds practical. How do we proceed?

B: We place an order with you for the embroidery machine and the value of the embroidered belts will offset in two years the payment for the imported machine. And we will also pay the interest based on business practices. In addition, all the relevant parties should sign an agreement on compensation trade including all the details of the two separate purchases.

A: Well, I need to contact the machine supplier, but personally I believe it's workable.

B: I hope the machine supplier will hold the same view. I look forward to seeing you again soon.

A：我们在东京的客户需要刺绣腰带，我带来一个样品，给点儿意见吧。

B：针眼又漂亮又整齐，但恐怕我们的生产商不能生产出这么漂亮的针线活，除非他们使用日本的设备。

A：你说的没错。我相信如果使用新型的设备，这个问题很容易解决。我已经意识到这一点，并从日本供应商那里拿到了设备的产品目录给你。

B：您真是太聪明了。但是您也知道安装新设备对我们的制造商来讲是一笔巨额的投资。我们可否进行补偿贸易？

A：嗯，您的建议很实际，该怎么操作呢？

B：我方和您签订进口刺绣设备的订单，而设备的价格通过我方提供刺绣腰带来抵偿，时间是两年。我们也会按照商业惯例支付利息。此外，相关各方签订补偿贸易协议，包括两次购买的所有细节。

A：好的，我需要和设备供应商联系，但我个人认为这是可行的。

B：但愿设备供应方持相同意见。期待我们早日再相见。

补偿贸易项目下的争执

A: Good morning, Madam. I come to your consultancy to inquire about the possibility of compensation trade for my company.

B: Sure. It is a great pleasure to help you. What do you intend to know about this transaction?

A: As you know, lack of enough currency and technology sometimes has hindered our development and expansion. But import of highly advanced machines is far more than what we can pay.

B: You are on the right path. The best solution is to look for competent partners to conduct compensation trade, since you have enough space and labor force.

A: But I have heard that compensation trade more often than not leads to disputes and even unpleasant lawsuits. Why is that?

B: Well, a compensation agreement is signed based on credit and trust and the subjective factors are not as reliable as hard stipulations in a contract. What's more, a compensation trade is more than machines and product. I mean, introduction of technology often causes the focus of conflict.

A: I see. The most developed nations are concerned with providing up-to-date techniques and devices. And the know-how and advancement of imported machines are the most sensitive part in the agreement, is it right?

B: You said it. And one more point, compensation product. In some cases the compensated products to device importers are in line with our export market. In such case it is unavoidable that

A：早上好，女士！我来您的咨询公司是想咨询一下我们公司开展补偿贸易的可能性。

B：当然可以，愿意为您效劳。关于这种交易方式您想了解点儿什么？

A：您知道，由于缺乏足够的资金和技术，我们公司的发展和扩展有时会受到制约。但是进口高技术性能的先进设备又远远超过了我们的支付能力。

B：那您选对了方向。最好的解决办法就是寻求有实力的合作伙伴进行补偿贸易，因为你方可以提供足够的空间和劳动力。

A：但是我听说补偿贸易经常导致争执甚至是令人不愉快的法律官司，为什么会这样？

B：嗯，一份补偿贸易协议的签署是建立在信贷的基础之上，而主观因素不像在合同里的硬性规定那么可靠。而且，补偿贸易不仅是设备和产品的交易。我的意思是，引进技术时经常构成双方冲突的焦点。

A：我知道了。大多数发达国家在提供先进技术和设备方面很保守。而引进设备的技术机密和先进性是协议中最敏感的部分，对吧？

B：你说的没错。还有一点，就是补偿产品。有时候补偿进口设备的产品和我们的出口市场相吻合，势必会

negative competition occurs.

A: There are so many factors to be taken into account before we come to compensation deal. It is far more complicated than I previously thought.

B: Hence, it is important to understand global technique condition and market situation as well before we come to the agreement.

造成对我方不利的竞争。

A：看来在我们着手进行补偿贸易前得考虑这么多的因素呢。这可比我之前想的复杂多了。

B：因此，重要的一点是要了解全球的技术状况和市场情形，然后再商谈协议事宜。

达人点拨

在协商和签署补偿贸易协议时，对于设备的引进是非常敏感和复杂的议题，常常构成双方日后争执的焦点。因为引进的不仅是设备本身，还有技术机密、专利、日后安装和维修等细节，所以在双方的谈判中常见这样的对白："If the equipment fails to give normal operation, you are to repair them at your cost, aren't you?"（如果设备不能正常运行，你方将付费维修，是吧？）。

文化点滴

如何与沙特阿拉伯人打交道

1．没有被邀请的非穆斯林不得进入沙特阿拉伯。您要想在此地做生意，有一个联系人或发起人非常重要。这个发起人将作为中间人以恰当的方式安排会面。

2．商业名片应该在背面翻译成阿拉伯文。

3．在这个国家，宗教对政治、社会行为和商业具有重要的影响。沙特人不愿意接受和伊斯兰价值观相悖的外部信息。

4．在沙特阿拉伯，商业活动的进展步伐非常缓慢，所以保持耐心是非常重要的。通常是，商务会议开始得很缓慢，人们会提问大量关于您健康和旅行方面的问题。

5．和沙特人说话时眼神接触很重要，要直视对方的眼睛。

6．在陈述某个观点时大声表达是正常的，提高语音语调在这里是表达诚意的信号。

7．要知道阿拉伯语是一种夸张的语言。比如，如果一个沙特人说"是"，他可能实际要表达的是"可能"。所以，尽管您会被类似的积极响应所鼓舞，但如果您认为谈判已经结束您就错了。

9．努力赞美而不是批评别人，无论对方性格如何。学习伊斯兰教的基本礼仪，着装得体，尊重长辈。女性商业访客如果不戴面纱是可以被接受的，只是她们着装要尽量保守。

10．你可能会遇到双方的会谈被对方的电话或是其他来访打断，你甚至会发现他们的商人会同时出席几个会议。

技术转让与合作
Technology Transfer and Cooperation

技术转移是指技术在国家、地区、行业之间或内部输入和输出的过程,包括技术成果、专利、信息的转让、交流和移植。

由于技术在不同国家和地区发展的不平衡性,导致了技术转移的定向性,一般是技术上先进的国家地区和行业向技术落后的国家地区和行业实行技术输出。但是与实物商品不同的是,知识性商品在交易完成后,虽然技术商品的使用价值已经让渡给对方,但溢出者仍然保留了这一技术知识的使用价值,所以技术转移只是使用权的转移,不影响溢出者对这一技术的拥有权。从这个意义上讲,技术的供给方能够不断重复出卖技术,而技术的购买者也可以连续不断地将技术转卖出去,直至所有人都掌握这种技术。

技术转移从技术内容的完整性看,可以分为"移植型"和"嫁接型"两种模式。"移植型"是指将技术的全部内容予以转移,这种转让对吸纳主体的原有技术依赖性小,成功率高;而"嫁接型"转移的是部分的技术内容,所以它要求匹配的条件较为苛刻,但是支付的成本较低。按照技术载体的差异性,技术转移又可分为"实物型"、"智能型"和"人力型"三种。

词语宝典

technology transfer	技术转让	improvement	改进
hard technology transfer	硬技术转让	agreed territory	契约区域
soft technology transfer	软技术转让	tangible materials	有形资料
human resources transfer	人力转让	favorable policies	优惠政策
transplantation transfer	移植性转让	exclusive license	独享授权
insert transfer	嫁接性转让	royalty	版税
patents	专利	show-how	技术演示
technical information	技术资料	lump sum payment	总付
know-how	技术秘密		

经典句型

- Party A agrees to acquire from Party B and Party B agrees to transfer to Party A the technical know-how for the contracted product. Such know-how shall be in exact accordance with the technology of Party B's latest product.
  A方同意从B方获得，并且B方同意转让给A方合同下产品的技术秘密。该技术应该与B方最新产品所运用的技术保持一致。

- Party B shall be responsible for providing Party A with documents relative to said technical know-how.
  B方有责任向A方提供与上述技术资料相关的文件。

- Party B shall send at its own expense technical personnel to Party A's factory for technical training and service.
  B方自费派遣技术人员到A方工厂进行技术培训和服务。

- Party B is obliged to train Party A's technical personnel so as to enable them to master Party B's mould design, performance test and technology in machining, erection and inspection of the contracted product.
  B方有义务对A方技术人员进行培训，使A方受训人员掌握B方该合同项目下产品的模具设计、性能测试、加工技术、装配技术和质量验收技术等。

- The technology doesn't merely refer to industrial property right. Actually, know-how is also included.
  技术所指的不仅仅是工业产权，还包括专有技术。

- You will pay for our technology in the form of royalties apart from a certain initial down payment.
  除了一笔首付费用，您还应该以版税的方式支付我方提供的技术。

- It would work if the first two years of production were exempt from royalty and if the rate comes down to 4% of the net sales price.
  如果头两年免版税，并且版税率降到净销售价的4%，还是可行的。

- You should suggest measures for improvement if the samples fall short of the requirements.
  如果样品达不到要求，你方应提供改进方案。

- The technology will enable the venture's products to achieve marvelous economic results.
  该技术应该使我们的产品获得丰厚的经济效益。

- Our technical division will make sure the product meet the necessary specifications.

我们的技术部门要鉴定产品是否达到规定的规格。

- The royalty rate is 5% of the net sale price of all licensed items made and sold during the terms of agreement.
  版税率是在协议期间所有许可产品净销售价的 5%。

- To be honest, buying the know-how will be much cheaper than making the machine with our patent.
  说实话，购买核心技术要比购买专利制造该设备便宜许多。

- We hope you will pay us $50,000 for buying the production right from us, as well as 5% of the sales price on each of the product sold.
  我们希望你方支付从我方购买的生产权 50,000 美元，此外对每件出售的商品支付我方销售价格的 5% 作为提成。

- We will guarantee the supplied machinery with latest world level and the technology we offer is full-packaged, perfect and reliable.
  我们将保证所提供的设备是世界最先进水平，提供的技术是全套的、完整的、可以信赖的。

时尚对白

讨论核心技术的转让

A: We'd like to buy your company's know-how.
B: Buying the know-how is better than the right to use the patent.
A: Why?
B: Because the know-how tells all the details of how to manufacture the machines, and buying the know-how will be capable of contributing to advancement of our scientific and technical level.
A: Then how much will you ask for?
B: Triple the price for the patent.
A: That's too high a price.
B: Oh, just the opposite, buying the know-how will be much cheaper than making the machine with

A：我方打算购买你们公司的核心技术。
B：购买技术核心当然好过购买专利使用权。
A：为什么？
B：因为核心技术包括设备生产的全部细节，而且购买技术会提高我们的科学技术水平。
A：那么，你方的报价是？
B：是专利的三倍。
A：这也太高了。
B：不，正好相反。购买核心技术要

our patent.

A: I am afraid your price is higher than we can afford. Is it possible for you to reduce it?

B: Well, for friendship's sake, we can consider reducing the price further by 5%.

A: A cut of 10% would be more realistic.

B: I think it is unwise for either of us to insist on our own price. Can we meet each other halfway in order to narrow the gap?

A: Right. You have a way of persuading me to agree to your terms.

比用专利制造设备便宜很多。

A：恐怕您的报价已经超出了我们的承受值。能否降低一下价位？

B：好吧，看在朋友的份上，我们可以把价格再降5%。

A：降低10%也许更实际些。

B：我看双方在价位上继续坚持是不明智的。我们彼此各让一半缩短差距好吗？

A：好的。您真会说服人，我同意了。

达人点拨

在商谈购买专利和技术时，常见这样的表达，"Buying the know-how is better than the right to use the patent."（购买核心技术要比购买专利好得多。）在这里要注意"know-how"和"patent"的区别。根据具体情形来决定您要购买的是"know-how"还是"patent"吧。

 购买专利

A: Welcome to New York, Mr. Yang. Did you have a good trip?

B: Yes. And I had a very pleasant night.

A: Shall we talk about the business now?

B: That's fine with me. I'm ready. As we have mentioned in our correspondence, we would like you to provide us with the equipment under the price agreed between us.

A: I'm afraid that we have to renegotiate that, because product costs have rocked up recently and actually we are losing money. However, we are quite willing to transfer our patent.

B: I am so sorry to hear that. Since this is the only way for us to go, in what form do you transfer your patent?

A：杨先生，欢迎您到纽约来，旅途愉快吗？

B：很好，而且我度过了一个愉快的夜晚。

A：我们现在可以进入正题了吗？

B：可以啊，我准备好了。正如我们在信件中提到的，我们希望您能在我们双方达成的协议价格下提供给我们那套设备。

A：恐怕我们得重新协商一下，因为最近产品成本飞涨，实际上我们正在赔钱。但是我们还是愿意转让我们的专利。

B：听到您这么讲，我很遗憾。既然我们双方没有别的选择，您打算

A: Do you accept it if we transfer the patent right in the form of license?

B: But the license only gives us the right to manufacture the equipment, not including technology, isn't it right?

A: Don't worry, we will provide all the information and five technicians to offer help during your manufacturing.

B: OK. How long will you allow us to use the patent?

A: Three years.

达人点拨

即使是购买专利，也不能保证买家购买到所有的权利，大部分的合同是"transfer the patent right in the form of license"（以许可证的形式转让专利权），即"license only gives the buyer the right to manufacture the equipment, not including technology."（许可证只授予买方生产该设备的权利，不包括转让技术。）所以，在谈判中一定要确定购买的专利的使用范围。

谈判专利转让价格条款

A: Now, since we both have agreed on the transfer of patent right, shall we come down to payment?

B: Well, how much will you ask for?

A: We hope you will pay us $50,000 for buying the production right from us, as well as 5% of the sales price on each of the products sold.

B: I'm afraid we could not accept the quotation. We prefer the possibility of reducing it down to 1% of the sales price.

A: Let's both make a friendly concession, what about 3%?

B: I agree. You are a tough bargainer. However you should train our workers how to use it.

A: No problem. I think half a year on-the-spot

training will be enough for the workers to master the skills.

B:Now we have come to an agreement on price. Why not take a rest before we go down to the other terms?

A:OK.

> A：没问题。我想半年的现场培训应该足以让工人掌握操作技巧了。
>
> B：现在我们在价格上达成一致了。在商讨其他条款前我们休息一下吧？
>
> A：好啊。

 技术转让

A:We would like to improve and innovate in our present product line and develop new ones. Can you provide us with a technique license?

B:Hopefully we can satisfy your requirement. We will guarantee the supplied machinery with latest world level and the technology we offer is full-packaged, perfect and reliable.

A:What right can we enjoy with the license?

B:It will guarantee rights of both manufacture and sales of our products.

A:Does the license include the patent?

B:Yes, of course.

A:How long would we be allowed to use the patent?

B:Up to five years. But you have to promise to keep all the technical information confidential provided by us within the stipulated duration.

A:Certainly. But if any third party questions the right to use the patent, you should bear full responsibility and explanation.

B:All right.

> A：我方想改造我们现有的生产线，还要开发新的生产线。你能提供我们技术许可吗？
>
> B：希望我们能满足你方的需求。我们将保证所提供的设备是世界最先进水平，提供的技术是全套的、完整的、可以依赖的。
>
> A：那我们会随着这个许可享受什么权利呢？
>
> B：该许可会保证您享受对我方产品生产和销售的权利。
>
> A：该许可包括专利在内吗？
>
> B：是的，当然。
>
> A：我们对专利的使用期限是多久？
>
> B：最多五年，但是您得保证在指定期间内对我方提供的所有技术资料保密。
>
> A：那是当然。但是如果任何第三方质疑对该专利的使用权，您得全权负责并解释。
>
> B：可以。

 技术转让协议细节

A:You know, this is the first time we are getting involved in a technology transfer transaction. As

> A：您知道，这是我们第一次接触技术转让贸易。作为一个在该领域

an experienced businessman in this field, what would you like to suggest in the technology transfer agreement? Is it a lot different from other contracts?

B: Yes. Technology transfer is rather complicated. It can be conducted by several means, such as licensing, consulting, technique assistance and co-operation, etc.. And in practice they are used together under one agreement. Therefore, it is never far enough to give full consideration before you sign the agreement.

A: So, what should be covered in a transfer agreement?

B: Let's take a licensing agreement for an example. As a commonly adopted transaction, a licensing agreement usually includes the following items: the scope of transfer, price and payment, confidentiality responsibility, technique continuing assistance and staff training, etc.

A: It seems we have lots of work to do for a transfer agreement. By the way, you have mentioned payment. What should I pay attention to in terms of price terms?

B: The pricing and payment are quite different from commodity trading since what is traded is know-how, patent and intellectual knowledge. And payment under this agreement usually is via lump sum payment, royalty and initial payment plus royalty.

A: Oh, my goodness. It seems we have so many terms to learn before we have a full understanding. Thank you so much for your information.

的资深人员，您能不能给我们的技术转让合同提些建议？这种合同与其他合同有很多不同吗？

B：是啊。技术转让相当复杂。它包括许可转让、咨询、技术支持和合作等。在实践当中，它们会并在一个合同中。因此，在签订该种协议之前一定要给予充分的考虑。

A：那么，在一份技术转让协议中通常都包含那些条款呢？

B：我们以许可协议为例。作为一种普遍采用的贸易方式，许可协议包括如下内容：转让范围、价格、支付方式、保密责任条款、持续性技术支持和人员培训等。

A：看来我们在达成一个转让协议前得做许多工作呢。对了，您刚才提到了支付方式。在价格条款中我该注意哪些问题？

B：这个项目下的定价和支付完全不同于实物的贸易，因为在该形式下交易的是技术机密、专利、知识产权等。而付款方式是通过转让总付款、版税，或是首付款加版税等形式来实现。

A：天哪，看来我们要想全面了解还有许多术语要学呢。非常感谢您提供的信息。

达人点拨

在签署技术转让协议时，最好要考虑全面，包括"the scope of transfer, price and payment, confidentiality responsibility, technique continuing assistance and staff training, etc."（转让范围、价格、支付方式、保密责任条款、持续的技术支持和人员培训等。）。

技术转让谈判

A: Now, can we come down to the details of payment?

B: Sure. We hope to get all of the contracted payment once the delivery of the basic technical document is effected.

A: I am afraid we couldn't accept it. It is preferred that we pay 60% of the agreed payment upon receiving all the demanded technical information. Then after the products produced with imported technology meet the quality standard agreed upon in the contract, the other part of the payment will be conducted immediately.

B: That's too long before we collect a full payment. You know, we are so short of money right now. Can we make concession on both sides by increasing to 80% of the contracted price as initial payment?

A: Well, for the sake of long friendship between us, let us fix it to the percentage you have mentioned. But you have to promise to provide in technical documentation full package of technical literature, drawings, diagrams, operation instructions and computer programs and so on.

B: Sure, no problem. We will do our best to meet your requirements.

A: And a detailed time schedule of documentation delivery should be drafted by you as soon as possible.

B: No problem. As a matter of fact our people are working on it now.

A: In addition, it is contracted in the agreement you should also deliver us a clear document specifying technical assistance with the names, specialties, working period and duties of the

---

A: 现在，我们可以谈谈支付条款的细节吗？

B: 当然可以。我们希望在基本技术文件发送之后就得到合同规定的全部款额。

A: 恐怕我方没法接受。我方建议在收到所需的所有技术资料后支付协议款项的60%。而在使用引进技术生产的产品达到合同规定的标准后，马上支付剩余款项。

B: 那我们收齐全部款额的周期太长了。您也知道，我方现在很缺乏资金。我们能不能双方做个让步，将首付款提高到合同总价的80%？

A: 好吧，既然我们双方一直很友好，就按照您提到的比例支付。但是您得承诺在技术文件里提供全套的技术资料、图纸、图表、操作指南、电脑程序等。

B: 当然，没问题。我们将尽力满足您的要求。

A: 请尽快发给我们文件发送的详尽时间安排。

B: 一定。事实上我们的人员正在处理。

A: 此外，如合同所规定的，你方应发给我方一份清晰的文件提供技术支持人员的名字、专长、工作期限和相关职责。

involved technicians.

B: Of course, a detailed timetable of documentation delivery and a full package of technical service personnel will reach you within one week.

B：当然可以。详细的文件发送时间表和完整的技术人员资料会在一周内让您收到。

达人点拨

在技术转让协议的履行中关于支付条款的执行也相当重要，常见的例句有："We hope to get all of the contracted payment once the delivery of the basic technical document is effected."（我方希望基本的技术文件发出后就得到所有的合同款项。）但是对方往往不会接受，他们会这样建议，"It is preferred for us to pay 60% of the agreed payment upon receiving all the demanded technique information. Then after the products produced with imported technology meet the quality standard agreed upon in the contract, the other part of the payment will be conducted immediately."（我方建议在收到所需的技术文件时，支付对方 60% 的合同款项。余额将在按照所得技术生产的产品达到合同规定的质量要求之后支付。）所以，学会一两句讨价还价的表达吧。

文化点滴

如何与德国商人打交道

1．在您的商务名片上写全您的职务或职称，以及您所获得的大学的学位。您的名片可以采用英文表述。
2．在德国商业文化中客观事实是真实与否的基础。
3．当您在准备推广材料时，要知道德国商人不会被广告和印象深刻的标语所打动，产品宣传手册应该语气严肃，内附详尽的细节。
4．如果您未能履行合同或条款，德国人会公开批评您。要准备好道歉并期望给予补偿。
5．在德国，制定的规则要严格遵守，德国商人是不会轻易让步的。一旦合同里的某一项条款确定下来，是不可改变的。
6．在德国的商业文化里，变通和冲动都不可行。
7．在德国的商业中做决定的过程是缓慢的，任何和你方案相关的细节都会被不辞辛苦地审查。
8．会议结束后，德国人有时通过用关节轻轻敲击桌面来表示同意或感谢，而不是鼓掌。
9．任何企图和一个大型德国公司进行争执和有过激的行为通常都会得到适得其反的效果。

合并与兼并
Merger and Acquisition

合并和兼并是指两个或两个以上的企业合并在一起经营。合并通常是发生在同样经营规模的企业之间，而兼并的情况多出现在一个企业以更大的优势和规模来吞并另一家弱小的企业。20世纪末以来，兼并合并在全球发展迅速。

合并和兼并，简称并购，通常有以下几种类型：水平并购是指处于同一行业和生产阶段的两家公司合并成一个更具有市场竞争力的企业；纵向并购涉及同一产品的不同生产和经营阶段的相关企业的联盟，旨在获取更加稳定的市场或者是扩大产业力度和规模。此外，还有多元化并购，在这种情况下两个或两个以上完全不同行业的企业合并在一起，以开发新的市场机会或降低经营风险。

导致并购的原因很多，首先它是扩展企业的一种快捷而简便的方式。另外，合并企业比单独发展成本降低，而与其他国家的企业合并又是打入外国市场和实现全球化战略的有效途径。同时，合并可以使企业获得规模化的经济效益。

词语宝典

takeover	兼并	horizontal integration	横向并购
acquisition	兼并	strategic alliance	战略联盟
merger	合并	complimentary skills	互补技能
globalization	全球化	means of settlement	结算方式
shareholders	股东	economy of scale	规模经济
management	管理（层）	friendly takeover	友好兼并
asset stripping	资产剥离	hostile takeover	敌对兼并
vertical integration	纵向并购		

经典句型

- What are the possible benefits of this merger to our company?
  这个新的并购企业可能给我们公司带来什么好处？
- Alliance may take looser forms of management than joint ventures.
  联盟与合资相比可以采取更宽松的管理模式。

- Why might a company need diversity?
  一个企业为什么需要多元化？

- It is possible for disagreements to occur about the management of the merged firm.
  很可能一个合并企业的管理中会有诸多不同意见的现象发生。

- Mergers may take place for defensive reasons.
  兼并之所以会发生是出于自我防御的考虑。

- Our merger can enhance our competitiveness in the global market.
  我们双方的合并会提高我们在全球市场的竞争力。

- To join together will mean the integration of our complementary skills and advantages.
  合并意味着我们互补技能和优势的融合。

- The firm may be struggling because it has cash flow problems.
  该公司正因为现金流问题陷入困境。

- Forward vertical integration involves merging with a firm which is the next stage of production, such as a merger with a retailer of bikes.
  向前纵向融合就是和一个位于下一个生产阶段的公司的联合，比如和自行车零售商的合并。

- In negotiation of M&A projects, both parties should be clear about their counterparty's purpose.
  在合并兼并项目的谈判中，双方要搞清对方的目的。

- What might be the motive for a reverse takeover?
  反向兼并的动机是什么？

- What factors gave rise to the significant increase in M&A in recent years?
  是什么因素导致了今年合并兼并的显著增长？

- Why might external growth be quicker than internal growth?
  为什么外部发展比内部增长要快？

时尚对白

兼并的价格和结算方式

A: Now, let's discuss the issue of price and settlement method for the acquisition program.

B: All right. Our bidding price is $10 billion. Do

A：现在，让我们讨论一下项目兼并的价格和结算问题吧。

B：好的。 我们投标的价格是一百亿美

you agree?

A: Yes, we do. Our board of directors has voted for it. But, concerning the means of settlement, there are still different ideas.

B: What different ideas?

A: Some shareholders think that settlement by cash payment is their best choice because they can immediately get the visible money. But others prefer to settle it by means of shares so that they will continue to be the owners of the new firm who can still have some influence over the firm.

B: I see. What is your current plan for the settlement method?

A: Our party would like to solve the problem by means of payment with half in cash and half in shares. Is it acceptable to your party?

B: Yes, it is.

元，您同意吗？

A：我们接受。我方董事会已经投票表决通过了该价格。不过，关于结算方式，我们仍然存在不同的意见。

B：有什么不同意见？

A：一些持股人认为现金结算是他们最好的选择，因为他们想立刻得到现金。但是有人打算通过股票方式结算，因为他们打算通过持股继续成为新公司的所有者，继续对新公司施加影响。

B：我明白了。那么您当前计划的结算方式是什么？

A：我方想通过一半以现金支付，一半采用股票的方式来解决这一问题。您接受吗？

B：好的，我们接受。

达人点拨

在兼并的协商中，通常会有股票和现金两种不同的结算方式，它们的目的也不一样，所以要记住这样的表达"Some shareholders think that settlement by cash payment is their best choice because they can immediately get the visible money."（一些股票持有者选择现金支付是因为他们可以马上拿到现钱。）但是有的人宁愿采用股票方式达成交易，因为他们可以继续成为新公司的股东，并对新公司施加影响。

讨论兼并的动机

A: Good morning.

B: Good morning. Pleased to see you again.

A: I've reviewed the proposal for the merger between our two firms. But I am still not very clear why we should join together?

B: There is an obvious key reason for this merger program. It is to say, our firms will both benefit a lot from it and a win-win situation will occur.

A：早上好。

B：早上好。很高兴再次见到您。

A：我已经审阅了您那份关于我们两家公司合并经营的建议书。不过我仍然不太清楚我们为什么要合并。

B：这个合并计划有一个明显的关键原因。那就是，我们双方会从中

A: What win-win situation can we achieve then?

B: Both of us are now facing fierce competition pressure in the global market, so our merger can increase our competitiveness.

A: How can we become a stronger competitor if we join together?

B: As all of us know, your company is good at operation in the Chinese local market, but you lack advanced international management experience. In contrast, our firm performs better in global market management, but needs more business accesses and sales networks in the Chinese market. Thus, to join together means the integration of our compensational skills and advantages. In that case, we will be more competitive in both domestic and foreign markets.

A: You are right. Such a strategic alliance between us, if based on such an obvious motive, will allow a quicker expansion of your company towards Chinese markets, and also push ours more rapidly into the global market. Is it right?

B: You said it.

获取诸多好处而且会有一个双赢的局面出现。

A：那么，我们会出现什么样的双赢局面呢？

B：目前我们双方都面临着严峻的国际市场竞争压力，因此我们的合并会增强我们的市场竞争力。

A：如果合并，我们怎么才能成为更强大的竞争者呢？

B：我们都知道，您的公司擅长中国本土市场的运作但是缺乏先进的国际管理经验；而我们公司精于国际市场的企业管理但是缺乏在中国市场的经营经验和销售网络。这样一来，双方的合并意味着双方技术互补和优势的合并。那样，我们在国内外市场将更具有竞争力。

A：我明白了。我们双方的战略联盟可以建立在这样一个显而易见的动机上，那么您的公司可以更快地拓展中国市场，而我们可以更快地向全球市场挺进。我说的对吧？

B：完全正确。

咨询并购类型

A: What can I do for you, sir?

B: Well, we are planning to take over other companies as our expansion strategy. We came to your consultancy firm for your advice on this issue.

A: We are pleased to offer you any possible help. What do you want to know?

B: We are not clear enough about types of mergers

A：先生，可以为您效劳吗？

B：嗯，我们打算兼并其他公司作为我们的扩展战略。我到你们咨询公司来是想听听您对这一问题的建议。

A：很乐意尽可能地提供帮助。您想了解什么情况？

B：我们目前对并购的类型不太了解，

so far. Could you first introduce this to us?

A: Sure, no problem. Mergers can be divided into horizontal integration, vertical integration, and diversified integration.

B: How are they different?

A: Horizontal integration occurs when two companies in exactly the same line of business and the same production stage join together, such as two auto firms, or two mobile companies, or two oil refinery plants, etc.

B: What about vertical integration?

A: Vertical integration means that one firm, for instance, a manufacturer, joins together with another firm in the previous production stage such as raw material supplier or in the next stage such as a retailer.

B: Then, how can we understand diversified integration?

A: Diversified integration involves two or more businesses who are dealing with two different lines, where the new merger is usually aimed at new and different market opportunities and reduced operation risks.

B: I see. Thank you so much for the help. Your explanation really enlightens me.

A: You are welcome.

您能首先向我们介绍一下这方面的知识吗？

A：没问题。并购可以分为以下几种类型：水平并购、纵向并购和多元化并购。

B：它们的不同之处在哪里？

A：水平并购是指处于完全同一行业或者完全同一生产阶段的两家公司的融合，比如两家汽车经营公司、两家手机公司 或者是两家炼油企业，等等。

B：那么纵向并购又是怎么回事儿？

A：纵向并购是指一家公司，如一个制造商和另一个处于上游生产阶段的公司，如原材料供应商，或一家处于下游阶段的公司，如零售商，联合成立新公司的情况。

B：那么，又该如何理解多元化并购呢？

A：多元化并购涉及两家或两家以上完全不同行业的企业，而新的合并公司旨在开发新的不同的市场机会，降低运营风险。

B：我懂了。非常感谢您的帮助，通过您的解释我全明白了。

A：不用客气。

达人点拨

您如果想了解兼并这个市场，得明确几个基本概念"Horizontal integration, vertical integration, and diversified integration."（水平并购，纵向并购和多元化并购。）"horizontal integration" 通常是指出于相同地位和规模的两家公司的合并重组；而"vertical integration"多是一个行业内部的上下游业务之间的兼并；至于"diversified integration" 是指跨行业的兼并。

合并和兼并

A: Hello, Professor Swift, are you free now? I have some questions to consult with you if you don't mind.

B: Surely not. What is it about?

A: In our last class, I noticed that sometimes you used the term "Merger", but some other times you used the word "Acquisition". Are they the same terms to express integration of two or more companies?

B: Well, that is a tough question. Theoretically they are different. Merger is also called absorption occasionally, that is, one company incorporates another one and hence deprives the latter of legal person status. It usually occurs when two firms of the similar size and capacity, strong or weak, both intend to enlarge their own scales and expand into a bigger market or continue smooth operation in a fierce competition.

A: So, acquisition refers to the integration of two companies of unparallel level, am I right?

B: Yes. Acquisition means literally to obtain something, hence usually involves the action that an enterprise obtains the actual ownership and administration and management through buying the other's capital or shares. Another expression of this integration is "take over." I think this word can teach you a lot about acquisition.

A: I see. As I understand it, takeover must occur when one firm is weak and the other is strong.

B: That's right in most cases. A business, say, can acquire a public limited company by buying 51% of the shares.

A：您好，斯威夫特教授。现在您有时间吗？如果不介意我有几个问题想咨询一下。

B：当然不介意。什么问题？

A：上次课，我注意到您有时用"合并"一词，有时又用"兼并"一词。它们在表达两家或两家以上公司的整合时是同样的意思吗？

B：嗯，这是个棘手的问题。在理论上它们不同。合并有时又叫吸收。也就是说，一个公司吸收了另一个公司而剥夺了后者的法人地位。这经常发生在两家具有同样规模和实力的公司之间，同样强大，或同样弱小，而双方都想扩大经营规模，开拓更大的市场，或在激烈的竞争中继续平稳发展。

A：所以，兼并是指两家实力不均衡的公司之间的融合，是吗？

B：是的。兼并在字面上的意思就是获得，因此经常包括这样的行为，如一家企业通过购买另一家的资本或股票获得实际的所有权和管理经营权。这种融合的另外一个表达是"接收"。我想这个词会对你理解兼并有帮助。

A：我明白了。我是这样理解的，"接收"一定发生在一个公司弱小而另一家实力强大时。

B：在大多数情况是这样。比如，一家企业可以通过购买51%的股份获得一家上市的股份有限公司。

A: But why did you mix them up in your lectures, sometimes using merger, while other times applying acquisition?

B: That is what I'm going to talk about. Although the initial intention of merger and acquisition might differ, the results in reality are basically the same, a new legal person, and a set of new administrations. So there is no necessity to give them strict distinction. That's why I blend them at times.

A: I'm so pleased to get it clear, thank you Professor Swift.

B: You are welcome.

A：那么，您为什么在讲课的时候混合在一起用呢？您有时用合并，有时又用兼并？

B：我正要讲到那儿。虽然合并和兼并的最初含义不同，但实际的结果基本是相同的。都是新的法人，全新的管理机构，所以没有必要对它们进行严格的区分。这也就是为什么我有时会把这两个词混淆。

A：能弄明白我很开心，谢谢您斯威夫特教授。

B：不必客气。

 ## 母国和东道国

A: Nice to meet you again, Mr. Johnson. How did you like your trip?

B: Really nice. After a full rest last night, I am refreshed again. I cannot feel any better now.

A: We invited you to come to our company in order to confirm the issue of belonging of our new merger. I am wondering why the new company belongs to your country, since we are foreign invested venture.

B: The case is like this. There is a difference under merger between the mother country and the host country.

A: That is pretty new to me. Could you give me a further explanation?

B: If a domestic company in Country X. for instance, intends to incorporate another local enterprise in Country Y, we say Country X is the mother country, and Country Y is the host country.

A：很高兴再次和您见面，约翰逊先生，您的旅途还好吧？

B：好极了。经过昨晚的休息，我现在精神焕发，感觉非常好。

A：我们邀请您来是想确认一下我们合并的新公司的归属地的问题。我想知道为什么这个新公司属于您的国家，我方是国外投资企业啊。

B：情况是这样的。在合并项目下，存在着母国和东道国的区别。

A：这对我来讲太新鲜了，您能进一步解释一下吗？

B：如果一个在X国注册的本地公司，要合并另一个在Y国注册的当地公司，我们称X国是母国，而Y国是东道国。

A: Then what if a domestic company in Country X takes over a foreign company registered in the same country, just like our case?

B: Under this situation, both the mother country and the host country are the same, Country X. That's because both of the two companies are registered in the same country. Hence our new firm is still a Chinese corporation under the governess of Chinese laws.

A: I got it. What plays a decisive role is where the firm is registered. And the mother country is related to the company conducting the merger or the takeover, while the host country is the place where the firm being merged or taken over registered.

B: Absolutely right.

A：那么如果一个在X国注册的本地公司想合并在同一个国家注册的外资企业呢，就像我们这种情况？

B：这种情况下，母国和东道国是一个国家，都是X国，因为两个公司都是在同一个国家注册的。这样我们新的公司仍然是适用于中国法律的一家中国公司。

A：我懂了。不论是母国还是东道国，起决定作用的是公司在哪里注册。母国就是和执行合并或接收的公司相关，而东道国就是被接收的公司注册的国家。

B：完全正确。

达人点拨

被兼并或重组后的公司的归属国的问题也相当敏感和复杂。这里要认清两个术语，"host country"（东道国）和"mother country"（母国）的区别。"Mother country is related to the company conducting merging or takeover."（母国和实施合并和接收的公司注册国相关。）"Host country is the place where the firm being merged or taken over registered."（东道国是指被兼并的公司的注册地。）。

跨国公司的优势

A: Good morning, sir. I come here to consult about the chance of expanding our company. As you know, our company has been keeping rapid development over the recent years. How can I make it larger and more popular?

B: Why not consider the possibility of merger & acquisition? It is particularly favored by international corporations, and most of them are from North America and EU.

A：早上好，先生。我来是想咨询一下我们公司扩大的可能性。您知道，我们公司在最近几年一直保持快速增长的态势。我怎么才能扩大其规模和知名度呢？

B：为什么不考虑一下并购的可能性？国际大公司特别喜欢这样做，而绝大部分都来自于北美和欧盟国家。

A: Why are they so keen on integration or takeover?

B: It offers a rapid route to enter into overseas market and expand market shares. Normally a firm adopts two ways to open international markets: direct product export or "Greenland Investment." But they both have to bear lots of negative factors.

A: What are the bad factors for the two methods?

B: Direct product export is often challenged with high cost in delivery and tariff barrier, and "Greenland Investment" refers to establish a new factory in another country, at the cost of long preparation periods.

A: So, many companies choose to take the manner of merger. How convenient and easy is it?

B: Compared with the aforesaid modes, merger & acquisition guarantees a company's access to a new international market at the fastest speed.

A: Are there any other benefits?

B: Certainly. It is an effective way to make use of current resources of the target corporation, including mature sales networks, existing patents, know-how, brands and reputation. It also contains established management and human resources.

A: That looks great. Perhaps I will make a plan to incorporate some companies abroad. Thanks a lot. I hope next time I come here you can tell me detailed information about merger agreements.

B: Glad to be at your service. You are always welcome to come here.

A：为什么他们如此热衷于并购？

B：这样做可以提供一条快速通道进军海外市场，扩大市场份额。通常情况下，一个公司采取两种方法开拓国际市场：直接产品出口，或是"绿地投资"。但是这两种做法都得承受许多不良因素。

A：哪些不良因素呢？

B：直接产品出口经常面临运输上的高成本和贸易壁垒问题，而"绿地投资"是指在另一个国家建立一个新的工厂，代价是准备时间太长。

A：所以，许多公司选择并购，这样做又方便在哪儿？

B：和之前提到的贸易模式相比，并购可以确保一个公司以最快的速度进军国际市场。

A：还有别的好处吗？

B：当然。它可以有效利用目标公司的现有资源，包括成熟的销售网络，现有专利、技术、商标和信誉，以及成熟的管理体制和人力资源。

A：看起来不错。或许我该计划一下兼并海外公司的可能性。太谢谢了。我希望下次来的时候您可以告诉我一些关于合并协议的具体内容。

B：很高兴为您服务，欢迎您随时来咨询。

> **达人点拨**
>
> 最近几年来兼并如此盛行，主要原因是其能使一个公司迅速地并且无需费力就可以进军一个新兴市场，而传统的直接产品贸易或是在另一个国家投资建厂都是耗时又耗力。想表达兼并的好处可以记住这样的句型，"It is an effective way to make full use of current resources of the target corporation, including mature sales networks, existing patents, know-how, brands and reputation."（这是一个有效的方法，可以充分利用目标公司的现有资源，包括成熟的销售网络，现有专利、技术、品牌和知名度。）。

文化点滴

如何与法国商人打交道

1．强烈建议您学些基础法语，尽管大多数法国商人都懂英语。
2．绝大多数的法国商人都懂英语。但是如果你的名片采用了法语，应该在上面用法语标明你的职位和大学学历。
3．法国人非常直接，好质疑且一针见血，所以和他们交往时准备一份完备的计划书是非常重要的。
4．他们会迅速批评任何不合逻辑的部分。
5．法国人会根据您在和他们辩论时或是讨论新颖观点时您的表现来评价您的能力。
6．法国人不愿意承担风险。
7．通常来讲，在法国，遵循政府和行政部门的一系列手续要比效率或灵活性重要得多。
8．法国人不会接受任何和文化理念相悖而驰的观点。
9．法国人倾向于长远的目的，力图同合作方建立牢固的私人关系，但是，他们不太相信过于迅速的友谊。
10．法国的商业礼仪中一贯注重程序化，在谈判中会有所保留。

合作经营
Joint Venture

合营企业又称合资企业，是当代国际间直接投资的主要形式之一。合营企业包括股权式合营，即我国的中外合资合营企业；契约式合营，即我国的中外合作经营企业。

合资经营，就是有关各方共同投资、共同经营、共负盈亏。合资的各方以现金实物或无形财产折价后，各按一定比例的股份出资，共同组建一个具有法人地位、在经济上独立核算、在业务上独立经营的企业。

与合资经营企业不同，中外合作经营企业是一种建立在合约基础上的合营关系。缔约各方的权利和义务、合作条件、产品分配、风险的分担、经营管理方式等事项，都通过合作企业合同予以约定，而不像合资企业那样以各方的认股比例为准。

词语宝典

dividend	红利	simple majority	简单多数
ownership	股权	special majority	特别多数
contribution	出资	market arrangement	市场布局
premise	房屋	equity joint venture	股权式合营企业
unanimity	一致意见	contractual joint venture	契约式合营企业
joint venture	合营企业	preferential treatment	最惠待遇
capital structure	资本结构	tax exemption	税收减免
board of directors	董事会	registered capital	注册资金
transfer of shares	股票转让	legal person status	法人地位

经典句型

- Last time we talked about the establishment of a joint venture to produce wooden floors. Through the consultation with my company, we'd like to establish an equity joint venture. Each of the two sides will put in a certain portion of the capital and share profits or losses in proportion to their respective contributions.

上次我们探讨了建立合资企业生产木质地板的事宜。通过与我方相关人员的咨询，我们有意建立股份制合资企业，双方各按一定比例投资资金，并按照投资比例共享收益或共担亏损。

- Many of your suggestions have been incorporated into the new plan.
  贵方的许多建议已经被纳入这项新计划中。

- How much would you like to invest in this project, anyway?
  但是，你们打算在这一方案中投资多少？

- What regulations does Chinese government have on the foreign proportion of investment?
  中国政府对于外商投资比例有何规定？

- Then our capital contribution will include production equipment, testing instruments and technology.
  那么我方投入的资金总额包括生产设备、试验仪器和技术。

- Now let's talk about the duration of the joint venture. How long can we run it?
  现在我们来谈谈该合营企业的期限问题。合营期限多长？

- Usually the composition of the board of directors is in proportion to the capital contributed.
  董事会成员组成按照各方的注入资金成比例分配。

- The term of office for the directors is set for a four-year term.
  董事的任期是四年一届。

- The law precisely states the legal status of the joint venture and protects the lawful rights of the foreign participants.
  该法律明确规定了合资企业的法律地位，保护了合营外方的法律权利。

- As we have informed you previously, it is our opinion that we make investment on 50%-50% basis and wonder if this is practical.
  正如我们之前告知的，我方的意见是各投资50%，不知是否可行。

- After the authorizations have been obtained, A and B shall establish, in accordance with the whereas clauses, a joint stock company under the laws of P. R.China for the purpose of manufacture and sale of transition radios.
  经授权后，A、B双方应根据条款要求建立一个符合中国法律的合资股份公司，目的是生产和销售半导体收音机。

- The board of directors of NEWCOMP shall consist of six directors, three of whom shall be persons nominated by A and three of whom shall be persons nominated by B.

All the directors shall be elected in the general meeting of the shareholders.

新公司的董事会成员将由六位董事组成，其中三位由A公司提名，另外三位由B公司提名。所有董事都通过股东大会选举产生。

- All business administration of NEWCOMP shall be decided by a majority of the board of directors. The quorum for the meeting of directors shall not be less than a majority of the total number of the directors.

  新公司的行政管理应由董事会的大多数决定。董事会议的法定人数应不少于全体董事的大多数。

- A shall supply NEWCOMP with technical know-how regarding the processes of production and render technical assistance regarding the operation of machines and tools.

  A方负责提供新公司与生产过程相关的技术机密，在设备和工具的操作方面给予技术支持。

- B shall provide NEWCOMP for the successful operation of this enterprise with necessary land, facilities and local labor.

  B方负责向新公司提供为了企业的顺利运行而必需的土地、设施和当地的劳动力。

- The share of NEWCOMP shall not be mortgaged by either party without prior written consent of the other party.

  新公司的股份如果没有另一方事先的书面同意，任何一方不能用作抵押。

- A and B agree to keep strictly secret and not to disclose to any third party any technical, financial or marketing information acquired from the other or from NEWCOMP.

  A、B双方同意严格保守机密，不向任何第三方泄露来自于另一方的或是新公司的任何技术、财务或是营销信息。

时尚对白

询问中国的合资优惠政策

A: I'm thinking of joining hand with you to set up a mobile phone construction factory which would furnish China with the latest technical cellphones.

B: It sounds a good idea. There is no doubt we will make each effort to cooperate with you. And you

A：我正考虑和您联手建立一个手机组装工厂，生产面向中国客户的含有最先进技术的手机。

B：听起来不错。毫无疑问我们会竭尽

will enjoy preferential treatment for this joint venture in China.

A: What privileged treatment can we get for a Sino-foreign joint venture?

B: According to the related laws and regulations of the Chinese government, a joint venture in China pays lower income tax, or even no income tax at all under some conditions, during the first five profit-making years.

A: But the profit-making year is different from the year the factory is in operation, right?

B: You said it. This is the year when the factory gets profits. Furthermore, if you have paid income taxes on your net profits in China, you are exempted from taxation at home country as long as you meet relative requirements.

A: It's encouraging. That is the avoidance of double taxation. Since it is our first time to invest in China, what concerns me is how long the advantages of paying lower taxes would last.

B: Please don't be worried about it. Since it was incorporated into the Chinese constitution, the policy would remain stable for a long period.

A: Then I can rest assured of it.

中国的中外合营企业经营模式

A: Furthermore, China is a big country with a large population and low wages, together with abundant natural resources and land. All these are favorable conditions for direct investment.

B: What China needs to deal with is the import of advanced equipment, technology and mature management experience. In addition to this, I'd like to know how profits and risks are shared in a joint venture.

A: Basically there are two types of joint venture: equity joint venture and contractual joint venture.

B: What's the difference between them?

A: In an equity joint venture, the profits and risks are shared according to the partners' capital contribution in the venture. While in a contractual one, everything is stipulated in a contract, including the profits and risks.

B: I see. Are there any regulations regarding foreign investment proportion in the registered venture?

A: Generally speaking, the foreign partner should invest no less than 25%, but no upper limit.

B: Thanks. How long is the duration of a joint venture?

A: No rigid rules. The contract could be extended if the sides involved agree.

B: How would a joint venture be administrated?

A: A joint venture is under the guidance of the board of directors. And the number and the rights of directors, based on certain regulations, are determined by the investment they have made in the business.

B: It sounds rather reasonable. You have certainly enlightened me quite a lot about establishing a joint venture in China. I will hold a discussion with my company's management and let you know the result as soon as possible.

我想知道合资企业里利润和风险是如何分配的？

A：基本上有两种合资方式：股权式合营和合约式合营。

B：有什么区别？

A：在股权式合营里，利润和风险根据合伙人投资资金的多少来分配；而在一个合约式合营企业，一切按照合同规定，包括利润和风险。

B：我明白了。关于外资在注册的合资企业里的投资份额，有什么规定吗？

A：一般来讲，外商投资额度不少于25%，但是没有上限。

B：谢谢。合资企业的合作期限呢？

A：没有硬性规定。如果各方同意，合同可以延长。

B：合资企业怎么管理？

A：合资企业是在董事会的领导下。董事的人数和权利 根据一定的规则，取决于各方在企业里的投资。

B：听起来比较合理。关于在中国建立合营企业您给我提供了很多信息，我会和我公司的管理层讨论，尽快让您知道讨论结果。

达人点拨

在进行"joint venture"（合营企业）的谈判中，首先要确定两种合营企业的区别，即"equity joint venture"（股权式合营）和"contractual joint venture"（合约式合营）；其次要理清双方的"profit and risk share"（利润和风险分配）。如果是在中国境内建立合资企业，外商要咨询中国政府要求的"the minimum requirement for foreign share"（外方投资最低比例）。

股权式合营与合约式合营的区别

A: I'm interested in the business structure of Sino-foreign joint venture. You mentioned two types of joint venture: equity joint venture and contractual joint venture. What are the differences between them?

B: You see, there are a few legal distinctions between an equity joint venture (EJV) and contractual joint venture (CJV). First, in an EJV, the rofit distribution and management responsibility are determined by the proportion of investment by each party. While in a CJV, the profits and rights and obligations are distributed according to the joint venture contract.

A: I see.

B: Also, a CJV may distribute profits both in cash and in venture output, but an EJV is restricted to making cash distribution.

A: So a CJV has more flexibility, right?

B: Yes. A CJV can adopt a non-legal person status, which distinguishes itself from an EJV. This allows foreign CJV partners to contribute less than 25% of the total investment capital of the joint venture.

A: You mean in an EJV the foreign partner has to contribute at least 25%?

B: Sure. The third difference is that the CJVs are not required to survey Chinese sources before importing supplies or raw materials from abroad, while EJVs must give first priority to Chinese suppliers.

A: I see. If I understand it right, the EJV is very rigid and the CJV is much more flexible. If I have to choose between them, I'd prefer the CJV format.

B: Well, it depends.

A：我对中外合营企业的结构很感兴趣。您刚才提到了两种合资类型：股权式和合约式。它们有什么区别？

B：你看，二者有几点法律上的区别。首先，在股权式合营企业里，利润的分配和管理职责是由参与方的投资份额决定的。而在合约式合营企业里，利润和权利义务是根据合营合约来分配的。

A：我明白了。

B：而且，一个合约式合资企业可以以现金或产品的方式分配利润，而股权式合营企业仅仅限于现金分配。

A：也就是说一个合约式企业有更大的弹性，对吧？

B：是的。一个合约式合资企业可以采用无法人体制，这一点是有别于股权式企业的。这也允许合约式企业的外商可以投资少于25%的份额。

A：您的意思是在一个股权式合资企业里，外商投资应不少于25%，是吗？

B：对。第三点区别是，合约式合资企业在从国外进口原材料时，不需要调查中国的原材料市场情况；而在一个股权式合资企业里，原材料的优先供应权应给予中国供应商。

A：我明白了。如果我理解正确的话，股权式合营比较僵硬，而合约式就有更大的弹性。如果可以选择的话，我倾向于合约式。

B：哦，这得依情形而定。

> **达人点拨**
>
> 在协商建立合资企业期间，双方会分析股权式合营和合约式合营的区别和利弊。常见的表达方式有："A contractual joint venture may distribute profits both in cash and in venture output, but an equity one is restricted to making cash distribution."（一个合约式合营企业可以通过现金和产品的方式分配利润，而一个股权式合营企业仅限于现金分配。）此外，在两种不同的合资模式下，外方的投资比例要求也不一样。不仅如此，在进口原材料方面，"A contractual joint venture doesn't have to take into account China's domestic raw material market, but an equity one has to give the priority to China's local market."（一个合约式合营企业不用考虑中国的国内原材料市场；而一个股权式合营企业必须要优先考虑中国的本土市场。）

 讨论建立合资企业的细节

A: We'd like to establish a refrigerator joint venture. Is there any regulation on the foreign proportion of investment?

B: Yes. The lowest proportion shall be 30%, but there is no upper limit.

A: We are ready to pay a contribution of 60%. Must we invest in cash only?

B: The parties to the joint venture may contribute cash, capital goods and industrial property rights, etc. as their investment.

A: Good. We'll invest machinery and equipment estimated at about 45 % of the total investment.

B: We then provide the factory building, premises, some machinery and equipment. The right to use the site is also a part of our investment.

A: How will the value of contribution other than cash be determined?

B: The machinery and equipment shall be assessed by a Chinese assessment organization according to their prices in the current world market.

A: How shall they be evaluated if there is not such a world market price?

B: They will be estimated based on actual cost plus freight and insurance.

A：我们想建立一个生产冰箱的合资企业。在外商投资方面有什么规定吗？

B：好的，外商投资的最低比例是30%，没有上限。

A：我们准备投资60%，一定得用现金投资吗？

B：合作各方可以投资现金、生产资料、产权等。

A：很好。我们要投资的设备估计占总投资额的45%。

B：那么我方提供工厂地点和建筑物，以及部分机械设备。对场地的使用权也是我们投资的一部分。

A：那么，非现金部分的投资该怎样进行估价？

B：机械设备的估价将由一家中国评估公司根据现行的国际市场价格估测。

A：在没有国际市场价格的情况下该如何进行估价？

B：那就根据实际成本费用加上运费和保险进行估价。

A: How long will the joint venture be?
B: We can tentatively fix the term for 5 years first. And the duration can be extended as long as we can run the plant well.
A: Good, we're very much interested.

A：合资企业的年限有什么规定吗？
B：我们可以首先暂定五年，只要工厂运行良好，期限就可以延长。
A：很好，我们很有兴趣。

达人点拨

在双方投资建立合营公司的过程中，双方参与投资的不只限于"cash or share"（现金或股票），根据具体情形，还可以投资"building, premises, equipment and machinery, and even technology."（建筑物、场地、设备设施，甚至是技术），这些统称为"non-cash investment"（非现金投资）。

合资企业的出资分配

A: Now, Mr. Brown, we were talking last time about your idea on forming a joint venture for the Morpan Project. Our head office has agreed to your proposal and I am authorized to discuss it.
B: That's very good news, Mr. Cheng. Do you have something specific in your mind?
A: First, we have to make clear our purpose in this cooperation. That is, both sides agree to jointly prepare and submit a bid for the Morpan Project.
B: How much funding would you be prepared to provide for this purpose?
A: Are there any regulations regarding the foreign party's share in a joint venture in this country?
B: No, not really. But as a usual practice, the leading party shall be the one who provides the most funds.
A: We'd like to act as the leader of the joint venture and lay out more than half of all required funds for it, say, 55%.
B: That includes cash, construction equipment and other temporary facilities, if I understand correctly,

A：布朗先生，我们上次讨论时，您提过要为墨畔项目建立一个合营公司。我们总部已经同意您的建议并授权我来和您协商。
B：这真是个好消息，程先生。您有什么具体的建议吗？
A：首先，我们想表明这次合作的目的。也就是说，双方同意共同准备投标墨畔项目。
B：那么你方打算出资多少呢？
A：你们国家对外商在合营企业的出资份额有什么规定吗？
B：那倒没有。但是按照惯例，牵头公司应该提供大部分资金。
A：我方愿意做牵头方，我们会出所需资金的一半以上，比如55%。
B：如果我理解的没错，程先生，您说的资金里包括现金、建筑设备和其他临时设施，对吧？

Mr. Cheng?

A: Of course.

B: Then how do we arrive at the true value of them?

A: That's a good question. We could ascertain such value through joint assessment. In order to have an impartial evaluation, we might also invite a third party to attend, if necessary.

B: That's good. So, we will provide 45% of the funding. I think we should make it clear that we can provide the funding in local currency only, as we don't have foreign currency.

A: Accordingly, you will share the profit, if any, in local currency only. The exchange rate for the currency conversion will be the same as stated in the owner's bidding documents.

B: I agree. All the profits, losses arising out of the contract shall be shared out between us based on the funds proportion to what both sides contribute.

A: That's the basis of our agreement.

A：当然。

B：那我们怎么知道它们的实际价值呢？

A：问得好。我们可以通过共同评估来确定这些价值。为了公平评估，如果必要，我们甚至可以请第三方参与。

B：很好。这样我方提供45%的资金。我想讲清楚，我们只能提供本地货币，我们没有外汇。

A：那么，你方也只是以本地货币的形式分享利润。汇率和业主招标文件中表明的一致。

B：我同意。有关合同发生的所有利润、损失都按照双方出资的比例分配。

A：这是我们协议的基础。

在新合营公司中双方的管理责任划分

A: How about the management of a joint venture?

B: I am thinking about establishing the Joint Venture Executive Committee as the highest authority to decide on the general policy and to deal with such important matters as the appointment of the general manager and the approval of financial statements.

A: What about the appointment of the chairman of the committee?

B: It is sensible to say that the chairman shall be nominated by the leading company.

A: So, how do you identify responsibilities of each party during the execution of the project if we win

A：合营企业的管理该怎么进行呢？

B：我正在考虑成立一个合营执行委员会作为最高权力机关，执行委员会将决定总体决策，处理重大事宜，比如任命总经理，对财务报表予以批准。

A：那么如何任命委员会的主席呢？

B：主席应由牵头公司任命，这样做是符合常理的。

A：如果我们中标，项目实施中的双

the contract?

B:I haven't thought of that. Considering you are a local company with good connections, why don't you take responsiblity for recruiting and dealing with the external affairs?

A:And if we are in charge of purchasing the materials and equipment. I'm sure we will do a good job. We know the market well.

B:Why not leave the issue to our next meeting, Mr. Brown?

A:All right. I do say that we have had a fruitful discussion today.

方职责该怎么划分呢？

B：这个问题我还没有细想。既然你方是本地公司，有很多社会关系，负责招聘和处理外部事务如何？

A：还有，如果让我们负责材料和设备的采购，我们同样会做得很好。我们对市场了如指掌。

B：布朗先生，这个问题我们留到下次会上再谈论，好吗？

A：好呀，我们今天的磋商成果颇丰。

合资企业的合作方选择

A:Since there are so many advantages in operating a joint venture in China, I have great interest in cooperating with others. But there is at least one foreign company in a joint venture, is it right?

B:Well, traditionally two companies from the same country join together in a foreign market and the new organization is called a joint venture.

A:Really? I thought it should be the establishment of a local company's combination with a foreign one.

B:To be honest, that is the most popular business mode, although there are some other permissions in terms of partners.

A:Do you mean in addition to what we have talked about, there are still other unusual collaboration patterns?

B:Sure. We have companies from different countries form a joint venture in a third country. And it is not uncommon that a local government,

A：既然在中国建立合资企业有这么多的好处，我还真有兴趣和别人合作。但是在一家合资企业里至少得有一家外资企业，对吗？

B：是这样，传统上讲，来自同一个国家的两个公司可以在国外市场组合，组合后的新企业也叫做合营企业。

A：真的吗？我还以为必须是一家本地公司和一家外方公司的合并才有效。

B：老实说，这也是最流行的经营模式，当然在合作方上还有其他的许可形式。

A：你是说，除了我们刚才讨论的，还有别的不常见的合营模式吗？

B：当然。还有的是来自不同国家的公司在第三方国家建立合营企

if necessary, is also allowed to join in a private company.

A: That's far more than what I thought before I came here. It seems I have lots of choices in finding an ideal business partner.

B: Keep it in your mind: the more companies are involved, the more complex the ownership arrangement will be.

A: Thank you for your warning. I will talk with our administration about the possibility of seeking potential cooperators.

业。如果出于需要,当地政府也可以加入合营公司,这也不少见。

A:这可跟我之前理解的合资企业有很大的差别。看来,我在选择理想的合资方上有很大的选择余地呢!

B:记住一句话:涉及的公司越多,在所有权分配上越复杂。

A:谢谢您的提醒。我会和我们的管理部门讨论,看看有没有可能寻求到潜在的合作方。

文化点滴

如何与英国商人打交道

1. 如果可能,请派年长的代表前往英格兰。长者能更好地营造出权威的氛围。
2. 先例在英格兰人做决定上起到一个重要的作用。也就是说,您的建议如果和过去曾经经营的业务在方法上是一致的,将会拥有更大的胜算。
3. 幽默在英格兰的商务谈判中起到重要作用,包括不点破显而易见的结果,所以应注意在欣赏这种幽默时什么不该说不该做是很必要的。
4. 尽管英格兰的企业文化是高度等级化的,但团队精神也很重要。通常,一个最终决定会在达成一致意见后才向最高级领导汇报。
5. 在决策上,英格兰人倾向于从已经成熟的法律和规则中寻求指南,而不是依靠他们的个人经验和感觉。
6. 直接的问题可能会导致间接的回答。
7. 强硬的销售技巧,比如"硬性销售",或者是贬低其他公司的产品或服务的做法是不被认可的。
8. 英格兰人更注重短期效果而不是长期的目的。在与他们交易当中要知道英格兰人是"低调大师"。
9. 一旦英格兰人决定要和你做生意,他们会很直接,甚至可能毫不犹豫地直抒心意。
10. 公司政策对一个公司各个级别的商务代表来讲具有绝对的权威。

进出口许可
Import and Export License

　　进口许可证是一国政府规定某些商品的进口必须有指定部门所签发的进口文件方能进口的一种进口管理体制。

　　进口许可证可分为一般许可证和特种进口许可证。 一般许可证又称为公开进口许可证或自动进口许可证。它对进口国别和地区没有限制，凡属于一般进口许可范围内的商品，进口商只要填写一般许可证后，即获准进口，因此这类商品实际上是可以"自由进口"的商品。而在特种进口许可证下，进口商必须向政府有关当局提出申请，经有关当局审查批准后才能进口。这种许可证多数都指定进口国别和地区。

词语宝典

import license	进口许可证	import formality	进口手续
license-issuing organization	发证单位	quantity limitation	数量限制
hold good	有效	place an order	订货
be null and void	无效	fulfill an order	执行订单
general license	一般许可证	on hand	在手边
special license	特殊许可证	in effect	有效的
application form	申请表	be designed to do	旨在，打算

经典句型

- How can we get the import license?
  我们怎么才能获得进口许可？

- We are required to present a copy of the contract, and a copy of a letter of credit together with an application form to the license issuing department.
  我们需要向许可证签发部门提交合同副本、信用证副本和申请表格。

- It is the responsibility of the buyers to deal with import license affairs.
  买方有责任办理进口许可证事宜。

- What the government issued to us this year is a special license.
  政府今年签发给我们的是特殊许可证。

- The import license of this kind of product holds good only for half a year in our country.
  在我们国家，这种商品的进口许可有效期只有半年。

- Under such circumstances, we had to declare this agreement null and void.
  在这种情况下，我们不得不宣布该协议无效。

- We have no other way out but to accept it.
  我们只有接受，此外毫无选择。

- They have only a limited stock on hand.
  他们现在手头的货存有限。

- Is there any quantity limitation for the import of silk goods from China?
  对来自中国的丝绸商品贵国在进口数量方面有限制吗？

- Last year's regulations are no longer in effect this year.
  去年的规定今年不再有效了。

- This contract has become null and void owing to Party C's failure to carry out their obligations.
  这份合同失效了，因为 C 方未能履行他们的职责。

- We have sufficient stocks on hand to meet your requirement.
  我们有足够的库存来满足你方的需求。

- The newly adjusted prices will be in effect from the first day of next week.
  这批调整后的价格将从下周第一天起生效。

- As a result of the rush of orders, our stocks have been nearly used up.
  由于订单激增，我们的库存几乎用完了。

- Our government is so strict on the control of imports of silk goods probably for the sake of protecting local silk textile industries in Japan.
  我们政府在丝绸制品的进口上控制如此之严格，很可能是为了保护日本的本国丝绸产业。

时尚对白

进口许可对订单的影响

A: I'm sorry to say that I didn't bring any good news with me this time?

B: Well, how bad is the news?

A: This year our government has adopted a special license system for the import of silk goods.

B: As I understand it, from now on, silk goods can be imported only from the countries or regions nominated by the government.

A: Yes.

B: Is there any quantity limitation for the import of silk goods from China?

A: I'm not sure. It all depends upon the government's regulations. And the importers have to apply for an import license for each specific purchase.

B: I know the import license was also required last year. How did you place an order for 6 million US dollars of silk goods last year?

A: Last year's regulations are no longer in effect this year. What the government issued to us last year was a general license.

B: Right. As I remember, you placed an order of 6 million US dollars of silk goods last year, but in fact only 3 million US dollars worth of silk goods were shipped. And as a result, we could not fulfill your order completely.

A: Yes, that's true.

B: Is it possible to transfer the remaining part of the order of last year's import license to that of this year's import license?

A：对不起，这次我们带来了不利的消息。

B：哦，什么样的坏消息？

A：今年我们政府对丝绸品的进口采用了特殊许可证制度。

B：按照我的理解，从现在起，丝绸商品只能从政府指定的国家或地区进口，是吗？

A：对。

B：从中国进口丝绸有数量限制吗？

A：我还不确定。这完全取决于政府的规定。进口商得为每一笔交易申请进口许可。

B：我知道去年我们的商品也需要进口许可，去年你方价值600万美元的丝绸订单是怎么签订的？

A：去年的规定对今年是无效的。去年政府发给我们的是一张一般许可证。

B：好吧。去年，我记得您的订单是600万美元，但是实际上只发运了300万美元的货，因此，我方不能完全履行订单。

A：是的，没错。

B：有没有可能把去年进口许可的订单的剩余部分转化为今年进口许可的那部分？

A: No, it is impossible. It is the same as in China, the import license holds good only for one year in my country.

B: That's to say, the license of last year is null and void now.

A: Right. If you want to import again this year, you will have to apply for a new license.

B: Why is your government so strict on import control of silk goods?

A: It's probably designed to protect the silk textile industries in my country.

B: OK. There's no point in discussing further. Whatever amount of an order from you is welcome.

A：不行，那不可能。和中国一样，在我们国家，进口许可有效期只有一年。

B：也就是说，去年的许可现在已经期满无效了。

A：没错。如果您想今年继续进口，您得重新申请许可证。

B：为什么你们政府对丝绸的进口控制得如此严格？

A：这可能是为了保护我国的丝绸纺织业。

B：好吧，再谈下去也毫无意义。我们欢迎您的订单，无论量多量少。

达人点拨

在进出口业务中，交易双方不能控制的是政府会掌控 "import and export license"（进出口许可）。更郁闷的是，同样的商品在不同时间段会被发放不同的许可证。即便今年政府发放给你的是 "general license"（一般许可证），明年很可能就是 "special license"（特殊许可证）。而且，在去年通用许可证项目下的合同，即使当年没有履行完，进入第二年，如果该进出口商品已经转为特殊许可证，就要按照特殊许可证的要求进行交易。

进口许可申请程序

A: I have been taking a course on international trade recently. But I met some difficulties when I was studying the chapter "Import License". I wonder if you can help me with some questions.

B: No problem. What do you want to know?

A: Does China have an import licensing system for importing commodities?

B: Sure. Like many countries in the world, China practices licensing system to stabilize and develop home industries and strengthen government planned control.

A: Who is responsible for releasing import licenses?

A：我最近正上一门国际贸易课程，但是学到"进口许可"这一章时我遇到了困难。您能否帮助我解答一些问题？

B：没问题。你想知道点儿什么？

A：中国进口商品需要进口许可证吗？

B：当然。中国同世界上其他国家一样，也实行进口许可证制度来稳定和发展国内产业，加强政府规划和控制。

B: The Ministry of Foreign Economic Relations and Trade is the organ in charge of issuing import licenses on behalf of the state.

A: I see. Then, how can companies get the import licenses?

B: The companies applying for the import licenses can submit to the above mentioned organization application letters and perfect import certificates signed and approved by relative department or bureau.

A: If my company has completed the application format, how long can we wait before getting it?

B: After receiving the application letter and relevant documents, the issuing institute may issue the license within three workdays, if the import formalities are perfect.

A: I got it. Thank you very much.

 进出口许可证申请的准备工作

A: I really have no idea as to what to get ready for the import & export license application, could you do me a favor?

B: My pleasure. An enterprise entitled to foreign trading should submit to issuing authority an application form stamped on with the applicant's company. And it is also necessary for you to provide an approval document signed by provincial authorized departments under Ministry of Commerce. And don't forget to bring your business license in case of trouble.

A: I see. And I have already got a copy of application form. But there are still some terms I'm not so clear. Say, what is the difference between "Importer" and "Consignee"?

A：什么部门负责发放进口许可呢？

B：对外经济贸易部代表国家签署进口许可证。

A：我知道了。那么，公司怎样才能拿到进口许可证呢？

B：申请进口许可证的公司应该向上述机构递交申请书以及由相关部门批签的完整的进口证书。

A：如果我们公司已经填写了申请表，多久才能拿到许可证？

B：在接到申请书和相关文件后，如果进口手续齐全的话，签发部门会在三个工作日内予以签署。

A：我知道了。非常感谢。

A：我真不知道在申请进出口许可证方面该做哪些准备工作，帮帮忙吧。

B：乐意为您效劳。一个拥有进出口权的企业应该向发证机关提交一份盖有申请人单位公章的申请表。同时还要提交一份由商务部授权的地方主管部门签发的批准文件。别忘了带上您的营业执照，以防万一。

A：我知道了。我已经拿到了一份申请表。但是表上有一些项目我不太明白。比如说，进口商和收货人这两者有什么不同？

B: Well, if your company has been authorized to import or export, you just fill in your own company, otherwise you have to assign an importer to deal with it and you should put its name; while the "Consignee" refers to the company who finally acquires the licensed quota.

A: Then, what should I put in under "Terms of Trade"? I mean I have no idea as regards "Terms".

B: The commonly practiced trading terms include ordinary trade, barter trade, compensation, export process, international bidding, international fair, international auction, donation, foreign investment import, etc. So before you write down the term, you had better determine the nature of your business.

A: So, under the "Function" I am supposed to fill "for self-consumption", is it right?

B: Yes, that's right under your circumstance. But that can change based on different purposes. Some companies import licensed products for production; while some others for serving local markets. So it depends.

A: I'm so much enlightened by your explanation. I really appreciate your patience.

B: It is my great pleasure to offer some help. You are welcome anytime.

B：是这样。如果您的公司拥有进出口权利，您在两个栏目内只需要填写您公司的名字，否则您得指定一个进口商处理进出口事务，那么您得在"进口商"一栏内填写该进口商的名字；而"收货人"是指最终获得进口配额的公司。

A：那么，我应该在"贸易模式"一栏中填写什么，我是说我不懂所谓的"模式"。

B：常见的模式有普通贸易、易货贸易、补偿贸易、来料出口加工、国际投标、国际展卖、国际拍卖、捐赠、外商投资进口等，所以在你写下模式前，您得事先确定您的贸易性质。

A：那么，在"用途"一栏内我应该填写"自行消费"吧？

B：对，在您这种情形下是这样的。但是这一栏根据不同目的会有变化。有的公司进口许可项目下的产品是为了生产，有的是用于当地市场。所以，这一栏依情形而定。

A：您这一解释我明白了，真感谢您如此有耐心。

B：很高兴能有所帮助，随时欢迎您。

 建立进出口许可证制度的必要性

A: Excuse me, Professor Wang, may I have you for a minute? Some of the terms you have covered in class are still confusing to me.

B: Sure. What's worrying you?

A: You told us that many countries in the world

A：王教授，打扰了。能占用您几分钟吗？您在课上讲的几个术语我还不太明白。

B：当然可以。哪里不明白？

practice import & export license policy. Since nowadays the world market is featured with globalization and internationalization, why do governments take such measures?

B: Good question. Although the world is unavoidably to be contacted and mingled, an individual country has to try its best to protect its domestic business development. Any trading transaction, if found to pose threat to local companies' expansion, would be under the control of government.

A: Is it really that serious? Could you give me an instance for my better understanding?

B: Let's take an example here. As you know, China is well known for its quality textile products, and therefore makes a handsome profit every year thanks to the large amount of export to other countries. By contrast, those countries who import our low-priced quality clothes, if they let it develop as market demands, would definitely damage their local garment factories or related textile industries.

A: I see. And a threatened business might be faced with bankrupt and finally lead to unemployment and social instability, am I right?

B: How smart you are! That's exactly what the government worries about. In addition, we implement foreign trade license strategy sometimes for the purpose of social security, such as the import of nuclear products, chemical commodities, and dual-use goods, which are under strict control by Ministry of Commerce.

A: I didn't think up to that point just now. It seems that import and export are far more than pure

A：您告诉我们世界上许多国家都在实行进出口许可政策。但是如今全球市场的特点是全球化和国际化，为什么各国政府还要采取这种手段呢？

B：问得好。尽管整个世界不可避免地存在着联系和融合，每一个国家都在尽力保护本国的行业发展。任何外贸形式，一旦发现对本国公司的发展构成威胁，都会受到政府的控制。

A：这么严重吗？您能否给我举一个例子帮助我更好理解？

B：比如说，你也知道，中国因为质优的纺织品而闻名于世，因此每年都由于大量的出口而获得丰厚的利润。相比之下，那些进口我们质优价廉服装的国家，如果按照市场的需求发展下去，势必会损坏本国服装厂和相关纺织企业的利益。

A：我明白了。而一个受到威胁的企业可能会面临着破产，最终导致失业和社会不稳定，是吧？

B：很聪明。这正是一个政府所担心的。此外，我们执行对外贸易许可策略有时出于国家安全的考虑，比如进口核产品、化学商品、（军民）两用产品等，这些商品的进出口受到商务部的严格控制。

A：我之前没想到这一点。看来进出口不仅仅是纯粹的商务行为。这就是

business matters. That's why governments of most countries have formulated license system and put sensitive commodities under their control.

B: You are absolutely right. And I will go on to specific categories under control by next class.

A: Thank you for your time, Professor Wang. I can't wait to know what items are under license. See you next class.

为什么大多数国家的政府制定许可证制度，对敏感的物品实行控制的原因啊。

B：完全正确。下次课我将讲解到具体的管控类别。

A：谢谢您，王教授。真想早点知道都有什么项目在许可范围内。下次课见。

达人点拨

在进出口许可证方面，要理解政府的决定。而在与外商进行谈判或是业务往来中，您也许会不可避免地同对方解释许可证的发放缘由。一般来讲，国家采取许可证制度在经济层面有以下主要原因："Every country issues import or export license so that domestic industries would develop under such protection."（每一个国家发放进出口许可证为的是可以保护本国的国内行业的发展。）另外，在双方的交流中，您也可以这样解释，"We carry out foreign trade license system sometimes for the purpose of social security, such as the import of nuclear products, chemical commodities, and dual-use goods."（我们有时采用外贸许可制度是为了确保社会安全，比如对核产品、化学物品和（军民）两用产品的进口。）。

文化点滴

如何与墨西哥商人打交道

1．墨西哥的商业文化氛围是温暖的、友好的，但是节奏缓慢。他们在解决问题时通常不遵守规则或法律。他们更注重于在特定情形下私下解决。

2．主观感受是墨西哥商业文化中确定真假的基础，所以要向您的墨西哥商业伙伴强调他将如何在您的建议中获得个人利益。

3．墨西哥人避免直接说"不"。您也要在商业活动中采用这种间接手段。否则，对方会认为您粗鲁。

4．墨西哥商人有时会非常具有等级意识，所以在您的团队里有一位高级管理人员是非常重要的。

5．在墨西哥的商业文化中用言语展现很重要，不要只是把文件扔在谈判桌上。

6．要注意到墨西哥的商人对他们的商业对手经常了如指掌。

7．在谈判中，你方要对该商务项目非常了解，在整个过程中保持权威和果断的气势。

8．您在商业交往中所出示的信件、备忘录、报告书、促销文件或是其他的文件资料都被视作重要的，因此要仔细核实。

9．在墨西哥的商业文化中，交际技巧在赢得别人好感方面是最重要的因素，有时比专业能力和经验更重要。

进口配额
Import Quota

进口配额，又称进口限额，是一国政府在一定时期内，对某些商品的进口数量或金额加以直接的限制。在规定的期限内，配额以内的货物可以进口，超过配额不准进口，或者征收较高的关税或罚款才能进口。

进口配额通常表现为两种类型，即全球配额和国别配额。全球配额属于世界范围内的绝对配额，对于来自世界任何国家和地区的商品一律适用。主管当局通常按照进口商的申请先后或过去某一时期内的实际进口额批给一定的额度，直至总配额发放完为止，超过总额度就不准进口。而国别配额是在总配额内按照国别和地区分配给固定的额度，超过规定的配额就不能进口。为了区分来自不同国家和地区的商品，在进口商品时进口商必须提交原产地证明书。实行国别配额可以使进口国根据它与有关国家的政治经济关系分配给不同的额度。

词语宝典

import quota	进口配额	be applicable to	适用于
global quota	全球配额	individual importer	个体进口商
country quota	国别配额	to be frank with you	老实讲
make a handsome profit	获利丰厚	our concerted efforts	我们双方的共同努力
total quota	总配额	to bridge the price gap	填补价格差
national quota system	国别配额制度	samples of products	产品样本
tariff barrier	贸易壁垒		

经典句型

- Thanks to the Global Quota System adopted by our government this year, I immediately applied for the quota upon receiving the information.
  由于我国政府今年采用了全球配额体系，我一得到这一消息就马上申请了配额。

- What is the total quota of your country for men's shirts?
  你们国家对男士衬衫的进口配额总量是多少？

- Our government adopts a country quota system for each country.
  我国政府对每一个国家采用国别配额制度。

- I haven't known how big the quota for China is.
  我还不知道对中国的配额是多少。

- Exporting companies can apply for quota from the quota administration department.
  出口公司可以向配额管理局申请配额。

- Companies can also buy from others, but the price may be higher.
  公司也可以从其他商家那里购买，但是价格会贵一些。

- Please feel free to contact us concerning this product and other articles.
  关于这项商品和其他商品，如有问题请随时与我们联系。

- I am sure your exporting the goods will bring you handsome profits.
  我相信你们出口这些商品会获利丰厚的。

- Since your company is big and prominent, you'll get the quota anyway.
  因为你们公司是一家重要的大公司，您们无论如何都会拿到配额的。

- I can assure you more orders will be forthcoming in the near future.
  我确信很快你就会收到更多的订单的。

- All goods must have markings and labels required by the applicable laws.
  按照适用法律的要求，所有的商品都应该有标识和标码。

- The manufacture of the goods is in hand, but not finished, so we couldn't ship the goods at once.
  该商品的生产还在进行中，尚未完成，所以我们不能马上发货。

- We assure you that all your enquiries will receive our prompt attention.
  我们向您保证我们会迅速处理您所有的咨询。

- Apart from this order, please offer us another 50 tons.
  除了这份订单，请再给我们提供 50 吨。

- He doesn't know yet how big the country quota for China is for cotton and woolen goods.
  他还不知道在棉制品和羊毛制品上对中国的国家配额到底会是多少。

时尚对白

讨论全球配额体制

A: It's good to see you again, Mr. Sherlock, what do you want to order this time?

B: I have a lot of things to buy. The main items I want to order are men's shirts, and cotton jerseys, embroidered shirts, and things like that.

A: That sounds great. You are welcome to place bigger orders. Would you tell me the quantity you intend to buy?

B: Men's shirts, a minimum of 200,000; cotton jerseys, a minimum of 80,000. You know, thanks to the Global Quota System adopted by our government this year, I immediately applied for the quota upon receiving the information. The Global Quota is applicable to men's shirts and cotton jerseys. I got the quota in January.

A: You are lucky indeed. Once you have the global quota in hand, you are free to import men's shirts and cotton jerseys from whatever countries you like, right?

B: Sure. This is indeed a precious chance for me.

A: And you will more likely make a handsome profit.

B: Not necessarily. It all depends on how the market situation develops.

A: How many do you want to order for embroidered shirts?

B: It is hard to confirm right now. Our government adopts a country quota system for each country. But for the moment I haven't known how big the quota for China is.

A：很高兴再次见到您，夏洛克先生，这次您想订购些什么？

B：我有许多要订购的。主要想购买男士衬衫、棉质套头衫、刺绣衬衫等。

A：太好了。我们欢迎您加大订单量。您能告诉我您想要购买的数量吗？

B：男士衬衫，最少二十万件；棉质套头衫，最少八万件。您知道，因为我国政府最近采用了全球配额制度，而我一听到消息马上申请了配额。这个全球配额制度针对男士衬衫和棉质套头衫。我在一月份拿到了配额。

A：您真是太幸运了。一旦您拥有了全球配额，您将按照您喜欢的国家自由进口男士衬衫和棉质套头衫，是吧？

B：没错。这对我来说的确是宝贵的机会。

A：很可能您又要大赚一笔啦。

B：不一定。这得取决于市场运行状况。

A：您想订购多少刺绣衬衫？

B：现在很难确定。我们政府对每个国家都采取了配额制度。到目前为止我还不清楚分配给中国的份额是多少。

第一部分 贸易实务

A: Since your company is big and prominent, you'll get the quota anyway.

B: It's really hard to say anything definite at the moment. There are more than 150 companies dealing with this goods in our country, and some of them enjoy good reputation and sell well.

A: No matter how long it is before you get the quota, would you please let us know it as soon as possible?

B: OK. No problem. I can assure you more orders will be coming in the near future.

A：你们公司是一家重要的大公司，无论怎样您都会拿到配额的。

B：现在真的很难说。在我国目前有150个公司在从事此类商品的贸易，而有一些享有良好声誉，并且销路很好。

A：不管多久您获得配额，您能尽快地告诉我们吗？

B：当然，没问题。我保证很快就会有更多的订单发送给您。

达人点拨

一个国家的政府会根据实际情况限制某种产品的进出口数量，这种对外贸的干预行为叫做"import and export quota"（进出口配额），所以一家精明的公司会在最早的时间内拿到政府发放的"quota"（配额）。如果你抢不到你理想的配额量，只能从其他已获得配额的人员手中购买，那代价就大了。所以，想法设法在第一时间拿到配额吧。

如何为一家中国公司申请配额

A: How are you?

B: Fine, thank you. What can I do for you?

A: I'm doing a survey about quota conditions of China since it entered WTO in 2001. Can you answer some questions?

B: Sure. I'm happy I could offer help.

A: What countries and regions are most of China's quota for?

B: The USA and Europe.

A: How can a Chinese garment exporting company obtain quota to the above regions?

B: There are three ways. First, exporting companies can apply for quota from the quota administration department. The quantity will be based on how much they had gained in the previous year. Second, they

A：你好吗？

B：很好，谢谢。能为您效劳吗？

A：我正在做一份自从中国在2001年加入WTO之后的外贸配额制度调查。您能回答我几个问题吗？

B：当然可以，乐意为您效劳。

A：中国的大多数配额是发配给哪些国家和地区的？

B：美国和欧洲。

A：一个中国制衣出口公司怎样才能获得上述地区的配额？

B：有三种途径。首先，出口公司可以从配额管理机构那里申请配额。数量取决于他们前一年的经营业绩。或者，他们可以为目标数量投标。

can bid for the aiming quantity. And last, companies can buy from others, but the price may be higher.

A: When will the quota system end?

B: The total quantity for quota has been decreased a lot during the past three years. We believe that there will be no quota by the end of 2018.

A: Some people are scared of the messy conditions in the future when there is no quota in international trade.

B: I'm optimistic with trading conditions because the demanding will adjust the market.

第三种方法，公司可以从其他商人那里购买配额，但是价格会高一些。

A：配额制度什么时候终止？

B：配额总量在过去的三年内已经大大降低了。我们相信到了2018年将不会再有配额限制。

A：有些人担心当将来在国际贸易上取消配额时会出现混乱局面。

B：我对贸易状况充满信心，因为需求决定市场。

 ## 如何解决配额问题

A: Good morning, I come to discuss about our order. We have decided to purchase more woolen sweaters from you next year.

B: I'm very happy to hear that. May I know the extra quantity you want to order?

A: I think the total order this year will double that of last year. That is, we will purchase another 10,000.

B: That sounds great. But I need to check what is the quota for your country next year.

A: Oh, the same problem again.

B: If you can offer a reasonable price, we can buy some from the markets.

A: Certainly we can, but you must guarantee the quantity and quality as well as the delivery time.

B: Sure we will.

A：早上好。我来是想讨论一下我们的订单。我们想明年从你处购买更多的羊毛衫。

B：很高兴听到这个消息。我想知道您额外想订购多少？

A：今年的订单总额是去年的两倍。也就是说，我们将另外订购一万件。

B：太好了。但是我需要查一下明年你们国家的出口配额。

A：哦，又是这个问题。

B：如果您能提供一个合理价位，我们也可以从市场上购买一些配额。

A：当然可以。但是你方要确保数量和质量还有发货时间。

B：没问题。

进出口配额类别

A: You know, our company has the intention to expand into mobile import. But I was told that mobiles are under strict quota management in China. May I have your information on that?

B: No problem. Import Quota indicates that within any stipulated period only those below quota are allowed to import. And it can be classified into absolute quota and tariff quota. The former releases a maximal import amount of some commodities. And the latter conducts management via tariff control.

A: Then how is global quota different from country quota?

B: Well, global quota and country quota are under absolute quota item. They tell one from the other in the countries receiving quota. Global quota applies to any countries and regions, the point being the amount under control rather than nations. While country quota takes into consideration both import maximum and specific countries, which might have much to do with non-economic reasons.

A: So the tariff quota takes duties as one of the measures to control import, is it right?

B: Absolutely. Sometimes the government prefers to adopt duty-free or duty-privilege policy to the goods beneath stipulated amount; while the imported commodity above requirement has to be faced with unpleasant tariff or fines.

A: It sounds too complicated for me. I will digest it slowly and talk with my partners about the possibility in stepping into this sector. Anyway, thanks lot!

B: To have a perfect understanding in quota is absolutely necessary before you get your foot in

A：您知道，我们公司打算进军汽车进口领域。但是我听说在中国汽车的进口是有严格的配额管理的。您能给我讲讲吗？

B：没问题。进口配额是指在规定的时间范围内只有在配额内的商品可以进口。可以分为绝对配额和关税配额。前者是指某些商品被指定最大进口额度。而后者通过关税管制进行管理。

A：那么全球配额和国家配额有什么区别？

B：是这样。全球配额和国家配额都处于绝对配额类别下。他们的区别在于获得配额的国家不同。全球配额适用于任何国家和地区，关键是受到控制的是数量而不是国家。但是国家配额既考虑到进口最大额度又考虑到具体国家，政府在国家配额政策上有可能会考虑到非经济因素。

A：因而关税配额把关税的收取作为控制进口的一种手段，是吗？

B：没错。有时政府对管制额度下的商品实行免除关税或优惠关税政策，但是对超过管制数量的商品提高关税或实行罚款。

A：对我而言太复杂了。我要慢慢消化这些政策，再和我的合伙人谈谈进军这个领域的可能性，不管怎样，多谢！

B：在进入相关行业之前对配额制度有

related industry. Don't hesitate to come to my place if you need me.

一个完全的了解是绝对必要的。如果需要就来找我吧。

> **达人点拨**
>
> 在进出口配额的分类上有几个特别的术语您要掌握。两大基本类别是 "absolute quota and tariff Quota"（绝对配额和关税配额）。所谓绝对配额，就是政府直接规定限制的进出口量。在关税配额制度下，对某种商品的交易限量是通过提高进出口关税来实现的。绝对配额又可细分为 "general Quota and country Quota"（通用配额和国别配额），通用配额适用于任何国家和地区，而国别配额是针对某个具体的国家实行的限量交易，可能出于商业目的，也可能是政治需要。

实行进出口配额管理的目的

A: I'm really exhausted with the import & export license policy, you know, every year I have to spend much of my time on struggling for quota, so fatigue!

B: You said my mind. But if we stand at the height of strategic administration, perhaps it is not difficult for us to find it reasonable.

A: What do you mean by that? Do you mean business performance is closely associated with government decisions and policies?

B: Sure. A government's stipulation on the maximal imported or exported amount is equal to the tariff barrier in foreign trade. This non-tariff barrier measure is adopted by developed countries for the sake of bargaining in negotiation and competing foreign markets; while the developing countries make use of it to protect national businesses.

A: That sounds more complicated than what I thought about. But it is so hard to obtain a quota approval recently since early 2008. The quota license is even harder than business. That's a big headache.

B: It is unavoidable under such a gloomy economy.

A：这个进出口配额政策搞得我筋疲力尽。每年我都得花大量的时间在争取配额上，太累了！

B：你说到我心坎里了。但是如果我们站在战略管理的高度看，不难发现其实这个制度是合乎情理的。

A：你说的管理是怎么回事儿？你是说商业行为与政府决策和政策有密切相关性？

B：当然。政府规定最大进出口额度，等同于在外贸里的关税壁垒。发达国家采用这种非关税的壁垒手段是为了在谈判中讨价还价，竞争海外市场；而发展中国家运用它来保护民族产业。

A：听起来比我原来想的要复杂。但是自从 2008 年以来，很难获得配额许可了，配额申请过程比生意更难做。真头疼。

B：在这种低迷的经济条件下，这是不可避免的。你也知道，每个国

As you know, since every country is making effort to protect national industries, what we can do is to wait for the revival of global economy.

家都在试图保护民族产业，我们能做的只是等待全球经济的复苏了。

 文化点滴

如何与俄罗斯商人打交道

1．建议您将商业名片的反面翻译成俄语。
2．重要的一点是确保和您打交道的是决策人，而不是"看门人"或是别的被指派接待来访人员的中间人。
3．让您的俄罗斯商业伙伴在私下场合了解您是在这个国家成功进行商业活动的重要一部分。
4．第一次会面通常被俄罗斯人当作评估您信用的最佳机会。
5．尽量表现得果断而得体，同时还要保持热情而平和的气势。
6．会议经常会被电话或是来访打断。很可能要花费很长的时间才能做出一个决定。
7．陈述要简单，易于理解。如果您是用英语陈述，要准备一份俄语的版本。
8．通常来讲，俄罗斯人认为妥协是软弱的象征。他们不会退步，除非对方表现得特别坚决。
9．俄罗斯人有时会坚持采用书面的议定书形式记录在会议上讨论过的内容。会议结束时，议定书当面宣读，获得一致同意后需要签署。
10．合同签订后，如果里面的条款没有被完全履行不要吃惊。俄罗斯人试图修改条款是很普遍的。

通关和报关
Customs and Clearance

通关是指出入境运输工具的负责人、货物的收发货人及其代理人、物品的所有人向海关申请办理进出口货物及物品的手续。海关对其呈交的单证和申请的进出口货物或物品依法进行审核、查验、征收税费、批准进出口的全过程。对不同类型的进出口商品和物品有不同的检查程序并征收不同的关税。如果出入境者携带需要申报的商品或物品，应向海关递交申报单据，报请海关办理出入境手续。

词语宝典

customs clearance	通关	supervision	监管
customs declaration	海关申报	free of charge	免费
customs officer	海关官员	customs clearing fee	报关费
item dutiable	应缴税物品	customs broker	报关行
personal article	个人物品	customs agent	报关代理人
civil servant	公务员	port of entry	报关港口
duty-free	免税	chargeable weight	计费重量
tariff	关税		

经典句型

- What formalities do we need to go through to clear the customs?
  我们得需要办理哪些通关手续？

- You have to make a declaration if you have brought something that has to be declared.
  如果您有需要申报的东西必须进行申报。

- Actually I have no idea about what stuff should be declared.
  事实上我不知道什么东西是需要申报的。

- Do you have anything dutiable?
  您携带了应缴税的东西吗？

143

- I have to fill in the declaration form for my belongings.
  我得为我携带的物品填写申报单。

- The importers or exporters or passengers need to make declaration in accordance with the regulations stated in the related law.
  进出口商或是旅客需要根据相关法律的规定进行申报。

- The basic principle is to stipulate different scope and duty limitations for different items.
  基本的原则是对不同的商品制定不同的税费范围和限制。

- Could you assign the personnel who are familiar with duty clearance to go together with us in handling related formalities?
  您能否指派熟悉通关的人员和我们一起办理相关的手续？

- What's the purpose of your visiting this time? For business or pleasure?
  您这次出访的目的是商务还是旅游？

- Would you please go to the duty counter and see if you have something dutiable next?
  您可以到关税柜台去咨询一下还有没有什么需要上税的物品。

时尚对白

 通关报关常识

A: To be honest, I am not so much interested in my major now, but I hold great passion in knowledge about customs. I dream to be a civil servant in the customs field. That's why I come to your lecture, Professor Wang.

B: That's a fantastic idea. What exactly would you like to know?

A: I'm especially keen on the customs clearance. Could you please first tell me the definition of customs clearance?

B: Yes, sure. It refers to the people in charge of cargo transport, the importers and exporters or their

A：老实讲，我对我现在的专业没什么兴趣，但是对于通关报关很感兴趣。我真想成为一名在海关工作的公务员。这也是为什么我来听您的课，王教授。

B：这是个不错的梦想。你具体想了解什么？

A：我特别想知道通关的事。您能先告诉我通关的定义吗？

B：当然可以。通关是指负责货物运输

agents, or the owner of personal items make a declaration to the customs to get approval for their goods to go through the customs. At the same time, in terms of customs officers, customs clearance also refers to the whole process in which the relevant customs officers carry out inspection, collection of a certain amount of duty, and release of permission of import or export goods or private belongings.

A: Then what are the detailed formalities in customs clearance?

B: The importers or exporters or passengers need to make declaration in accordance with the regulations stated in the related law, except for the exemptions from inspections. Passengers who bring with them articles to be declared ought to hand in the China Customs Declaration Form.

A: Amazing. There are so many formalities and stipulations. But I have one more question. On what basic principle is it based for customs officers to inspect the passengers' belongings or businesspersons' cargoes?

B: The basic principle is to stipulate different duty limitations for different items.

A: Thank you very much. I understand I still have a long way to go before I become a competent customs officer.

B: I have full confidence in you that you will make your dream come true.

的人员、进出口商或者是代理公司、私人物品的所有者在海关进行申报以获得批准确保货物通过海关的检查。同时，对于海关官员来说，通关是指对货物的审查、关税的收取、发放货物或个人物品的进出口许可证明等一系列过程。

A：那么，通关的详细手续是怎样的呢？

B：进出口商或是出入境旅客需要根据相关法律规定的规则进行申报，除非有免除审查特例。旅客如果携带需要申报的物品应该填写中国海关申报单。

A：不可思议。原来有这么多的手续和规定。但是我还有一个问题。海关官员根据什么原则审查旅客的物品和商人的货物？

B：基本的原则是针对不同的商品制定不同的税收限制。

A：非常感谢。我知道要想成为一个合格的海关官员，我还有很长的路要走。

B：我完全有信心你的梦想会实现。

达人点拨

几乎所有的进出口公司都会提供专业的报关员为您商品的进出口环节服务，但是作为一个开展进出口业务的公司应该掌握一些基本的报关术语，比如，进出口商或是委托人要填写"declaration form"（报关单），主动要求"customs declaration"（海关申报），而海关官员会对你的商品"go through customs clearance inspection"（进行通关检查）。如果一切顺利，海关会发放"permission of import and export goods"（进出口放行证），您的商品就会顺利通关了。

通关条款协商

A: Shall we get down to the issue of customs clearance?

B: OK. According to the terms in our contract, you have to take charge of all the stuff in customs clearance.

A: We get it. But in this respect we have some difficulty and lack enough experience.

B: If so, we can have a discussion to let it solved.

A: Thank you for your understanding. As you know, we are not quite familiar with the procedures of customs clearance here and this will waste a lot of time and energy. And you can see the low efficiency due to unfamiliarity will lead to losses on both sides.

B: That's true. What can we do to help?

A: Could you assign the personnel who are familiar with duty to go together with us in handling related formalities?

B: All right. That sounds acceptable.

A：我们能否讨论一下通关的事情？

B：好的，根据合同条款，你方负责通关的所有事宜。

A：我知道。但是在这一方面我们有些难度，而且缺乏经验。

B：既然这样，我们可以讨论一下解决方法。

A：非常感谢您的理解。您也知道，我们对通关手续不太熟悉，做起来会浪费时间和精力。而由于不熟悉引起的低效率会给双方都带来损失。

B：那倒是。我们可以做点什么？

A：您可以指定熟悉通关业务的人和我们一起办理相关手续吗？

B：好的，可以接受。

文化点滴

如何与美国商人打交道

1. 会议会以简短的闲聊开始。通常商务活动的进程是相当迅速的。美国商人经常会在首次会面期间就达成口头协议。
2. 在美国谈判期间，要尽量避免沉默。
3. 要相信他们国家是全世界最成功的经济实体，美国人对其他国家的常识没兴趣。
4. 美国人通常不知道什么是"留面子"，大多数情况下，他们会很直接地、毫不犹豫地否定您的想法。
5. 美国商人的另一个特征是前后一致。一旦他们同意达成协议，他们很少改变主意。
6. 美国人倾向于着眼未来。他们更关注创新而不是传统。
7. 在会议室以外，美国人很随意，并坚持对方称呼自己的名，省略姓。
8. 时间就是金钱这个观念在美国的商业文化中是相当严肃的，所以要开门见山。
9. 通常，美国人如果出现争执会采用投票的形式表决，而不是把时间花在寻求统一上。
10. 记住美国是一个全球最爱打官司的国家。

2 应对及处理

第一章 合同违约

Unit 1　品质违约　Quality Discrepancy
Unit 2　数量违约　Quantity Discrepancy
Unit 3　付款违约　Payment Discrepancy
Unit 4　交货期违约　Delivery Time Discrepancy

品质违约 Quality Discrepancy

词语宝典

consistent	一致的	as soon as possible	尽快
entrust	委托	batch	一批货
shipment	装船，出货	expiry date	有效期限，保质期
specification	规格	instead of	而不是
stipulation	规定	in person	亲自
singular case	特例	make up	弥补

经典句型

- It's clearly a breach of contract, and you should be responsible for it.
  这显然是违反了合同，你方应当负责任。

- The last batch of goods' quality and standards do not meet the requirement in our contract.
  上一批货的质量和规格都不符合合同规定。

- We ship our goods in accordance with the terms of the contract.
  我们按合同条款交货。

- You have not kept the terms of our contract.
  你没有遵守我们合同中的条款。

- This is the survey report by Beijing Commodity Inspection Bureau.
  这是北京商品检验局的检验报告。

- I'm here today to tell you that the cheese which arrived yesterday was not in conformity with the contract stipulations.
  我来这儿的目的是要告诉您昨天抵达的奶酪与合同规定的不一致。

- We entrust the local inspection authority to re-examine the goods.
  我们委托本地的商品检验局对这批货进行了再检验。

时尚对白

 房屋装修质量不合格

A: Excuse me. Can I see your manager?

B: I am sorry. He is not here for the moment. What can I do for you?

A: I just got my key of the new flat sold by your company, and there are some problems with the interior decoration.

B: I am sorry to hear that. What kind of problems does it have?

A: The color of tiles used in the bathroom are not consistent, and the color of some tiles are light yellow instead of white as stipulated in the contract.

B: Really? But all the flats have passed the examination after decoration.

A: Well, the difference is not very obvious, but it can still be found if you look at them carefully. So I think it's clearly a breach of contract, and I hope you can make it up.

B: OK, I see. We'll send someone to check it again and change the tiles with different colors as soon as possible.

A: Thank you.

A：对不起，我能见你们经理吗？

B：我很抱歉，他现在不在。我能做些什么吗？

A：我刚刚拿到你们公司销售的公寓的钥匙，发现内部装修有些问题。

B：我很遗憾听到这一点。有什么样的问题呢？

A：浴室瓷砖的颜色不一致。一些砖的颜色是淡黄色，而不是按合同规定的白色。

B：真的吗？但是，所有装修后的公寓都已经通过检查了。

A：色差不是很明显，但是如果你仔细看，仍然可以发现。所以，我认为这显然违反合同，我希望你们能够弥补。

B：好吧，我明白了。我们会派人去检查一下，然后尽快为您更换不同颜色的瓷砖。

A：谢谢。

 商品质量不合格

A: The second batch of goods' quality and standards do not meet the requirement in our contract.

B: Really, I can't believe it?

A: It is so pitiful that there is this kind of thing happening.

B: Could you tell us some particulars about it?

A: We entrust the local inspection authority to re-examine

A：第二批货的质量和规格都不符合合同规定。

B：是吗？怎么会有这样的事儿？

A：我们也很遗憾。竟然发生了这种事。

B：能不能介绍一下详细的情况。

A：我们委托本地的商品检验局对这

the goods. The result of the inspection indicates that the goods below the standard in smooth and color make up 30% of the goods.

B: Let me have a look over the test report.

A: OK, we request your party pay for the goods with bad quality.

B: We know that. I will contact the factory party to clarify at once. And if it is because of the unqualified products, we will properly deal with it.

批货进行了再检验，结果变色度、光洁度不够的约占总数的30%。

B：把商品检验报告给我看一下。

A：好的，请看。对不合格的产品我们要求赔偿。

B：我了解您所说的。我马上与厂方联系，弄清原因之后，若确实是产品不合格，我们一定负责妥善处理。

口语秘笈

"contact" 用做动词时是及物动词，直接接宾语，如："Please contact the person in charge of this business."（请与负责这笔业务的人联系。）如果做名词用时，则要与 "with" 连用，例如："I keep contact with Mr. Smith."（我与史密斯先生保持联系。）。

商品超过保质期

A: Good Afternoon! We have received the first shipment of our Order No. 009/08 for milk powder yesterday.

B: Good. Next shipment will be made next week.

A: I'm here today to tell you that the powder which arrived yesterday was not in conformity with the contract stipulations.

B: Oh? What happen? We ship our goods in accordance with the terms of the contract.

A: According to the contract, the expiry date of the milk powder is on April 1 next year. But unfortunately, upon examination of the goods, we found that the expiry date is on December 1, this year.

B: How can that be? We've never had complaints like this. It's rather a singular case.

A：下午好，我们已经收到了我们第009/08号奶粉订单的第一批货。

B：很好，下周将进行下一批装运。

A：我今天来这儿的目的是要告诉您昨天抵达的奶粉与合同规定的不一致。

B：嗯？怎么回事？我们按合同条款交货。

A：根据合同，奶粉的到期日是明年4月1日，但不幸的是，在我们检查货物的时候发现到期日是今年的12月1日。

B：怎么会是那样呢？我们从来没有接过这样的投诉。这绝对是特例。

A：但是到期日清清楚楚地印在包装

A: But the expiry date is clearly printed on the cartons.

B: Have you looked at the expiry date printed on the cans of the powder? Maybe the expiry date on the cartons is wrong.

A: Yes, we did look at the cans. The expiry date on them is the same as that on the cartons.

B: That's incredible. We even went to the factory to supervise in person the processing of the powder for your order.

A: But what I've said is fact. This is the survey report by the American Commodity Inspection Bureau. It certifies that the milk powder was made twelve months ago. You have to be responsible for it.

箱上。

B：您看了奶粉罐上印刷的到期日吗？或许包装箱上的到期日搞错了。

A：是的，我们的确查看了罐上的到期日，和包装箱上的一样。

B：真是难以置信，我们甚至到工厂亲自对你们订购的奶粉的加工进行监督。

A：但是我所说的是事实，这是美国商品检验局的检验报告。报告证明奶粉是12个月前生产的。你们要对此负责。

数量违约 Quantity Discrepancy

词语宝典

inadequate	不充分的、不足的	load on board	租船
issue	签发、出具	in transit	在途中，在运输中
moisture	潮湿	original commercial invoice	正本商业发票
shortage	短装	original policy	正本保单
stipulate	规定	quantity difference	数量增减，溢短装
at fault	应受责备的、错误的	short weight	短重
bulk goods	大宗货物		

经典句型

- We come here to lodge a claim against you.
  我们到这里来向你方提出索赔。

- The ship owner has issued a clean on board bill of loading as well as a standard certificate of weight.
  船主已经出具了一份标准的已装船清洁提单和一份货物重量说明。

- I'm sure they will compensate for your losses.
  我相信他们会赔偿你的损失的。

- I'm here today to discuss the matter of the short weight of the salt we ordered from you.
  我今天来此是想与您磋商我们从贵方订购的盐的短重问题。

- According to the contract, we sell our goods on shipping weight not on the actual landed weight.
  根据合同规定，我们按照离岸重量而不是实际的卸货重量出售商品。

- We hope you will take positive action towards settlement of the claim.
  希望你方采取积极行动解决索赔问题。

- When is the limit for loading?
  装运的最后期限是什么时候呢？

- At what price is the tolerance to be paid?
  差额如何偿付？

时尚对白

 食盐短重

A: I'm here today to discuss the matter of the short weight of the salt we ordered from you.

B: I was notified this morning and I hope we will settle the matter as amicably as possible because this is the first business deal between us.

A: I feel the same way. We ordered a total amount of 500 tons of your salt. But when we inspected the goods after its arrival at the destination we found there was a shortage of 1,000 kilos.

B: We had the goods checked and weighed by the Commodity Inspection and Quarantine Bureau when loading. Besides we had the weighing apparatus checked, too. There couldn't be any mistake.

A: But the fact is we didn't get the full amount of salt we ordered in the contract.

B: According to the contract, we sell our goods on shipping weight not on the actual landed weight. I think the weight shortage was caused by something else.

A: I think you should hold responsibility for it. Since the packing remains intact, there is no doubt that the shortage occurred prior to shipment.

B: We've sent you the certificate of weight issued by our Commodity Inspection and Quarantine Bureau. That shows the exact amount of goods. Maybe the shortage was caused by evaporation in transit.

A: Do you mean that we have to bear the loss?

B: Well, I must remind you that according to the contract, the maximum allowance for natural loss is

A：我今天来这儿是想与您磋商我们从贵方订购的盐的短重问题。

B：我今早接到的通知，我希望我们尽可能友好地解决这个问题，因为这是我们之间的第一笔交易。

A：我也这么认为。我们从贵方总共订购了 500 吨食盐，但是当货物到达目的地我们对货物进行检验之后，我们发现短重 1,000 公斤。

B：装船时我们通过商品检验检疫局对货物进行了检查和称重。另外我们也对承重器具进行了检测。这是不可能出差错的。

A：但是事实是我们没有得到合同中我们所订购的食盐的数量。

B：根据合同规定，我们按照离岸重量而不是实际的卸货重量出售商品。我想，短重可能另有原因。

A：我认为你们应该对此事负责。既然包装仍未开封，毫无疑问短重发生在装运之前。

B：我们已向贵方发出商品检验检疫局的重量证明书，上面有货物的准确重量。或许短重是因途中蒸发造成的。

A：您的意思是我们要承担这笔损失吗？

B：嗯，我们必须提醒您，根据合同，最大的自然损失限度是 0.2%。考虑到我们刚刚开始交易，我

0.2%. Considering that we have just started business, we'll give you 5% discount for your next order.

们将在贵方的下一次订购中给予5%的折扣。

 大米短重

A: Oh, I'm sorry to burst in on you like this, but I'm really upset. The last shipment of 100,000 tons of rice reached us last month. But as we examined them at this time of unloading we found there were only 95,500 tons. That is, there is a shortage of 4,500 tons of rice, for which we came here to lodge a claim against you.

B: I'm so surprised to hear you say that. You know, our goods have been weighed before shipment, and the ship owner has issued a clean on board bill of loading as well as a standard certificate of weight.

A: But we can show you the survey report, with evidence that there is a shortage of 4,500 tons.

B: I'm afraid the loss might have happened in transit. The transaction was concluded on FOB basis. We're not prepared to entertain your claim.

A: What shall we do then?

B: I think you'd better lodge your claim with the shipping company or the insurance company. If they were at fault, I'm sure they will compensate for your losses.

A: All right. I'll take your advice.

A：我很抱歉这么唐突地找你，但我的确很着急。最后一船100,000吨的大米已于上个月到达我方，但是我们在卸货时发现只有95,500吨，也就是说少了4,500吨大米，因此我们到这里来向你方提出索赔。

B：听你这么说真是太吃惊了。你知道，我们的货物在装船前就已经称过重了，而且船主已经出具了一份标准的已装运清洁提单和一份货物重量说明。

A：但我们可以向你方提供一份调查报告，以此证明少了4,500吨。

B：恐怕短重是在运输途中发生的，因为我们的交易是按照离岸价格进行的。我们不会答应你方的索赔要求。

A：那我们怎么办？

B：我认为你方最好向运输公司或者保险公司提出索赔。如果是他们的过失，我相信他们会赔偿你的损失的。

A：好吧，我听你的。

 商议货物数量增减幅度

A: Let's have a word about shipment. When is the limit for loading?

A：我们谈一下装运事宜吧。装运的最后期限是什么时候呢？

B: The loading period is from May to June.

A: Since you take delivery under FOB terms, your buyers are to charter a ship or book the shipping space. We'll see the goods pass over the ship's rail and our responsibility ends there.

B: For bulk goods, it's convenient for sellers to arrange the shipping space.

A: No doubt about that. But you insisted on FOB this time. Another problem, do you allow any quantity difference when the goods are loaded on board?

B: Yes, there may be some difference, but it can't exceed 5 percent of the quantity stipulated.

A: At what price is the tolerance to be paid?

B: It will be paid at the contracted price.

A: That's quite fair. The ship should be at the port of loading within 25 to 30 days after the goods have been ready.

B: If you can't get the goods ready by the time the ship chartered by us arrives at the port of loading, you will be responsible for the losses thus incurred.

B：装运期限是从5月到6月。

A：由于你们采用离岸的价格条款，你们买方应负责租船订舱。货物越过船舷，我们的责任就尽到了。

B：对于大宗货物，由卖方安排舱位更为方便。

A：是这样的，但是这次你们坚持采用离岸价。还有另外一件事，你们允许装船货物有数量增减幅度吗？

B：是的，允许有增减幅度，但不得超过规定数量的5%。

A：差额如何偿付？

B：按合同价格偿付。

A：十分合理。运输船只将在货物备好后25天到30天内驶抵装运港。

B：如果我们租的货船到达装运港时，你们还未备好货，由此可能造成的损失，你们应全部负责。

口语秘笈

在实际业务中，对于大宗散装商品，通常可在合同中规定溢短装条款，规定交货数量可在一定幅度内增减，常常设定允许溢短装的百分比。在以信用证支付方式成交时，按《跟单信用证统一惯例》（UCP）的规定，可有5%的增减幅度。溢短装更完整的表达方式为"with 5% more or less both in amount and quantity allowed at the seller's option"，"at the seller's option"指的是"卖方具有选择权"。

付款违约
Payment Discrepancy

词语宝典

amendment	修正，改正	promote	促进，提升
component	成分	replacement	代替物，替换品
consult	咨询	undertake	承担，承揽
defective	有缺陷的	in accordance with	符合，依照
forerunner	先驱	sales contract	销售合同
joint effort	共同努力	to some extent	在一定程度上
process	过程，程序，步骤		

经典句型

- Are you worrying about the non-execution of the contract and non-payment on our part?
  你是否担心我们不履行合同或者拒不付款？

- We always carry out the terms of our contract to the letter and stand by what we say.
  我们坚持重合同，守信用。

- No doubt that this will be the forerunner of closer ties in the interest of our two parties.
  毫无疑问，这是一个良好开端，它将我们双方有利。

- Our claim on your L/C No.84 has not been paid.
  我们对你方的第84号信用证收汇没有得到支付。

- You may rest assured that our L/C will meet your requirements in every respect.
  您尽管放心，我们的信用证将完全符合您的要求。

- We had to apply to the Bank of China for short-term loan to cover the rest.
  我们最终不得不向中国银行申请短期贷款来支付其余的支出。

- We cannot proceed the shipment if you fail to open the L/C on time.
  如果你们不能准时开立信用证，我们无法组织装运。

时尚对白

 变更支付条款违约

A: Hello, this is CNS Imp. & Exp. Co. Li Lin is speaking.

B: Oh, hello, this is Wilson. Glad to see that our joint efforts to promote trade have led to our sales contract.

A: So am I. No doubt that this will be the forerunner of closer ties in the interest of our two parties.

B: But there is one thing I want to mention. The date of the delivery is approaching, while the L/C has not come to us. So we cannot proceed the shipment.

A: Actually, we are considering to change the L/C payment to T/T payment 30 days after receipt of the goods.

B: What? I can't believe it. Why?

A: Due to the financial crisis, many of our customers have postponed the purchase of our products, so regarding our current cash flow, it will be more cost-efficient for us to effect the payment by T/T.

B: I understand your situation, but we can't accept that. The ship will leave the port in 7 days, and you must send us the L/C within 7 days, or you will breach the contract.

A: It is impossible for us to send you L/C in 7 days.

B: Well, we have to stop the supply and ask for compensation.

A：您好，CNS 进出口公司，我是李琳。

B：您好，我是威尔逊。很高兴看到经过我们双方的共同努力，终于签定了销售合同。

A：我也是。毫无疑问，这是一个良好的开端，它将对我们双方有利。

B：但是有一件事情我想提一下。发货日期就快到了，而我们还没有收到你方的信用证，因此我们无法组织装运。

A：实际上，我们考虑把信用证支付改为收货后 30 天电汇支付。

B：什么？我无法相信。为什么？

A：由于金融危机，我们的许多客户都延期了对我们商品的采购，所以考虑到我们公司目前的现金流，使用电汇支付更能节约成本。

B：我理解你们的情况，但是我们无法接受。船 7 天后离开港口，你们必须在 7 天内把信用证发过来，否则你们将属于违约。

A：我们不可能在 7 天内把信用证发给你们。

B：那么，我们不得不停止供货，并要求赔偿损失。

拖欠预付款违约

A: We had a hard time in finance since we undertook your order. You know the financial capability of our company is rather limited. A large order like yours really involves a great amount of money.

B: I think 20% of our advance payment will solve some problems for you.

A: To be frank with you, 20% advance payment is helpful only to some extent. According to the contract, the advance payment should be 50%. But finally we had to apply to the Bank of China for short-term loan to cover the rest. So you must know the reason why I am here.

B: Sorry for delay in payment. Just a few days ago, we found some of your parts and components were defective and we asked your Export Dept. to send some replacements for the parts. And we also want to purchase a large amount of accessories for the future use.

A: Such being the case, you mean to make these two payments as one? But we still have to pay interest on the loan from bank due to your delayed 30% advance payment, and I think you should make compensation on that.

B: Well, we will consider that. Anyway, the sooner you send us the replaced parts, the earlier you will get our full payment.

A: Maybe I'd better phone back to consult our manager.

A：自从接了你们的订单以后，在财务上我们一度比较紧张，你知道我们公司的资金能力十分有限，完成你们这样的大订单确实需要许多钱。

B：那么我们的 20% 预付款应该帮你们解决了一定的困难。

A：坦率地讲，20% 预付款只解决了一部分问题。按合同规定，预付款的比例应该是 50%。我们最终不得不向中国银行申请短期贷款来支付其余的支出。想必你已经知道我们此行的目的了。

B：抱歉未能及时付款。就在几天前，我们发现设备中的一些零部件有缺陷，就要求你们的出口部发来更换件，并想再购买大量的附件以备将来之需。

A：既然如此，你想将两笔付款合二为一吗？但是由于你们拖欠了 30% 的预付款，我们不得不向银行支付贷款利息。我认为你们应该对此做出补偿。

B：嗯，我们会考虑的。无论如何，只要你们快一点儿给我们发来更换件，你们就能早一点儿得到全部货款。

A：也许我得打电话请示经理。

达人点拨

关于各种付款方式（terms of payment），一般在合同中都有详细的规定。在一方发生付款违约时，另一方应明确要求其履行合同的付款义务。例如："You are supposed to effect the payment according to the contract."（你们应该按合同规定付款。）语气最强、最直接的表达方式为，"We demand prompt payment."（我们要求立即付款。）。

UNIT 4 交货期违约
Delivery Time Discrepancy

词语宝典

balance	余额	delivery time	交付时间
exceed	超出	force majeure	不可抗力
incur	招致、遭受	loading period	装运期
printer	打印机	microwave oven	微波炉
specify	具体说明	order number	订单号
urge	敦促	shipping schedule	船期
beyond one's control	超出某人能力范围		
cancel the order	取消订单		

经典句型

- The contract states that the supplier will be charged a penalty if there is a delay in delivery.
  合同规定如果供货商延误交货期，将被罚款。

- We must make it clear in the contract that you are obliged to complete the delivery of the goods within the contractual time of shipment.
  我们必须在合同中明确，贵方必须在合同规定的交货期内完成交货。

- I'm sure that shipment will be effected according to the contract stipulation.
  我保证我们能按合同规定如期装船。

- If you fail to make the delivery ten weeks later than the time of shipment stipulated in the contract, we shall have the right to cancel the contract.
  如果贵方延期交货超过合同规定的时间10周，我方有权取消合同。

- We should lodge a claim for all the losses incurred as a consequence of your failure to ship our order in time.
  你方未能及时装船造成了我们的损失，我方要提出索赔。

- I'm very sorry for all the losses you suffered, but it's due to force majeure.
  对于贵方遭受的所有损失，我们深表遗憾，但这都是由于不可抗力造成的。

时尚对白

延迟装运

A: Why haven't you effected shipment?

B: Owing to the shipping schedule, it will be impossible for us to ship the goods until the end of May.

A: As the shopping season is drawing near, buyers urge us for an immediate delivery of the goods, or the season would be over.

B: I am sorry to hear that.

A: Please do your very best to hasten the shipment.

B: As you know, there are three basic factors to be considered in shipment.

A: Which three factors?

B: Cost, time and safety. I'm afraid the cause of this delay of shipment was beyond our control.

A: Then, when is the earliest we can expect for the shipment?

B: By the middle of April, I think.

A: If the goods are not shipped within three weeks, we have to cancel the order.

B: We will do our best to ship the goods as early as possible. We don't want to breach the contract.

A: I believe what you said.

B: We're very sorry for the delay of shipment.

A：	你们为什么还未装运？
B：	因为船期的缘故，我方直到5月底才能运送货物。
A：	由于销售旺季即将来临，买主催我们立即交货，否则他们就赶不上旺季了。
B：	我非常抱歉。
A：	请尽最大可能加速装船。
B：	正如你所知道的，运输需要考虑三大因素。
A：	哪三大因素？
B：	运费、时间和安全。我担心延误装运的原因超出我方能力所及。
A：	那我们能期望最早什么时候装运？
B：	我想要到4月中旬吧。
A：	如果3周内还不装运，我们不得不取消订单。
B：	我方将尽力早日装运。我们也不希望违反合同。
A：	我相信你的话。
B：	我们对装运延误感到非常抱歉。

延迟交付

A: Hello, this is Li Ming calling from CNT Imp. & Exp. Co. I'm phoning about our order for the microwave ovens and the printers. We placed the

A：我是CNT进出口公司的李明。我打电话是想询问我们订购的微波炉和打印机的情况。我们两个月之前

order two months ago. We haven't received the printers yet.

B: Just a minute, could you tell me the order number?

A: It's NC367.

B: NC367. I'll check that. Yes, I'm very sorry, We're still waiting for the delivery of them.

A: But our customers are waiting, too. It is a breach of contract. We should lodge a claim for all the losses incurred as a consequence of your failure to ship our order in time.

B: I'm very sorry for all the losses you suffered, but it's due to force majeure.

A: What evidence do you have to support that this delay was caused by the force majeure? I am told the delay was due to your carelessness.

B: That's not true. We can show you the weather report of last month.

A: Well, now that no settlement can be reached between us, the case under dispute will have to be submitted to arbitration.

下的订单，我们还没有收到打印机。

B：请稍等，请告诉我您的订单号。

A：订单号是 NC367。

B：NC367，我马上查查。非常抱歉，我们还在等打印机的交货。

A：可我们的客户也在等啊！这是违约行为。你方未能及时装船造成了我们的损失，我方要对你们提出索赔。

B：对于贵方遭受的损失，我们深表遗憾，但这是由于不可抗力造成的。

A：但你有什么证据证明延迟发货是由不可抗力造成的呢？据我所知，延迟发货是因为你方的疏忽造成的。

B：不是的，我们可以给你们看上个月的气象资料。

A：那好吧，既然我们双方无法达成一致意见，我们只好进行仲裁。

口语秘笈

是否按时交付是检验是否履行合同的一项重要指标。货物未按时到达的表达方式为："delay in delivery"或"late delivery"。例如："There is 5% penalty for late delivery."（延期交付罚款5%。）未收到货物的表达方式可以为："do not receive goods"或"the goods do not reach us."在这里一定要注意，"receive"不能用"accept"替换，因为"accept"表示"接受"，如果替换则表示"接受货物"。

文化点滴

违约行为是指违反合同的强制性规定而做出的积极行为或消极不作为。违约行为主要指不履行合同的义务或履行的义务不符合合同的约定，具体指拒绝履行、延迟履行、质量瑕疵等。此外，当事人不按合同约定履行通知、协助、保密等附随义务时，也属违约行为。

解决合同纠纷有四种基本途径，即协商、调解、仲裁和诉讼。其中通过合同当事人根据法律和合同的有关规定自行协商解决，或者通过调解即由民间组织根据自愿和合法原则对合同当事人的纠纷加以解决，这两种方式最省时、最简便易行。其次，依据合同仲裁条款或事后达成的仲裁协议解决纠纷的方式，较之向法院起诉来讲，也利于案件的迅速解决和减少解决费用。当然通过诉讼解决虽然耗时长、费用高，但却是解决合同纠纷的一种最重要、最权威的途径。

国际贸易中买卖双方之间的违约包括：①买方违约，如不按时开立信用证；无理拒收货物；或在买方负责运输的情况下不按时派船接货等。②卖方违约，如不按时交货；不按合同规定的品质、规格、包装、数量交货；不提供合同、信用证规定的合适单证等。

在商务营销时，如果你想为你的英语口语表达道歉时，可以说："I hope you'll excuse my English. I'm a little out of practice/please excuse my rather poor English."

如果有听众打断你讲话，你可以说："I think, if you don't mind, we'll leave questions to the end."

与客户握手告别时，可以说："It's been a pleasure doing business with you and I look forward to seeing you again in the very near future."

2 应对及处理

第二章 解决争端

Unit 1　起因调查　Sorting out Problems
Unit 2　应对策略　Handling Strategy
Unit 3　解决办法　Finding Solutions
Unit 4　应对不同的客户　Dealing with Different Clients

起因调查
Sorting out Problems

词语宝典

double-check	仔细检查	control the situation	控制形势
outstanding	没付清	get it corrected	进行更正
track	追查	have the case settled	解决这个问题
adhere to	遵守	make an investigation	做一个调查
be held up at customs	被海关扣留	run through	记下来
consumer complaint	消费者投诉	sales ledger	销货账

经典句型

调查问题

- Can you hold on while I make a note of that? You say the shipment was delayed by rough weather?
  你别挂电话,让我做一下记录行吗?你说因为天气恶劣装船要推迟是吗?

- Let me just run through that again. You say some of the goods were damaged en route?
  让我查一下我记下没有。你说有些货物在运输中损坏了?

- Let me see if I have understood. You say that the last batch was held up at customs?
  让我看看我是不是明白了。你说前一批货被海关扣留了?

- I'm satisfied with the current situation after I've understood the event completely.
  了解事情的全过程之后,我对现状感到很满意。

- The lap top is incompatible with the electrical supply.
  笔记本电脑与供电不相容。

- The fire alarm system is not functioning.
  火警系统不发挥作用了。

- You service department has let us down again.

你们的维修部门又让我们失望了。

付款问题

- The total was $4,000 and you have only sent us $3,000. Can you send us the balance immediately?
  总额是4,000美元,而你们只给我们寄了3,000美元。你们能不能立刻把剩余部分给我们寄来?

- You have underpaid by $1,000. Please adjust accordingly.
  你们已少付1,000美元,请做相应调整。

- The agreed terms of payment have not be adhered to.
  议定的付款条件没被遵守。

- According to our records the amount of $1,500 is still outstanding.
  根据我们的记录,还有1,500美元的金额没付清。

时尚对白

交货与包装纠纷

A: I have something unpleasant to talk to you about. The goods you sent to us can't reach us in due time because of the bad weather.

B: Can you hold on while I make a note of that? You say shipment was delayed by rough weather?

A: Yes, and the shipper informed us that the packing of the goods were damaged seriously.

B: As far as I know, the goods were in perfect condition when they left here.

A: Please look into the matter and have the case settled immediately.

B: We'll get in touch with the shipping company and see what can be done.

A:和你谈件不愉快的事儿。你发给我们的货物由于天气恶劣不能及时到达我地。

B:您别挂电话,让我做一下记录行吗?你说因为天气恶劣装船要推迟了是吗?

A:是的,同时,船方告诉我们货物的包装严重损坏。

B:据我所知,商品在这儿起运时,状况很好。

A:请调查一下这件事,并立即予以解决。

B:我们会和船运公司取得联系,看看怎么办。

达人点拨

当你收到疑难问题的消息或投诉时，仔细检查情报资料并准确记录下来是非常重要的。这是一些可供你使用的表达法："Can you hold on while I make a note of that?"（请您别挂电话，让我做下记录。）或"I see. Just a moment."（我明白了，稍等。）如果对方发出抱怨，不要急于认可或否认，通常的策略是先进行调查，以事实为依据。可以说："We'll get in touch with the shipping company."（我们会和船运公司联系。）或"We'll check with the department concerned."（我们会向有关部门调查。）。

开错发票

A: Good afternoon, Mr. Lee, what is your hurry?
B: Oh, I'm sorry to burst in on you like this, but I'm really upset.
A: What on earth has happened to trouble you so?
B: Please look at this invoice. The shirts you estimated at three hundred dollars for three dozen have been invoiced to us for eight hundred!
A: Do you mean those striped shirts you ordered last month?
B: Yes, with two thousand dozen handkerchiefs, remember?
A: Yes, yes. May I see the invoice?
B: Certainly, here you are.
A: Well, the invoice does say eight hundred dollars for only the three dozen.
B: Right. The shirts are just the same as I ordered, but not at the price listed on the invoice.
A: Of course not. This invoice looks like a retail sales ledger. May I take this one to our Accounting Department to look up your account in the sales ledger?
B: Of course, please do.
A: Please wait here for a while. I'll look into it and try to get it corrected for you as quickly as possible.
B: That's very kind of you.

A：下午好，李先生，忙什么呢？
B：噢，很抱歉这么突然来访，但我真的不高兴。
A：到底什么事儿让你烦恼？
B：请看看这张发票。你把3打衬衫300美元的发票开成了800。
A：你指的是你上月订的条纹衬衫吗？
B：是的，还有2,000打手帕，记得吗？
A：是的，让我看看发票好吗？
B：当然可以，给你。
A：好的，发票上写着3打衬衫800美元。
B：对，衬衫和我订的一样，但不是发票上标的价格。
A：当然不是，这个发票看起来像零售账目。我把这张发票拿到我们会计部查一下你的销售账，好吗？
B：当然可以，请便。
A：请在这等一会儿，我仔细查一下并尽快给你把它更正过来。
B：太谢谢你了。

> **口语秘笈**
>
> "burst in on" 是 "突然到来，突然造访" 的意思。例如："It was very rude of you to burst in on him while he was working."（他在工作时你去打搅他，真是鲁莽。）。

 产品质量问题

A: Have you seen the report of consumer complaints? It got a lot of negative feedback from customers who purchased it.

B: I wasn't aware of that. What did they complain about?

A: Many said that it wasn't user-friendly and that the earphone cord wasn't long enough.

B: Let me see. Oh yeah! It does seem to be a bit short. Let's start to fill out our report before we forget something.

A: Looks like this MP3 player has more cons than pros!

B: Right! We'll have to advise the R&D Department and Quality Control.

A：你看到消费者投诉的报告了吗？此产品的消费者给了它很多负面的回应。

B：我没注意到那个。他们投诉些什么？

A：很多人说它用起来不够人性化，而且耳机线不够长。

B：我看看。真的！它似乎是真的有点儿短。趁我们还没忘记前，快开始填写我们的报告书吧！

A：看起来这款MP3的缺点比优点多！

B：是啊！我们得通知研发部和品管部。

UNIT 2 应对策略 Handling Strategy

词语宝典

cancel	取消	customer service manager	客户服务经理
feasible	可行的	delayed flight	延误的航班
inconvenience	不方便	different opinion	不同的看法
replacement	替换	international standard	国际标准
accept responsibility	承担责任	play for time	为争取时间而拖延
all-round view	全面的看法	rental agreement	租赁协议
compromise proposal	折中建议	workable suggestion	可行的建议

经典句型

拖延时间

- I've tried all possible ways, but none of them is feasible.
  我试过所有可能的办法，但是没有一个行得通。

- Leave it with me. I'll have to get permission from the accounts department.
  交给我吧，我需要得到会计部门的许可。

道歉

- What we can do now is to make an apology.
  我们现在唯一能做的就是道歉。

- Please accept our apologies.
  请接受我们的道歉。

- We have lost production time because of you.
  因为你们，我们失去了生产时间。

解释原因

- We're having trouble with our suppliers.
  我们与供应商有了麻烦。

- That package you sent was open when it arrived.
  你们发送过来的包裹到达的时候是打开的。

解决问题

- This is a really unfortunate accident.
  发生意外真是不幸。
- This comes as a complete surprise.
  这真令人吃惊。
- We have never had a complaint of this kind.
  我们从未收到过这样的投诉。

时尚对白

旅游投诉分析

A: Hello, I'm Angela. I'm the customer service manager. Would you like to come with me and take a seat, so you can explain to me what actually the problem is?
B: OK, OK, fine.
A: Can I take your name?
B: Yes, my name's Alison.
A: OK. Alison, if you'd like to make yourself comfortable. As I said, I am the customer service manager and I'd like to help you. I understand you are having a few problems.
B: Well, yes. I've just come back from one of your holidays. I went to Crete, in Greece, got back last week and the whole thing was a disaster.
A: Would you like to just explain from the beginning what's happened?
B: Well, yes. To start with, when we got to the airport, in Crete, we had a two-hour wait on the coach. I think there was a delayed flight or something,

A：您好，我是安吉拉。我是客户服务经理。您愿意和我一起坐下来吗？这样您可以向我说明一下问题。
B：好的。
A：可以告诉我您的名字吗？
B：可以。我叫艾利森。
A：好的，艾利森，不要拘束。正如我刚才说的，我是客户服务经理，我很乐意为您提供服务。我知道您有几个问题。
B：是的。我刚刚参加完你们组织的旅行回来，去了希腊的克里特岛，上周刚回来，整个旅程简直就是场灾难。
A：能从开始时解释一下到底是怎么回事儿吗？
B：好。开始时，当我们到达克里特岛的机场时，我们在长途汽车上等了2个小时。我以为是飞机延误和……

and… and…

A: Right, that's quite possible.

B: Yes. And I just can't work out why you didn't take us to our hotel and then come back to the airport to pick up the people from the delayed flight.

A: Right, I'm sorry for that wait. I don't know what the problem was. You mentioned a delayed flight there. As you can imagine, you probably weren't the only family on the coach waiting, and to ferry people to and from the resort to the airport would have been a lot of extra work and they like to try and keep everybody together who are going on the same flight. I can actually look into that for you …

A：是的，那是有可能的。

B：是的，但是，我想不明白你们为什么不能把我们送回宾馆，之后再回到机场去接延误的那个航班的人呢？

A：是的，我对您的等候深表歉意。我不知道问题出在什么地方。您提到了航班延误。正如您所想的，或许您并不是在长途汽车上唯一等候的家庭吧。如果先送人然后折回机场接其他人将会产生很多额外工作。他们希望能尽量把同一航班的人聚集到一起。我可以帮您了解一下该情况……

达人点拨

应对纠纷，需要具体的解决办法，需要表示歉意，"I'm sorry for that wait."（我对您的等候深表歉意。）或"I'm sorry for the inconvenience."（对此造成的不便我们深感歉意。）。

 解决快递纠纷

A: Hello!

B: Hello, can I speak to dispatch, please?

A: You're through to dispatch.

B: Right. Well, I phoned two days ago to say that I hadn't received delivery of my order and I'm ringing again to say it still hasn't arrived.

A: Can I just take your name, please?

B: Yes, it's Mark Anderson.

A: Ah! I think there's been a problem with that order, Mr. Anderson.

B: What kind of problem?

A: Oh, I don't know offhand. Let me check for you. Yes, part of the order didn't arrive here at the depot, so I

A：您好。

B：您好。是快递公司吗？

A：是的，请说。

B：好的。我两天前打过电话说我没有收到我的订货，现在我要重新跟您说一下，我的订货还是没到。

A：请问您叫什么名字？

B：马克·安德森。

A：嗯，安德森先生，我想是您的订单出问题了。

B：什么问题？

A：我现在还不知道。我帮您查一下吧。是的，一部分货物没有到达仓库，因此在我们收到所有东西之前我

couldn't send it out until we'd received everything.

B: Well, surely that was your problem to sort out without my having to call you back again. I did phone and draw your attention to this a couple of days ago. Look, I placed this order weeks ago. It's just not good enough.

A: Yeah, I'm sorry about this, Mr. Anderson. I'm sorry for the inconvenience, but I can assure you we'll do everything we can to send it out to you as quickly as possible.

们不能给您发货。

B：好吧，很显然这是你们的问题，你们不应该让我再打电话来催。我几天之前就给您打过电话，并请您注意一下这批物品。我是几周前下的订单。我想这样不好吧。

A：是的，抱歉，安德森先生，对此造成的不便我们深感歉意。我向您保证我们将尽最大努力将订货尽快发给您。

口语秘笈

"draw one's attention" 是 "引起……注意" 的意思，同类的表达方式还有 "invite one's attention, have one's attention"。

设备召回

A: Hello. This is Jenny Smith of BiB Systems.

B: Jenny, could you do something about this fax machine? We hired a fax machine from you and I would like to cancel our rental agreement.

A: What's wrong with it? I sent someone yesterday and I suppose everything is OK.

B: Yes, you sent someone yesterday but it still cannot work properly. I would rather just cancel the agreement...

A: Oh, I'm sorry.

B: Yes, could you send someone to collect it tomorrow morning, please?

A：你好。我是 BiB 系统公司的詹妮·史密斯。

B：詹妮，你能解决一下这台传真机的问题吗？我们在你公司租了一台传真机，我现在要取消租赁协议。

A：什么毛病？我昨天派人过去了，我想应该没问题了吧。

B：是的，昨天你确实派人来维修，但还是不能正常工作。我只想取消协议……

A：很抱歉。

B：是的，请你明天上午派人来取回传真机。

否认质量问题

A: The goods you sent us are below our usual

A：你发给我们的货物低于我们的一般

standard.

B:Our products are up to the international standard.

A:The quality of this lot of goods is so far below the standard that we cannot use them for our purpose.

B:This comes as a complete surprise. We have never had a complaint of this kind.

A:Our analysis was made on the retained samples .

B:Well, I'm afraid we'll have to have the retained samples re-checked before we settle it.

A:Here's the inspection report made by the health officers in London.

B:This is a really unfortunate accident. But, all our goods had been certified as good in quality and well-packed.

标准。

B：我们的产品是符合国际标准的。

A：这批货物质量与标准质量相距甚远，我们无法使用。

B：这真令人吃惊，我们从未收到过这样的投诉。

A：我们的分析是根据保留样做出的。

B：那我恐怕要将保留的样品再次检查后才能处理。

A：这是伦敦卫生检疫所官员的检查报告。

B：发生意外真是不幸。可是，我们的全部货物都经过检验，质量合格、包装也合格的。

口语秘笈

"the inspection report"（检查报告），"certify"（证明），"good in quality"（质量好）。

处理质量问题

A:I'd like to speak to the customer service manager, please.

B:Speaking.

A:Last week I bought a CD player from your company, but it doesn't work today.

B:I'm sorry about that, sir. I'll replace it for you if it was only bought within this week.

A：我想找客户服务经理。

B：我就是，请讲。

A：上周我从你们公司买了这个ＣＤ播放器，今天无法正常使用了。

B：抱歉，先生。如果是本周内买的我会给你调换。

UNIT 3 解决办法 Finding Solutions

词语宝典

compensate	赔偿	suspend	终止
lose	损失	old model	旧式样
modify	修改	redesign	再设计
outlet	出路	financial analyst	财务分析家
personnel	人员	international standard	国际标准
renew	续签		

经典句型

处理主要问题

- You should submit the bills to the Finance Department.
  你得把账单送到财务部。

- We are impossible to renew the contract under such conditions.
  我们不会在此条件下续签合同的。

- Some of the terms must be modified before we renew the contract.
  续约前必须更改其中的一些条款。

应急方案

- We should suspend all the shipments and , in the meantime, request the payment in US dollars.
  我们应该终止所有货物装运并且要求用美元付款。

- We should send in financial analysts as soon as possible and consider re-investing locally.
  我们应当尽可能快地派出财务分析专家并考虑在本地的再投资。

长期解决办法

- We must change our investment policy.
  我们必须改变我们的投资政策。

- You have to redesign the old model.
  你不得不对旧式样进行再设计。

时尚对白

 更正发票

A: We've made a very embarrassing mistake. Please forgive us.
B: That's all right. How did it happen, I wonder?
A: Well, they were awfully short of time last week, and one of the new young typists mixed up your account with another one.
B: Oh, I'm glad you found that out.
A: Our Accounting Department is now making out another invoice for you with the correct amount on it.
B: Thank you. I'm very pleased we were able to get this settled so quickly.
A: I think we must get a few more experienced typists for greater efficiency.
B: Ha, ha, but on the other hand, new typists may mean that your business is expanding right? That's a good sign.
A: Here you are, Mr. Lee. Here's the correct invoice.
B: Oh, thank you very much.

A：我们犯了个令人尴尬的错误，请谅解。
B：没事儿的，怎么回事儿？
A：上周他们时间特别紧，一个新来的年轻打字员把你的账和另一笔账弄混了。
B：噢，很庆幸你能查出来。
A：我们会计部正在给你另外开一张金额正确的发票。
B：谢谢你。很高兴我们能这么快处理这件事儿。
A：我认为我们应该找几个更有经验、效率更高的打字员。
B：哈哈，另一方面，新的打字员意味着你们的业务正在扩大？是个好迹象。
A：给你，李先生。这是正确的发票。
B：噢，非常感谢。

 宾馆房间调换

A: Can you change the room for me? It's too noisy. My wife was woken up several times by the noise of the baggage elevator made. She said it was too much for her.
B: I'm awfully sorry, sir. We'll manage it, but we don't have any spare room today. Could you wait until tomorrow?

A：能给我换个房间吗？这儿太吵了。我妻子被运送行李的电梯发出的嘈杂声弄醒了几次。她说这使她难以忍受。
B：非常对不起，先生。我们会尽力办到，但是今天我们没有空余房间。等到明天好吗？

A:I hope we'll be able to enjoy our stay in a quiet suite tomorrow evening and have a sound sleep.

B:And if there are any other things you need, please let us know.

A:The light in this room is too dim. Please get me a brighter one.

B:Certainly, sir. I'll be back right away.

A：我希望明天晚上我们能待在一个安静的房间里睡个好觉。

B：如果还需要别的什么东西，请告诉我们。

A：这房间里的灯光太暗了，请给我换个亮一点儿的。

B：好的，先生，我马上就回来。

 选择解决办法

A:There's an angry customer outside.

B:Why? What's up?

A:He is not satisfied with our after-sale services, which make him really furious.

B:We must work out a solution to this matter right away.

A:Yes, we must do something.

B:Do you have any suggestions?

A:There are four optional solutions to this complaint. Here you are.

B:I'd like to choose one of them.

A：外面有个生气的顾客。

B：为什么？怎么了？

A：他对我们的售后服务不满意，这使他很愤怒。

B：我们必须想办法立刻解决这个问题。

A：是，我们必须做点儿什么。

B：你有什么建议吗？

A：对于这类投诉有四个解决方案，给你。

B：我想从中选择一个方案。

口语秘笈

当我们提议一个解决办法时，可在动词前加上"should"表示提供建议或表示必要。如果我们认为十分必要，其他词你还可以使用"must"或是"have to"；如果我们不能绝对肯定或是我们在许多建议中只是提供一个选择就用"could"。

Unit 4 应对不同的客户
Dealing with Different Clients

词语宝典

disorganization	杂乱无章	in an orderly fashion	井井有条
reschedule	重新安排时间	red tape	繁文缛节
emergency meeting	紧急会议	wade through	费力地办理
get this straightened out	解决这个问题		

经典句型

- These guys are disturbing our business.
  这些人影响了我们的生意。

- I apologize for the delay, sir. Please have a seat here.
  非常抱歉耽误您时间了，先生。请坐。

- I understand what makes you angry, Mr. Grant.
  我知道您为什么恼火，格兰特先生。

- There is really no excuse for this. But I promise you this will not happen again!
  的确不应该如此。我向你保证这样的事情绝不会再次发生。

- I realize it appears simple enough, but there is a lot of red tape to wade through.
  我知道，这工作看上去是简单，却有许多公文手续需要办理。

- I didn't anticipate how long it would take Mr. Barkley. Let me see if I can reach him.
  我不知道巴克利先生会耽搁多长时间。让我试试能否和他联系上。

时尚对白

面对不耐烦的顾客

A: Excuse me, miss?

B: Yes, Ms. Li? May I help you?

A: I arrived here at 8:30 this morning, and I've been waiting since then for Mr. Gates! If I have to wait one more minute, I'm going to take my business somewhere else.

B: I'm very sorry, Ms. Li. Mr. Gates was called away to an emergency meeting. He should be back at any moment.

A: I wish you should let me know that earlier! I could have rescheduled my appointment rather than waiting for such a long time!

B: You're right, Ms. Li. I didn't anticipate how long it would take Mr. Gates. Let me see if I can reach him now.

A：打扰一下，小姐？

B：什么事儿，李女士？我能帮助您什么吗？

A：我今天早上8:30到的这里，一直等盖茨先生到现在！如果再让我多等一分钟，我会把我的生意拿到别的地方的。

B：十分抱歉，李女士。盖茨先生被召去开一个紧急会议。他随时会回来。

A：你应该早点儿告诉我！那样我可以重订我们的约见时间，而不是等这么长时间。

B：您说得对，李女士。我不知道盖茨先生会耽搁多长时间。现在让我试试能否和他联系上。

面对生气的客户

A: Look! I've had enough! If you can't get this straightened out, I'm going to a different company! I have never seen so much disorganization!

B: I understand why you got angry, Mr. Wang. There is really no excuse for this. But I promise you this will not happen again! We have spoken to the salespeople involved, and we can solve this problem soon.

A: Well, obviously, what you're doing is not good enough! I just don't trust your company to take care of business in an orderly fashion.

A：听着！我受够了。如果你们解决不了这个问题，我要去找另一家公司了。从来没见过这么混乱的。

B：我知道您为什么恼火，王先生。的确不应如此。我保证同样的事不会再发生。我们已经找有关的销售人员谈过了。我们很快就能解决这个问题。

A：可是，很明显，你们所做的还远远不够。我就是不相信你们公司能井井有条地做事儿。

177

B: If you could just give us a few more days, we should be able to get this problem ironed out. I do hope you'll reconsider.

B：如果您能给我们几天时间，我们一定能把这个问题解决好的。我也真诚希望您能重新考虑一下。

 文化点滴

在国际贸易中，当一方认为另一方没有执行合同规定的责任时，双方就会发生纠纷，也可能导致索赔。进口商和出口商提出索赔的类型包括：质量不好、质量差异、包装不好、损坏、短重、延迟到货、没有派船、没有及时开信用证、无理拒绝货物、货物丢失、发错货物。在处理顾客纠纷时，一般要从四个方面来进行：

1．详细倾听顾客的抱怨；
2．向顾客道歉，并弄清原因；
3．提出解决问题的方法并尽快行动；
4．改进工作，避免同样的问题再次发生。

2 应对及处理

第三章 应对索赔

Unit 1　提出索赔　Lodging Claims
Unit 2　接受索赔　Accepting Claims
Unit 3　拒绝索赔　Dismissing Claims

UNIT 1 提出索赔 Lodging Claims

词语宝典

consignment	货物	original certificate	原始证明
indemnification	补偿、赔偿	survey report	检验报告
to make a (one's) claim	提出索赔	to lodge a (one's) claim	提出索赔
damaged condition	损坏程度（状态）	to file a (one's) claim	提出索赔
inspection fee	检验费	up to the standard	合格，达到标准

经典句型

- This lot of goods is not up to the standard stipulated in the contract, and we are now lodging a claim against you.
  这批货未达到合同规定的标准，我们现在要向你方提出索赔。

- We regret to inform you that ten of the cases of your consignment arrived in a badly damaged condition.
  我们遗憾地告诉你发来的货物中有 10 箱受损。

- From the shipment of 1,000 cases of glassware, we find that a number of wooden cases and the contents have been broken.
  从 1,000 箱玻璃货物中抽查了一些，我们发现一些木箱以及其内装物已经破损。

- On examination, we have found that many of the sewing machines are severely damaged.
  检查时，我们发现许多缝纫机严重受损。

- We have to ask for compensation of £6,000 to cover the loss incurred as result of the inferior quality of the goods.
  我们不得不就劣质货物产生的损失索赔 6,000 英镑。

- We have to file a claim against you to the amount of $7,000 plus inspection fee.
  我们向你方索赔 7,000 美金外加检验费。

- We are willing to accept the shipment only if you allow a 30% reduction in price.
  只有你方降价 30%，我们才愿接收这批货。

时尚对白

 车床质量不合格

A: The consignments of the lathes have just reached us. We have to lodge a claim against you for inferior quality, I'm afraid.

B: Is there anything wrong?

A: We bought 100 sets from you, but there are 10 not up to the standard.

B: It's hard for us to believe it. We have been of the best quality for years. Do you have any reliable evidence?

A: Here is the survey report from a well-known public surveyor in Beijing. You may inspect the defective lathes personally.

B: Well, according to the contract we are responsible for repairing or replacing those defective lathes. We'll send our technicians to repair them.

A: 10 sets mean that 10% of the total account of the contract, as well as for the inspection fee.

B: I'm sorry about the quality problem, and I propose we compensate you for 10% of the total value apart from the inspection fee.

A: OK, in that case, we can continue to cooperate after all.

A：我们刚刚收到车床这批货。恐怕我们不得不就这些产品低劣的质量向你方提出索赔。

B：有什么不对吗？

A：我们从你们那儿购买了100套，但是有10套是不合格的。

B：我们很难相信会这样。我们的仪器多年来质量一直很好。你有什么可靠的证据吗？

A：这是北京的一家权威机构的调查报告。你们也可以亲自对这些次品进行检查。

B：好吧，根据合同，我们要对这些次品进行修理和调换。我们会派技术人员去修理。

A：10套不合格产品意味着10%的不合格率。你们应该向我们赔偿合同总价值的10%，还包括检验费。

B：对于质量问题我表示歉意。我提议我方除了赔偿检验费，再赔偿总价值的10%。

A：好吧，这样的话，我们以后可以继续合作。

 货物生锈

A: We found in the examination that 30% of the goods have rusted, please exchange them.

B: We think it quite probably derives from natural changes in the voyage.

A：我们在检验中发现有30%的货物已生锈，请给予调换。

B：我们认为很可能是航途中的自然变化。

A: But according to the checker's report, the packaging is half-baked, and therefore, you should be responsible for the damage.

B: We pledge there is absolutely nothing wrong with the packaging. Don't you think the damage was caused during the loading?

A: Please find out the cause.

B: OK. We will make an investigation.

A: Thanks for your cooperation.

A：但是根据检验员的报告，检查时货物的包装是不完整的，由此发生的损失应是贵方的责任。

B：我们保证货物的包装绝对没有问题。包装的破损是不是装船时引起的？

A：请你们查明原因。

B：好的，我们会展开调查。

A：谢谢你们的合作。

口语秘笈

在回复索赔要求时，如果能肯定责任归属，可以使用"ensure, guarantee, warrant"或"pledge"等表达方式给出明确回复，例如："We guarantee there is absolutely nothing wrong with the quality."（我们保证货物的质量绝对没有问题。）。

奶酪变质

A: You've probably been advised of the serious deterioration of the last consignment of 2,000 cases of cheese. Closer inspection of the health officers showed that the contents were considered unfit for human consumption.

B: Have you people in Seoul discovered the exact cause of the deterioration?

A: Here is the original certificate issued by the Seoul health officers. As to the causes, closer examination revealed that the deterioration was brought about by inferior quality of raw materials and improper packing.

B: I'd say we've never come across such an unpleasant case since we started exporting cheese 8 years ago.

A: Yet the fact remains that this has made it necessary for us to file a claim against you. We do hope you'd compensate us in some way or another so that the loss

A：你一定得到了上一批 2,000 箱奶酪变质的消息。卫生官员经过严格检查发现这些奶酪已不适合食用。

B：你方在首尔的人士是否查出了变质的原因？

A：这是首尔的卫生官员出具的原始证明。至于变质原因，严格检验表明变质是由于原材料品质低劣和包装不妥所致。

B：我们出口奶酪有 8 年了，从未遇到过这类令人不愉快的事情。

A：然而事实是我们要向你方提出索赔。我们希望你们想办法对我们进行赔偿，这样我们的损失也不

wouldn't be so hard on us.
B: But, it is first of all a matter of responsibility rather than a matter of loss.
A: I hope we'd have things straightened out as early as possible.
B: So do I.

过于惨重。
B：但是，这首先是个责任问题而不是损失问题。
A：我希望我们尽快把问题搞清楚。
B：我也是这么想。

 产品尺寸不合格

A: Part of goods do not coincide with standards described in the contract.
B: Really, what is the difference in size?
A: It should be 40mm in diameter according to the contract, but the material object is only 39.7mm in diameter.
B: Please let me have a look at the object.
A: (measuring) Look, it is only 39.7mm.
B: How many of these products are there?
A: There is 1,500 according to the contract, of which 500 failed to meet the standard. Please check it.
B: I am inquiring about this with headquarters. Please give me a sample to ask them to negotiate with the factory.

A：有部分货物与合同的规格不符。
B：是吗？尺寸差多少？
A：合同规定的规格是直径40mm，但是实物的直径只有39.7mm。
B：让我看看实物吧。
A：（边测量）看，只有39.7mm。
B：这样的货物有多少？
A：合同数量是1,500个，有500个不符合规格。请贵公司负责查清楚。
B：我们马上向总部询问。请给我一个样品，以便送到总部与工厂交涉。

口语秘笈

提出索赔的表达方式很多，能与"claim"的名词形式搭配的动词及词组包括"make，bring up，register，file，lodge，raise，put in"等；"claim"做动词时的搭配包括"claim for indemnity"和"claim on sb."。在商务英语的口语表达中，使用"lodge，register，file，raise"与"claim"的搭配表达较为正式。

UNIT 2 接受索赔 Accepting Claims

词语宝典

compensate	补偿，弥补	accept a claim	接受索赔
consumption	消费	accommodate a claim	接受索赔
leakage	渗漏	canned seafood	罐装海鲜食品
leak	渗漏	entertain a claim	接受索赔
singular	罕见的	in person	亲自
steamer	轮船	inspection report	检验报告
remit	汇款	rude loading	野蛮装运
verify	核实，证实	surveyor's report	检验报告

经典句型

- We accept the claim, but can you tell me how much you want us to compensate you for the loss?
  我们接受索赔，但你能告诉我赔偿你多少损失吗？

- We will get this matter resolved as soon as possible and hope to compensate you for your loss to your satisfaction.
  我们将尽早地解决此事，希望赔偿你方损失直到你方满意为止。

- We regret the loss you have suffered and agree to compensate you $800.
  我们为你方遭受的损失表示歉意并同意赔偿 800 美金。

- We agree to compensate you for the detective watches by 5% of the total value.
  我们同意就缺陷手表赔偿总金额的 5%。

- We will make you a compensation of 6% and give you some preferential terms later on.
  我们将赔偿 6% 并在今后给你方特别条款。

- Since the responsibility rests with both parties, we are ready to pay 50% of the loss only.
  既然双方都有责任，我们准备仅付损失的 50%。

时尚对白 🔊

 包装破损

A: I have something very unpleasant to talk with you about. Upon the arrival of the first consignment, it was found that about 50% of the 60 cases of canned pineapples were leaking.

B: It's rather an unusual case. Have you found the cause of leaking?

A: It's simply because the cans were damaged.

B: It appears to be the only case to us that the goods have been damaged on the way.

A: I am sorry to say it was not on the way, but during loading. The cans inside the cases were broken evidently through rough handling.

B: Could you offer us a certificate issued by your health department?

A: Certainly. Here you are. Our health authorities said they were no longer suitable for human consumption. I have to remind you that our terms are CIF canned pineapples. I hope you would indemnify us for the loss so that it wouldn't be so heavy on us.

B: Now we are prepared to settle the issue with you amicably.

A：我有一些很不愉快的事情要和你说。第一批货物发过来的时候，60箱菠萝罐头中有50%是漏的。

B：通常不会发生这种情况的。你发现泄露的原因了吗？

A：很简单，罐子坏了。

B：看上去只可能是在运输途中损坏的。

A：很遗憾，我想这不是在途中损坏的，而是在搬运过程中损坏的。箱子里的破碎罐子很明显是因粗鲁的搬运造成的。

B：你能提供你方卫生部门签发的证明吗？

A：当然。给你。我们的卫生当局称它们已经不能食用了。我不得不提醒你，我们的条款是菠萝罐头的到岸价格。我希望你们可以给予赔偿以减轻我们的损失。

B：我们会积极地为你处理这个问题的。

 品质与样品不符

A: Two cases of your product didn't coincide with your sample last time.

B: I don't know what has happened. There hasn't been such things with us. Maybe the factory sent

A：上次你们的货物中有两箱的品质和规格与样品不符。

B：这是怎么回事儿，我们从来没有发生过这样的事情。也许是工厂方面

185

the wrong samples.

A: Here is what differs from your sample.

B: I got it. I am contacting the factory right now. … I am very sorry and we are responsible for the mistake, and we'll exchange all merchandise that falls short of sample.

A: We will not get to the bottom since this is the first claim.

B: There won't be such things.

发错了样品。

A：这是与样品不符的东西。

B：这样，我马上和厂方联系。……这次的差错完全是我们的责任。非常抱歉。与样品不符合的货物我们全部无偿调换。

A：这次是第一次发生索赔，所以我们不再追究了。

B：以后一定不会再发生类似的事情。

 货物破损

A: Our investigation results tell us that the factory party is responsible for the cargo damage. We are so sorry for the inconvenience we brought to you in this matter.

B: Well, that's all right.

A: The factory party agreed to compensate for your damage.

B: Thanks. I would like to know details about the plan of compensation.

A: We are not going to carry these damaged goods back. Would you accept to buy these goods at half price? We'd like to use the payment as our compensation fee.

B: Thank you very much.

A: We are completely responsible for this accident. We warrant we won't make this kind of mistake again.

A：关于货物破损一事，我方调查的结果表明是厂方的责任。给贵公司添了很多麻烦，非常抱歉。

B：啊，不必客气。

A：厂方同意赔偿损失的要求。

B：谢谢。我想知道具体的赔偿方法。

A：破损货物就不打算运回来了，能以半价处理给你们吗？我想这部分款项就充当赔偿金了。

B：非常感谢。

A：这次事故完全是由我方失误造成的，我保证今后不再发生类似事情。

 货物渗漏

A: I have to say the recent consignment of 2,000 cases of canned seafood didn't turn out to our satisfaction. Upon its arrival in Canada, it was found 288 cases were leaking and unfit for

A：我不得不说最近这2,000箱海鲜罐头不能令人满意。货到加拿大后，我们发现有288箱渗漏，已

consumption. Here's the inspection report made by the health officers in Toronto.

B: But all our goods have been verified to be good in quality and well-packed. What's the exact cause of the leakage?

A: The surveyor's report shows that the goods are well packed. The leakage might be caused by the rude loading at your port.

B: That's quite a singular case.

A: You may think it is a singular case, yet the accident has brought us great losses. As we conclude the business on CIF basis, we have to file a claim against you for it.

B: I'm sorry for any inconvenience we have caused. To compensate for your losses, we will ship another 200 cases of canned seafood by the first available steamer. The freight as well as the inspection fee is for our account. What do you think of it?

经不能食用。这是多伦多卫生检疫所官员的报告。

B：可是我们的货物经过检验是质量合格、包装良好的呀。渗漏到底是由于什么原因引起的呢？

A：检验报告表明，货物包装完好，渗漏是由于货物在你方港口的野蛮装运造成的。

B：我们可是很少遇到这种情况的。

A：对于你们来说，可能是个别案例，可是这给我们造成了巨大的损失。因为我们是以 CIF 价成交的，我只能向你们索赔了。

B：我们对由此给你们带来的不便感到非常抱歉。为了弥补你们的损失，我们将在第一时间向你方再运去 200 箱海鲜罐头。运费和检验费由我们负担。你看怎么样？

口语秘笈

接受索赔时，要沉着冷静，使用礼貌语询问索赔的具体事宜。例如："We'd like to express our sincere apologies for..."（我们就……致以深深歉意。），"We regret the loss you have suffered..."（我们为你方遭受的损失表示歉意。）。

UNIT 3 拒绝索赔 Dismissing Claims

词语宝典

allowance	补偿	suppliers	供应商
crack	裂纹	waive	放弃
dampness	潮湿	in perfect condition	完好无损
mileage	里程	international convention	国际惯例
mishap	灾难	raw material	原料
porcelain	瓷器		

经典句型

- A thorough examination showed that the broken bags were due to improper packing, for which the suppliers should be held responsible.
  彻底检查表明袋子破损归因于包装不合适，供应商应该承担责任。

- As the shipping company is liable for the damage, your claim for compensation should, in our opinion, be referred to them for settlement.
  由于运输公司对货物破损有责任，依我方之见，你们货物的索赔就交由他们解决。

- Your claim, in our opinion, should be referred to the insurance company, as the mishap occurred after shipment.
  据我方所见，你们的索赔应提交保险公司，因为是运输产生的问题。

- Since the damage was due to the rough handling by the steamship company, you should claim on it for recovery of the loss.
  既然损坏是因轮船公司野蛮装运所致，你们应向它索赔来挽回损失。

- We are prepared to make you a reasonable compensation, but not the amount you claimed.
  我们准备给你方一个合理的赔偿，而非你方要求索赔的数字。

- The shortage you claimed might have occurred in the course of transit, which is

out of our control.
你方短交货物的索赔也许发生在运输中，那不在我们掌控范围内。

- The shipping documents can prove that the goods, when shipped, were in perfect condition. They must have been damaged en route.
装船单据表明装船时货物是完整的，它们一定是在运输途中受损的。

- I'll try to find out why the shirts we sent you are a smaller size and inform you of the result as soon as possible
我将试着找出为何我们发给你的衬衫是小尺码，我将尽早告诉你结果。

时尚对白

不可抗力

A: On examination, we find a shortage in the shipment.
B: Because the shortage occurred after shipment, you may raise a claim against the ship owners.
A: We can't make a claim against the ship owners because the short weight was due to excessive moisture.
B: We'd like to have your present proof.
A: Here is our on board bill of lading to claim a settlement.
B: Sorry, the evidence you have provided is inadequate, therefore, we cannot consider your claim as requested.
A: What else must we obtain?
B: A statement from the vessel's agents certifying that the goods were actually loaded on the vessels at the time the vessel sailed out, and the full original set of ocean bills of lading, original policy and the original commercial invoice.

A：经检查，我们发现货物短重。
B：因为短重是装运后发生的，你们可向船东提出索赔。
A：我们不能向船东提出索赔，因为短重是由于过度潮湿所致。
B：我们想看一下贵方出具的证明。
A：这是我们用来要求索赔的已装运提单。
B：抱歉。贵方提供的证明是不充分的，因此我方不能考虑贵方的索赔要求。
A：我们还须出具什么证明？
B：你需要出具一份船行报告证明货物确实准时装船出运，再就是全套的海运装运提单正本，保单正本和商业发票正本。
A：希望你方采取积极行动解决索赔问题。

A: We hope you will take positive action towards settlement of the claim.

B: We shall not be responsible due to force majeure. And that is international convention. Every country follows this rule. Force majeure is exempt from claim.

B：如因不可抗拒力的事故，我们不负任何责任。这可是国际惯例，每个国家均遵循这一原则。不可抗力造成的损失不属于索赔之列。

 瓷器裂纹索赔

A: I want to have your opinion on the quality problem of the goods.

B: We regret for this but we guarantee there is nothing wrong with our products.

A: Well, there is crack with two boxes of porcelain and I think it's natural for us to ask for compensation.

B: It is hard for my company to accept compensation if it happened in the course of transportation. What is more, the quality of the goods was confirmed when loading under the standards of C&F, we are therefore not responsible for the quality problems when arriving.

A: That means we should ask for compensation from the insurance agent.

B: I think so.

A：我想听听贵方对这次货物品质问题的解释。

B：出现这样的事情我们感到很遗憾。但是，我们敢保证产品本身质量没有问题。

A：总之，有两箱瓷器出现了裂纹是事实，我们要求赔偿也是理所当然的吧。

B：对运输途中造成的损失进行赔偿，我公司是难以接受的。而且C&F价格条件下，品质以装船时为准，货物到达时的质量问题我们不负责。

A：就是说要我们向保险公司要求赔偿了？

B：我认为应该是这样。

 打印机索赔

A: Good morning. I'm here to settle the claim for the laser printer.

B: What is the matter with those laser printers?

A: Some of them are damaged so seriously that they became unsuitable for the requirement of this market.

B: How many?

A: About 180. Here is the video of those damaged ones.

B: You should believe me, all the goods had gone

A：早上好！我是为激光打印机索赔事件而来的。

B：那些激光打印机有什么问题？

A：有些激光打印机损坏严重，根本无法投放市场。

B：有多少？

A：大约180台。这是那些损坏品的影像资料。

B：你应该相信我，所有的货物在包

through rigid inspection before packing and the carrier received them in apparent good order, so, they must have been damaged in the course of transit.

A: Do you reject this claim?

B: Yes. You should refer the claim to the carrier or the insurance company.

A: But the inspection certificate shows that the goods are not packed properly.

B: Sorry, but I can't agree. I still believe we shall not be held liable for the damages.

A: This seems to be a very clear case. You should consider our claim seriously for protection of your own reputation.

B: I apologize deeply for this matter. Then, we could only submit the case to an arbitration organization.

A: 你们拒绝索赔?

B: 是的。你们应该向承运人或者保险公司索赔。

A: 但是检验证明书表明货物包装不当。

B: 很抱歉,我无法同意你的意见。我仍认为我们对此损坏不负责任。

A: 这件事情已很清楚。为了你们自己的声誉,你们应该认真考虑我们的索赔。

B: 对这件事情,我深表抱歉。那么我们只有把此案提交仲裁机构了。

 破碎险理赔

A: Good afternoon, Mr. Li. I was to come at 4 o'clock, wasn't I?

B: Yes, Mr. Smith, we have been expecting you. Mr. Smith, this is Mr. Bai of the People's Insurance Company of China. He has come to explain that unfortunate affair about the insurance.

A: Thank you for your coming. Mr. Li, as you may recall, the February consignment arrived at Manila seriously damaged. The loss through breakage was over 30% of the consignment. We've presented a claim to the underwriters through your firm, but the insurance company refused to admit liability, as there was no insurance against breakage. We naturally were not satisfied with such a reply.

B: I would like to hear what Mr. Bai has to say

A: 李先生,下午好。我应该在4点钟到,对吗?

B: 是的,史密斯先生。我们一直盼着你。史密斯先生,这是中国人民保险公司的白先生。他是来解释有关此次事故的保险事宜。

A: 感谢您的到来。李先生,你也许记得,这批2月份发运的货,到马尼拉时,破损严重。损失超过这批货的30%。我们已通过你公司向保险公司提出索赔,但保险公司拒绝负责,因为没有投保破损险。我们当然对这种答复是不满意的。

B: 我想听听白先生有什么看法。当然,

about it. You know of course that we, the sellers, are merely acting as mediators in this matter. The underwriters are responsible for the claim, as far as it is within the scope of cover.

C: That's just the point, gentlemen. The loss in question was beyond the coverage granted by us. According to your instructions, we made out an insurance certificate covering W.P.A., and the risk of breakage wasn't mentioned in it. We rang up the Ceramics Section of the Light Industrial Products Corporation but were told that their customer had not asked for a cover of the risk of breakage.

B: In the letter of credit only a cover for "all marine risks" was requested. I would like to point out that our prices were calculated without insurance of any special risk. So we applied for the usual W.P.A. cover, and let our customers deal with the matter of breakage. Since the validity of the letter of credit was to expire in two days, there was no time to write for more detailed instructions. If the letter of credit had been valid for a longer period, we should have had time to make the matter thoroughly clear.

A: Mr. Li, our import license was only running up to the middle of February, consequently we were not able to extend the validity of the letter of credit. But we presume that the wording of our L/C implies covering the risk of breakage. Besides, when I take a W.P.A. insurance, that is, with particular average, I should think the risk of breakage is included. Breakage is particular average, isn't it?

C: Not every breakage is a particular average. It is a particular average when the breakage is resultant from natural calamities and maritime accidents, such as stranding and sinking of the carrying vessel, or is attributable to fire, explosion or collision. Without the occurrence of any such fortuities, breakage is often considered as an ordinary loss and represents what we call "inherent

你是知道的,我们卖方对这件事只是个调解人。只要在保险责任范围内,保险公司就应负赔偿责任。

C:先生们,问题就在于这一点上。你说的损失并不包括在我方承保的责任范围之内。根据你方要求,我们出具了承保水渍险的保险凭证,没提破损险。我们曾经打电话给轻工业品公司陶瓷器部,但他们说客户并未要求承保破损险。

B:信用证只要求投保"综合海运险"。我想要指出的是,我们的价格没把任何特殊险计算在内。所以,我们只投保了通常的水渍险,而让我们的客户自行办理破损险事宜。由于信用证两天内就要到期,来不及写出更详细的说明。如果信用证有效期较长的话,我们就会有时间把事情彻底弄清楚。

A:李先生,我们进口许可证的有效期到2月中旬截止,因此,我们无法延长信用证有效期。但是,我方认为信用证的措辞包含了要投保破损险。此外,当我投保水渍险时,是单独海损赔偿,我认为是包括破损险的。破损险属于单独海损赔偿,对吗?

C:并不是所有的破损险都属于单独海损。只有自然灾害和海运事故所造成的破损,例如船只搁浅或沉没,或由于着火、爆炸或碰撞所引起的破损才属于单独海损。如果没发生上述事故,破损险便认为最普通损失,也就是我们所说的由于"投保

vice or nature of the subject matter insured", which is outside the scope of the cover.

A: But the risk of breakage is covered by marine insurance, isn't it?

C: Certainly, but it is a usual practice to make specific mention in the insurance policy or certificate that the risk of breakage is included. The inclusion of this special risk

will be subject to an additional premium, which will normally be higher than the basic insurance for the ordinary marine risks. The rate for such kind of risks will vary according to the kind, or, as in ceramics, according to the fragility of the goods. I think you know all about it.

A: Well, I have heard something about it, but I can't say that it is very clear to me.

C: Then let me explain this insurance…

B: Mr. Smith, would you care for a cup of tea? Or a cigarette?

A: A cup of tea, thank you. Let me hear more about it.

货物内在缺陷或特性"所引起的损失，它不在承保范围之内。

A：但破损险是包括在海洋运输货物险之内的，对吗？

C：当然，可是按照惯例要在保险单或保险凭证上特别注明破损险包括在内。包括这种特殊险就必须加付保险费，一般比通常的海洋货物运输险的基本险的费用高。保费率将根据货物种类，比如陶瓷器，就根据货物的易碎性而有所不同。我想这一切你都是知道的。

A：哦，我听说过，但我对保险条款不很清楚。

C：那我来解释一下这种保险……

B：史密斯先生，想喝杯茶吗？还是抽支烟呢？

A：谢谢，来杯茶吧。还请你多多指教。

口语秘笈

"refused to admit liability"（拒绝负责），"be liable to do sth."（能做某事），相当于"be likely to do sth…"。但是"liability"在法律中指的是应当承担的责任。

文化点滴

索赔是指在合同履行过程中，对于并非自己的过错，而是应由对方承担责任的情况造成的实际损失向对方提出经济补偿和（或）时间补偿的要求。在提出或受理索赔时，在正确利用国际贸易惯例和有关法律、力争友好协商解决的同时，要沉着冷静，坚持"有理、有利、有节"的原则。要注意选择灵活的解决方案，尽可能避免将索赔案件提交仲裁或诉诸于国际法庭。

索赔方应注意分清责任。质量问题如属于货物内在的缺陷、包装不当，责任在卖方。在这种情况下，买方可要求降价、赔偿，或解除合同。但是任何索赔都应该以事实为依据。受损方要详细陈述事实的经过，出示有关证明材料，提出索赔意见。

2 应对及处理

第四章 保险理赔

Unit 1　要求理赔　Claiming for Settlement
Unit 2　同意理赔　Promising the Settlement
Unit 3　拒绝理赔　Refusing to Settle the Claim

UNIT 1 要求理赔 Claiming for Settlement

词语宝典

extraneous risk	外来风险	proximate cause	近因原则
insurance policy	保单	subject matter insured	保险标的
insurable interest	保险利益	sue and labor expense	施救费用
insured amount	保险金额	salvage charge	救助费用
perils of the sea	海上风险	total loss	全部损失 / 全损
principle of indemnity	补偿原则	utmost good faith	最大诚信

经典句型

- The underwriters are responsible for the claim as far as it is within the scope of cover.
  只要是在保险责任范围内，保险公司就应负责赔偿。

- The extent of insurance is stipulated in the basic policy form and in various risk clauses.
  保险的范围写在基本保单和各种险别的条款里。

- May I ask what exactly insurance covers according to your usual CIF terms?
  请问根据你们常用的 CIF 价格条件，所保的险别究竟包括哪些？

- It's important for you to read the "fine print" in any insurance policy so that you know what kind of coverage you are buying.
  阅读保单上的"细则"对你是十分重要的，这样就能知道你要买的保险包括哪些项目。

- The rates quoted by us are very moderate. Of course, the premium varies with the range of insurance.
  我们所收取的费率是很有限的，当然，保险费用要根据投保范围的大小而有所不同。

- W.P.A. coverage is too narrow for a shipment of this nature; please extend the coverage to include T.P.N.D.
  针对这种性质的货物只保水渍险是不够的，请加保偷盗提货不成险。

- What kind of insurance are you able to provide for my consignment?
  贵公司能为我的这批货保哪些险呢？

时尚对白

 要求理赔须知

A: Once an accident takes place, what shall we do to claim the compensation of insurance premium?
B: You shall hand in the claim report to the insurance company first. It is your responsibility to notify and explain the accidents.
A: Then you get the insurance premium according to the insurance clause?
B: Various kinds of investigations have to be performed. There are situations causing the contract to be invalid due to the refusal of paying the insurance premium. It won't be that fast.
A: It is really troublesome.
B: Yes.

A：一旦发生了保险事故，索要保险金时该怎么办呢？
B：要先向投保的保险公司提交报告。你有通知和解释事故发生的义务。
A：然后按照保险条款就可以拿到保险金了吧？
B：还要进行各种调查，也有因为拒付保险费而引起的合同失效的情况，不会那么快的。
A：真麻烦呀。
B：是的。

口语秘笈

投保之初可以使用下列句型询问了解保险的相关事宜："I want to ask about general insurance."（我想请教一下有关保险事宜。）"Could you please tell me the insurances that People's Insurance Company of China undertakes?"（请问中国人民保险公司承保哪些险别？）。

 要求破损理赔

A: A few days ago, the porcelain shipped in February had a 20% breakage.
B: The porcelain was tied up very firmly. What's the problem?

A：前几天，2月份发运的瓷器，出现了20%的破损。
B：包装捆扎得很牢，问题发生在什么

A: This is the photo of the damaged product. Please take a look. Judging from these pictures, I guess the goods have been improperly conveyed.

B: It is possible that the goods fell from the crane.

A: If it has nothing to do with the packaging, the owner of the goods has no responsibility.

B: So this is to say the insurance company will compensate?

A: The insurance company is undertaking investigation at the moment. It can be compensated according to the inspector's suggestion. The exporting principle from China to Japan is CIF term, so the People's Insurance Company of China will pay the indemnity.

B: A breakage rate of 20% is very high. I feel I am very unlucky at this time. If all risks aren't covered, there will be a huge loss.

地方呢？

A：这是破损品的照片，请看。从照片来判断，我认为是货物搬运时出了差错。

B：很可能是货物从吊车上掉下来造成的。

A：捆包没有问题的话，货主就没有责任。

B：就是说保险公司给赔吗？

A：眼下保险公司正在调查中。根据检验员的意见不久就可以得到赔偿。中国对日本出口原则上是CIF，所以会由中国人民保险公司支付赔款。

B：破损率达到20%是相当高的比率。我觉得这次很不走运。如果没有投保一切险的话，损失会相当大的。

口语秘笈

"improperly conveyed"（货物搬运差错），其中"improperly"可以替换"inappropriately"；"undertake an investigation"（实施调查）；"breakage rate"（破损率）；"pay the indemnity"（支付赔款）；"cover all risks"（投保一切险）。

同意理赔
Promising the Settlement

词语宝典

average	海损	air transportation risk	航空运输险
co-insurance	共同保险	breakage of packing	包装破碎险
franchise (deductible)	免赔额，免赔率	clash and breakage	碰损，破碎险
premium	保险费	constructive total loss	推定全损
risk	保险，保险额	floating policy	浮动保险单
actual total loss	实际全损	freight policy	运费保险单
additional premium	附加保险费	General Average (G.A.)	共同海损
additional risk	附加险		

经典句型

- We have covered insurance on these goods for 10% above the invoice value against all risks.
  我们已将此货物按照发票金额加 10% 保了一切险。

- We shall effect the insurance of the goods for 110% of their CIF value.
  我方将按照货物到岸价金额的 110% 对这批货物进行投保。

- We have effected marine insurance on your behalf for the gross amount of the invoice plus 10%.
  我方已代表贵方按照发票金额加 10% 投保了海洋运输险。

- The marine insurance shall be covered by us.
  海上保险的费用将由我方承担。

- Do you know the percentage of the damaged portion?
  你们知道残损部分的百分比吗？

- We should require a survey report, with that we may know the extent of the damage.
  我们将要求出具检验报告，以便我们能了解损坏的程度。

- You can see yourselves the damaged condition and the reason why they are unsaleable.
  你们可以亲眼看到残损情况以及货物无法销售的原因。

- We should make it clear whether the damage was caused in transit or during the unloading process, or by other reasons.
  我们要弄清楚货物是否在运输途中受损，还是在卸货过程中受损，或者是由于别的什么原因。
- The goods were carefully packed and shipped here in excellent condition.
  货物包装得很仔细，装船很小心，到这儿完好无损。
- Then the damage must be caused at somewhere along the line where the goods weren't handled properly.
  那么残损一定是在运输途中的什么地方对货物处理不当造成的。

时尚对白

水渍险与平安险理赔

C: You see, Mr. Smith, the situation would be somewhat different if you had put in your letter of credit the words "all risks" instead of "all marine risks". Under an "all risks" cover, loss by breakage would have been recoverable, because, though by the word "risks" is meant that any loss occurring must be due to some fortuitous happening and through external cause. When a loss does arise in transition, it will be often rather difficult to distinguish between accidental and ordinary loss, especially as far as breakage or leakage is concerned. In such cases, ordinary loss will quite possibly be included in a claim and met by the insurer.

A: Then "all marine risks" means less than "all risks"?

C: The English understand by "marine risks" only risks incident to transport by sea, such as collision, stranding, fire, penetration of sea water into the holds of the ships, etc. In other words, under the "all marine risks", losses recoverable

C：史密斯先生，你知道，如果你在信用证上注明"一切险"而不是"一切海洋运输货物险"，情况就有所不同了。按"一切险"投保，破损损失就能得到赔偿，因为虽然这个"险"字是指：必须由于某些偶然事故或外部原因所造成的损失，但当货物在运输途中发生损失时，常常很难区分是意外的或是普通的损失，特别是有关破损或渗漏。在这种情况下，普通损失很可能就包括在索赔之列而得到承保方的理赔。

A：那么"一切海洋运输货物险"是否意味着比"一切险"范围小一些呢？

C：英国人对"海洋运输货物险"只理解为海运中的意外风险，诸如船舶碰撞、搁浅、起火、海水进入船舱等。换句话说，以"一切海洋运输货物险"投保，其损失的赔偿只限

will only be confined to those arising from perils of the sea and maritime accidents, whereas the "all risks" cover will admit all losses occurring at any time throughout the whole currency of the cover, irrespective of whether they are caused by accidents at sea or on land. In this sense, "all marine risks" provides a more limited cover than "all risks". In insurance parlance, the term "all marine risks" is liable to be misinterpreted and its use should be avoided in letters of credit. Now let us turn to losses through "inherent vice or nature of the subject matter insured", such as deterioration of food, leakage of liquid and breakage of glass or ceramics. These are not considered marine risks. Risks of this kind must be specifically applied for and explicitly accepted by the insurer.

A: That seems clear enough, now that you have explained it. But what I don't understand at this moment is the advantage of W.P.A. cover. I thought that the W.P.A. insurance should cover all principal risks whilst, according to what you say, this W.P.A. cover means very little. It seems to be a phrase without much substance. Just what is the difference between W.P.A. and F.P.A.?

C: Your question is very much to the point, Mr. Smith. It is a very common but mistaken idea that a merchant has done everything that is required to protect himself against losses when he has taken out a W.P.A. insurance. There is, perhaps, no mistake more detrimental to his interests.

A: That interests me very much. I must confess that I was under the impression that a W.P.A. insurance was quite sufficient and that losses due to breakage were covered. I know that the F.P.A. insurance dose not cover losses on consumer goods, but I did think that the W.P.A. insurance covered more risks than the F.P.A.

B: Actually it is like this. There is some difference between W.P.A. and F.P.A. The F.P.A. clause does not cover partial loss of the nature of particular average, whereas the W.P.A. clause cover such losses when they exceed a pre-arranged percentage. For instance, when W.P.A. 3% cover is taken out, a particular average loss under 3% of the insured amount will not be recoverable but one amounting to or exceeding 3% of the insured amount will be paid. This is the only difference between W.P.A. and F.P.A. Otherwise, the protection under the F.P.A. clause will be almost identical with that offered by the W.P.A. clause, because in the event of maritime accidents being encountered in transit, such as stranding, fire, explosion or collision, both clauses will cover particular average losses in full. In present day particularly, a WPAIOP cover, that is, "With Particular Average Irrespective of Percentage" is not infrequently granted, in which case all particular average losses of an accidental nature will be recoverable and the protection will be much wider than the F.P.A. clause.

A: I don't mean to annoy you, Mr. Bai, but I don't quite grasp this, couldn't you say it in more understandable terms?

C: I'll try. Neither the W.P.A. nor the F.P.A. mentions the risks covered or the risks excluded. The extent of insurance is stipulated in the basic policy form and in the various risk clauses. Look

安险并不包括消费品的种种损失，但我的确认为水渍险承保的范围比平安险要宽得多。

C：实际上是这样的。水渍险和平安险是有些不同。平安险条款不包括单独海损性质的部分损失，而水债险条款当超过事先商定的百分比时，则包括此类损失。譬如：投保了"3%的水渍险"，当单独海损的损失在所保金额的3%以下时，不赔。但是损失达到并超过所保金额的3%时，则赔偿。这是水渍险和平安险唯一不同之处。除此之外，平安险所承担的责任与水渍险所承担的责任几乎相同，因为一旦在运输途中遭遇海上意外事故，诸如搁浅、着火、爆炸或碰撞，这两种保险条款都全部赔偿单独海损的损失。现行惯例，投保 WPAIOP 即"无免赔率的水清险"是常常承保的，在这种情况下，属于意外性质的单独海损的所有损失都将给予赔偿，承担的责任范围比平安险要宽泛得多。

A：白先生，我并不想麻烦你，不过我还抓不住要领，你能否用更易懂的语言谈一谈呢？

C：我试试看。无论水渍险还是平安险都不指明包括那些险别，或不包括那些险别。保险范围是写在基本保险单内和在各种险别的条款里。看一下保险凭证，你看，对偷窃险、淡水险、沾染油渍险、油污险、

at the insurance certificates and you will find that the risks of theft and pilferage, freshwater, oil, grease, hooks, breakage, leakage, contamination, deterioration, etc. are specifically mentioned, and must be specifically applied for. These are special risks. F.P.A. stands for "Free from Particular Average" while W.P.A. or W.A. stands for "With Particular Average".

A: Mr. Bai, I must say that you have corrected my thoughts about the insurance. I see now that this is far more complicated than I ever imagined.

B: Now I know why you often point out to us the wording of some letter of credit which you don't feel happy about. But what are we to do about it? We must keep to the stipulations of the contract and the letter of credit.

A: The blame rests not alone with the letter of credit. I think the Light Industrial Products Corporation should have understood from our letter of credit that we wanted the cover of all risks, including the risk of breakage. So the error was on both sides. I think the loss ought to be shared by both parties-let us say half and half.

B: Our price calculation could hardly admit that, besides, we acted upon your instructions so this is not our fault.

C: I sincerely hope that you gentlemen will settle to our mutual satisfaction.

A: It goes without saying that both parties must abide by the contract terms which we have agreed upon and signed. This blunder, which is due to my ignorance, costs me a pretty penny.

B: We also have learned a lesson from this.

A: To compensate a part of the loss, may I ask you

破损险、破碎险、渗漏险、沾污险、变质险等，都是特别提出来的，必须特别投保。这些就是特别险。FPA（平安险）代表"Free from Particular Average"而WPA或WA（水渍险）代表"With Particular Average"。

A：白先生，我该说你已经纠正了我对保险的想法。我现在明白，保险问题比我以往所想象的要复杂得多。

B：现在我才了解为什么你经常向我们指出对某些信用证的措词你感到不愉快。不过，我们该怎么办？我们一定要遵守合同和信用证的规定。

A：不单是信用证的过错。我想轻工业品公司理应从我们的信用证中领会到我们要保的是一切险，包括破碎险在内。所以双方都有错误。我认为损失应由双方承担，我们就各负担一半吧。

B：根据我们所出的价格，难以接受你的提议。此外，我们是按照你们要求办理的，所以这不是我们的过错。

C：我衷心希望你们两位把这件事解决好，使双方都满意。

A：毫无疑问，双方必须遵守已经同意并已签署过的合同条款。这次疏忽是由于我的无知，使我破费了不少钱。

B：我们也从这件事吸取了教训。

A：为了补偿部分损失，可否请你们报给我们一个实盘，50,000块釉瓷砖，

to make us a firm offer for 50,000 pieces glazed wall tile CIF Manila including the risks of breakage, November shipment?

B: We'll make you an offer tomorrow. Come and see us at 9 a.m.

CIF 马尼拉，包括破碎险，11月装船？

B：我们明天给你报盘，请上午9点来和我们碰头。

A：谢谢你，明天9点再见。

口语秘笈

"as far as breakage or leakage is concerned"（有关破碎或渗漏）。"As far as ...be concerned" 相当于 "regarding, concerning, as to"，意思是 "对于……而言"；"be confined to…" 局限于……，相当于 "be limited to"。

拒绝理赔
Refusing to Settle the Claim

词语宝典

indemnity	损害赔偿	loss ratio	赔付率
survey	查勘	time limit for filing claims	索赔时限
recheck	核对	notice of loss	损害通知书
reinsurance	再保险	deposit premium	预付保险费
particular average	单独海损	natural losses	自然损耗
cargo damage survey	货损检验	natural calamities	自然灾害
obligation of compensation	赔偿的义务		

经典句型

- As you know, the claim concerning insurance or transportation should be referred to the insurance company or the shipping company.
  而你知道，有关保险或运输的索赔应向保险公司或船运公司提出。

- Only after receiving the detailed report, can we work out the way to handle the problem.
  只有接到详细报告以后我们才能找出这一问题的处理办法。

- Have you received the surveyor's report?
  你收到了检验报告吗？

- I'm sure we can settle the problem amicably through negotiations without resorting to arbitration.
  我相信，我们可以通过磋商友好解决这个问题，而不是诉诸仲裁机构。

- They are simply useless.
  它们简直没有用了。

- It appears that the damage was caused sometime during the transhipment.
  看来残损是在转船期间造成的。

- We are faced with the problem that part of the consignment is unacceptable.
  我们面临的问题是部分货物不被接受。

时尚对白

 证明缺失拒绝理赔

A: We can't process your damage claim.
B: Why not?
A: You didn't note the damage on the bill of lading.
B: I see. What else?
A: Do you have any certification that can testify the quality of the goods when delivered and upon delivery?
B: No, we don't.
A: That's why the insurance company refused to admit the liability.

A：我们无法办理你的索赔。
B：为什么？
A：你没有在提货单上注明损坏情况。
B：我知道了。此外的原因呢？
A：你们有证件证明这些货的出厂与到货质量吗？
B：没有证明。
A：这就是保险公司不负责赔偿的原因。

口语秘笈

当保险公司拒绝理赔时，投保人要求保险公司出具调查与检验证明可以这样表达："Could you please show me the results of your survey and investigations?"（能出具一下您对此案调查检验的结果吗？）。

 拒绝破损理赔

A: There is a 10% breakage in this batch.
B: We are so sorry about that.
A: I would like to know why your company will not compensate for the loss.
B: If you insured for damages in the first place, the insurance company surely would have compensated for the loss.
A: Since we have already arranged W.P.A., isn't it reasonable to say the loss caused by damage is within the compensation range?
B: This is a misunderstanding. The compensation range of W.P.A. is only limited to natural calamity and accidents. Not all damage qualify its compensation range.

A：这次的货物发生了10%的破损。
B：我们感到很遗憾。
A：我想知道贵公司不予赔偿的理由。
B：如果当初您投保了破损险的话，保险公司当然会赔偿这次的损失。
A：既然我方已经投了水渍险，那么由于破损造成的损失在其赔偿范围内不是理所当然的吗？
B：这是误解。水渍险赔偿范围仅限于自然灾害和偶发事故。并不是所有的破损都属于它的赔偿范围。

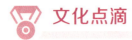

文化点滴

货物运输保险理赔知识汇集

在货物抵达时,请立即进行检验。 当发生保单承保范围内的货物损毁或丢失并由此产生运输保险理赔时,运输保险理赔者必须立即用书面或口头方式通知保险人。

运输保险理赔知识一:当货物抵达时,出现损害或有异状

1. 切勿将未加批注的交接回单交给承运人或货代公司,除非后者出具保函。
2. 取得承运人或货代公司签发的损坏货物证明或短装记录或货物残损清单,或者在提单或承运人送货回单上注明损坏／灭失。
3. 当投保了集装箱保险的货物由集装箱运送时,如集装箱运达时被损坏或铅封破损、遗失、铅封与运输单所列不符,请保留所有残缺或异常之铅封以做进一步鉴定并确保此集装箱的理货员在他的理货单上注明损失或异常,并从该理货公司获得一份损失／残损报告副本,再进行集装箱保险索赔。
4. 如果估计货损价值超过免赔额(如有免赔额),立即申请授权的检验员和承运人检验员或其代表进行联合检验,同时通知保险人。
5. 立刻以书面形式及时通知承运人和／或责任方货物损坏／遗失情况,并告知,你将在承运合同所规定的期限内追究其责任。

运输保险理赔知识二:货物抵达外观完好无损,但之后发现隐藏的损害时:

1. 立即申请检验,同时通知保险人。
2. 如果估计货损价值超过免赔额(如有免赔额),立即以书面形式告知承运人和／或责任方货物损坏／遗失情况,并告知你将在承运公司所规定的期限内追究其责任。

在赔案处理时为理赔进程顺利,应及时取得并提供下列文件给保险人:

1. 保单正本或者保险凭证;
2. 海运提单正本／空运提单正本或副本;
3. 商业发票及装箱单副本;
4. 注明损坏／损失的送货回单的复印件或异状证明;
5. 给承运人的书面索赔函及后者回复的复印件;
6. 检验报告正本及其账单;
7. 附有详细计算的运输保险理赔清单;
8. 当地警方的报告(如果发生被偷、被盗或被抢的理赔);
9. 交通事故报告(如果发生车辆翻车和碰撞事件的理赔);
10. 其他根据具体情况所需的文件。

2 应对及处理

第五章 申请仲裁

Unit 1　仲裁事由　Reasons of Arbitration
Unit 2　提请仲裁　Resorting to Arbitration
Unit 3　受理仲裁　Processing of Arbitration

仲裁事由 Reasons of Arbitration

词语宝典

arbitrary	强制性的	resort to	诉诸于
arbitration	仲裁	secretary-general	秘书长
dispute	争议	arbitration agency	仲裁机构
enforcement	执行	arbitration agreement	仲裁协议
penalty	罚金	contractual dispute	合同上的争议
proceeding	程序	panel of arbitrator	仲裁员名册
refer to	提交	reach a settlement	达成一致的意见

经典句型

- But if we apply for the court, it will cost almost equal and still take energy and time.
  但是如果我们提交法庭，要花相当的费用，而且还消耗精力和时间。

- Your late delivery has caused great losses to us, and if you are not prepared to compensate our loss, we suggest the case be submitted for arbitration.
  贵方货物没有按期到达已经给我方造成巨大损失，倘若贵方不打算赔偿我方损失的话，我方建议由仲裁来解决。

- If you don't accept our proposals, we may submit the matter to arbitration.
  如果你方不接受我方建议，我们也许要将此事提交仲裁。

- In case no settlement can be reached, the dispute shall then be submitted to China International Economic and Trade Arbitration Commission (CIETAC) for arbitration in accordance with its rules in effect at the time of applying for arbitration .
  如果协商不能解决，争议应提交中国国际经济贸易仲裁委员会，按照申请仲裁时生效的仲裁规则进行仲裁。

- In case of damage of the goods incurred due to the design or manufacture defects and /or in case the quality and performance are not in conformity with the contract , the buyer shall , during the guarantee period , request party…to make a survey .

在质保期内，如果货物由于设计或制造上的缺陷而发生损坏或品质和性能与合同规定不符时，买方应委托某方进行检验。

时尚对白

 仲裁问题广义咨询

A: Carl, I want to ask you a few questions about arbitration. First, if your company and the trade partners have some sort of dispute, and will bring it to arbitration, must the arbitration go only through China?

B: No. Arbitration can be performed either in China or in other countries. It depends on the stipulations in your agreement reached by you and your partners.

A: If it is performed in China, must we apply the Chinese rules of procedure?

B: Of course. But if arbitration takes place in a foreign country, then the rules of the foreign corresponding institution will be applied.

A: What kinds of disputes do you usually handle?

B: Well, many different kinds of disputes arising from foreign trade, transportation of goods, cargo insurance, transfer of technology, leasing and so on.

A: What about patent and trademark infringement?

B: Yes, some.

A: Are there foreign citizens in the arbitration panel if arbitration goes through China?

B: Yes.

A：卡尔 我想问你几个有关仲裁的问题。第一，倘若你们公司与你们的贸易伙伴之间有纠纷，需要求助于仲裁，那么仲裁必须在中国进行吗？

B：不是的，可以在中国，也可以在国外进行，这要看你们双方达成的协议是如何规定的。

A：如果在中国进行，只能运用中国的规则程序吗？

B：当然。但是如果在外国进行，就应该运用该国仲裁机构的仲裁规则。

A：你们通常处理哪些类型的纠纷？

B：很多。由对外贸易、货物运输、货物保险、技术转让、租赁等所引起的纠纷。

A：专利和商标侵犯呢？

B：有一部分。

A：中国进行的仲裁有外国籍的仲裁员吗？

B：有。

 详细询问仲裁条款

A: There's a particular clause in our contract which I'd like to discuss with you.

A：我们合同中有个特别条款我想和您谈谈。

B: You mean, the arbitration clause?

A: Right. I'm really pleased to say that we've never had the chance to invoke this particular clause.

B: It's nice to hear that.

A: But could you please give me some idea as to how conciliation is conducted?

B: With pleasure. The first stage in conciliation is to find out where the problem is and what the liabilities are.

A: And if they succeed? What if it fails?

B: The case is solved to the satisfaction of all concerned and if it fails, the case will be referred to arbitration according to the arbitration clause.

A: Thank you very much for being so informative.

B: My pleasure.

B：你是说仲裁条款？

A：是的，很高兴我们从来没有机会使用这一条款。

B：听您这么说我很高兴。

A：那您能不能给我讲一下调解是怎么进行的？

B：可以。调解的第一步是找出问题所在并明确责任。

A：如果调解成功了呢？如果失败了呢？

B：成功的话案情就解决了，大家都满意。如果调解失败，那就要根据仲裁条款提交仲裁。

A：感谢你让我增长了很多知识。

B：不客气。

达人点拨

在商务谈判中，尽管谈判双方都希望合作能够顺利进行，但是在签订合同时，一些违约、理赔和仲裁条款是必须提前协商好的，否则一旦出现纠纷，会给双方带来不必要的麻烦和损失，甚至影响再次的合作。本对话中"I'm really pleased to say that we've never had the chance to invoke this particular clause."（很高兴我们从来没有机会使用这一条款。）不但表达了对以往合作很满意，对未来合作也充满信心，而且把谈话顺利衔接到具体仲裁条款的探讨中。由于仲裁只是解决问题的有效手段之一，在询问仲裁条款时，不但要询问调解成功时如何处理，更要询问调解失败时如何应对。

口语秘笈

双方约定的仲裁条款中暗含了关于仲裁地的约定，如果你还不清楚，可以询问："Could you please tell me where the arbitration will be conducted?"（能麻烦问您能告诉我仲裁地一般在哪里吗？）。

提请仲裁
Resorting to Arbitration

词语宝典

appeal	上诉	arbitration court	仲裁庭
compromise	和解，协调	arbitration procedure	仲裁程序
conciliation	调解	arbitration sample	做判断用的样品
final	终局的	arbitration tribunal	仲裁庭

经典句型

- The issue has been taken to arbitration.
  争议已提交仲裁。

- They desired that the dispute be submitted for arbitration.
  他们要求把争端提交仲裁。

- They submitted their disagreement to arbitration.
  他们把他们的不满提交仲裁。

- Then the case may be submitted for arbitration.
  那只好将案件提交仲裁了。

- Disputes may be submitted for arbitration in case no settlement can be reached through negotiation between both parties.
  若争议无法通过双方谈判解决，可提交仲裁。

- The dispute shall be submitted for arbitration by a mutually nominated arbitrator.
  这起纠纷应由一位双方共同指定的仲裁人仲裁。

- Upon receipt of a copy of the arbitration application, the respondent shall, within the time limit prescribed by the Arbitration Rules, submit its defense to the arbitration commission.
  被申请人收到仲裁申请书副本后，应当在仲裁规则规定的期限内向仲裁委员会提交答辩书。

- The case shall then be submitted to the Japanese International Economic and Trade

Arbitration Commission for arbitration in accordance with its arbitration rules.
此案应提交日本国际经济仲裁委员会根据该会仲裁规则进行仲裁。

时尚对白

提请仲裁前提条件

A: In spite of the unfortunate incident, we hope we could settle this dispute amicably by negotiation.
B: We hope so, too. But what if negotiation fails?
A: In case no settlement can be reached between the two parties, the case under dispute shall be submitted for arbitration.
B: Do you permit arbitration in a third country?
A: Yes. Let me reassert the relevant stipulations in our contract: arbitration can be conducted in third countries and in China.
B: And the third countries are…
A: As stipulated in our contract, the third countries are Switzerland and Holland.
B: If in China?
A: In China, the Arbitration Commission of the China Council for the Promotion of International Trade will execute the arbitration. The decision of the arbitration shall be accepted as final and binding upon both parties.
B: We prefer to settle disputes in the end amicably and come to an understanding.
A: Sure.

A：尽管出现了不幸事件，但是我们愿意通过谈判友好解决这次争端。
B：我们也希望如此。可是如果谈判破裂怎么办？
A：如果双方协议不能解决，争执可以提交仲裁。
B：贵方允许在第三国进行仲裁吗？
A：是的，让我们重申合同中的有关规定：仲裁既可以在第三国也可以在中国进行。
B：第三国是……
A：按照合同中的规定，第三国指的是瑞士和荷兰。
B：如果在中国谁来执行仲裁？
A：在中国，由中国国际贸易促进会仲裁委员会进行仲裁。仲裁决定是终局的，对贸易双方均具有约束力。
B：我们希望双方经过和平调解，达成谅解而最终解决争端。
A：当然。

口语秘笈

如果某方认为有联合调解的必要，可以实事求是地说："As a matter of fact, we do want a joint conciliation."（事实上，我们确实需要联合调解。）。

双方签约商定仲裁

A: I made a very close study of the draft contract last night.
B: Any questions?
A: Yes. There are a few points which I'd like to bring up. First, the packing it's stipulated in the contract that all the machine parts should be packed in wooden cases. This can be done with the machine parts, but it's impossible to pack a truck base like that.
B: I see.
A: Second, about the terms of payment. Your draft contract says that payment is to be made by D/P. This is not our practice. We prefer to have the payment made by L/C through a negotiating bank in France.
B: And...
A: And the third point is about arbitration. It's stipulated that arbitration shall take place in China. In all our past contracts signed with you, it was stipulated that arbitration took place in a third country.
B: Yes, that's right.
A: But why do you wish to have it carried out in China this time?
B: Shall we take up the matter point by point?
A: That's a good idea.
B: Now, the first point is about packing. We agree to a different packing for the truck bases.
A: That's great. It saves a great deal of time.
B: Second, about terms of payment by L/C.
A: Thank you.
B: As for arbitration, in our dealings with many

A：昨晚我仔细审阅了合同草案。
B：有什么问题吗？
A：有，有几点我想提一下。首先，是包装。合同规定机器零件用木箱包装。机器零件可以，而汽车底座用木箱包装则是行不通的。
B：我明白了。
A：第二点是付款的有关条款。你们的合同草案规定付款方式为付款交单。我们不这么做。我们希望经法国的一家议付银行用信用证付款。
B：还有呢……
A：第三点关于仲裁。合同规定仲裁应在中国进行，在我们过去和你们签订的所有合同中都规定仲裁在第三国进行。
B：对，是这样。
A：那么，为什么这次你们希望仲裁在中国进行？
B：我们逐点研究一下，好吗？
A：好主意。
B：首先，第一点有关包装，我们同意汽车底座换用不同的包装。
A：太好了，这样可以省去很多时间。
B：第二，我们同意用信用证付款。
A：谢谢。
B：至于仲裁，在我们和许多国家的

countries, arbitration is to be carried out in China. The Arbitration Commission of CCPIT enjoys a high prestige among friendly companies. Personally I hope you'll accept this clause. Furthermore, the disputes that have arisen from our business transaction were all settled through friendly consultations. Very rarely was arbitration resorted to.

A: I see. OK. The new arbitration clause is acceptable. Is there anything else?

B: As far as the contract stipulations are concerned, there is nothing more. Thank you very much.

A: When should we sign the contract?

B: We'll revise the contract this evening, and have it ready to be signed tomorrow morning at ten. How's that?

A: Perfect.

交易中，仲裁都在中国进行。中国贸促会的仲裁委员会在各友好公司中享有崇高的声誉。从我个人来讲，希望你们接受这一条款。此外，我们生意中出现的争端均通过友好协商解决了，很少进行仲裁。

A：我明白了，新的仲裁条款可以接受，还有别的吗？

B：至于合同方面的规定，没别的了。非常感谢。

A：我们什么时候签合同？

B：今晚我们修改一下合同，准备明天早上10点签约，怎么样？

A：太好了。

口语秘笈

签约时若倡议仲裁条款，可以运用下列说法："I suggest we stress the arbitration clause in the contract. I know an old saying 'preparedness averts peril.' Is it right?"（我建议我们应该强调合同的仲裁条款。有句古话叫做"有备无患"，对吧？）。

受理仲裁
Processing of Arbitration

词语宝典

arbitrator	仲裁人	temporary	临时的
binding	受约束的	arbitral award	裁决
bias/partiality	偏见	conciliatory statement	调解书
negotiable	可以谈判的	equality and mutual benefit	平等互利
nonbinding	无约束力的	friendly negotiation	友好协商
plaintiff	申诉人	independence and initiative	独立自主
proposition	建议		

经典句型

- We refuse to accept the suggestion. It's unfair to put the responsibility on us.
  我们拒绝接受这个建议。把责任推到我们身上不公平。

- But we need evidence. You cannot show us your evidence.
  但是我们需要证据。而你们却拿不出证据。

- We sincerely propose both parties make a certain concession.
  我们郑重建议双方分别做出让步。

- The goods that have been delivered to us are quite different from what we have ordered.
  抵达我方的货物与我方事先的订货差距很大。

- They notified us a punctual delivery, but we have suffered a lot of breakage.
  对方通知我方货物会及时送达，然而货损极其严重。

- The late delivery of the raw materials have caused dramatic losses to our production.
  原材料的延期到货使我们的生产蒙受了极大的损失。

- We have the proof that our partner didn't send us a notice in time.
  我方有证据证明对方没有及时通知我们。

时尚对白

合同履行争端解决

A: We should settle the dispute through negotiations without resorting to legal proceeding.

B: As a matter of fact, most disputes can be settled in a friendly way, with a view to developing a long-term relationship. If you are not prepared to compensate for our loss, we suggest that the case be submitted for arbitration.

C: Where do you want to have arbitration held? As far as the place for arbitration is concerned, the customary practice is to hold arbitration in the country of defendant.

A: If we submit the case for arbitration, the place for arbitration is to be in Japan and if you submit the case for arbitration, the place for arbitration is to be in China.

B: We require you to compensate us with an amount of losses totaling ￥700,000 caused by your failure to execute the contract and with all the expenses arising from this arbitration.

C: We may discuss to agree upon a temporary arbitral body when needed.

B: We think that the court consisting of arbitrators from both sides must be fair and able to handle the dispute without bias or partiality.

C: No problem. The decision made by the arbitration commission shall be accepted as final and binding upon both parties. The losing party shall bear the cost for arbitration according to the contract. Shall we listen to A Company's statement?

A：我们应该通过协商来解决争议，而不应该诉诸法律程序。

B：实际上，本着发展长期关系的原则，大多数争议都可以通过友好的方式来解决。如果贵方不打算赔偿我方损失的话，我方建议提交仲裁。

C：你们想在什么地方进行仲裁？通常的做法是在被告方的国家进行仲裁。

A：如果我们提交仲裁，仲裁地应该在日本，而如果你们提交仲裁，仲裁地应该在中国。

B：我方要求你方赔偿由于不履行合同义务所造成的损失700,000元，并承担由于进行仲裁所引起的一切费用。

C：需要的话我们可以协商讨论成立一个临时的仲裁机构。

B：我方认为由双方指定的仲裁员组成的仲裁庭才会公正，而且能够不偏不倚地处理争议。

C：放心。仲裁委员会作出的仲裁决定为终极裁决，对双方均具有约束力。根据合同，败诉方将承担仲裁费用。我们来听一下A公司的陈述吧。

> **口语秘笈**
>
> "Shall we listen to …?" 和 "Could we listen to …?" 在仲裁调解中表示中断、转折以控制谈话的发展。例如："Now, could we listen to the report about the project's cost?"（现在我们能听一下这个工程的成本报告吗？）。

 延期货损争端解决

A: OK. Could both of you state your problems again?

B: According to the contract, the goods should be delivered to us on May 1st, but in fact we got them on July 15th—a late delivery over two months, which has caused great losses to our project. Accordingly, we ask for a million yuan remedy.

A: Shall we listen to C Company's statement?

C: We are really sorry about the delayed delivery. We failed to deliver the goods in time because of force majeure circumstances—our vessel had run a ground and we had to put it under repairs. Here's the certificate.

B: But you didn't notify us about it in time.

C: We did. We had sent a fax to your company. And we also checked with our secretary. It's your fault.

B: No, you didn't.

A: Well, shall we ask both of you to present the evidence?

B: OK. Now here are our contract, bill of lading, photos of the goods on arrival, acceptance report signed in the presence of the C company's experts.

C: Here we have the contract, the original of the fax, and the clean bill of lading.

A: All right. Now we'd like to pass on the

A：好的。双方能再陈述一下自己的问题吗？

B：根据合同，货物应该于5月1日运抵我方，可是我们7月15日才收到货物，整整晚了两个多月，给我方工程造成了巨大损失。因此我方要求100万元赔偿。

A：我们来听一下C公司的陈述。

C：我们对延误供货表示道歉。我们没有及时给贵方提供货物是因为不可抗力——我们的船搁浅了，我们不得不修理船只。这有证明。

B：但是你们没有及时通知我们货物延误。

C：我们通知了。我们还和秘书核实过了，没有收到通知应该是你们的过错。

B：你们根本没有通知我们。

A：双方能出示一下你们的证据吗？

B：好的。这里有我们的合同、海运提单、货物到达时的照片及C公司专家在场所签的验收证书。

C：我们这里有合同、传真原件和海运清洁提单。

A：好。现在，我们把你们的证件转给你们，读过后若对此证据有疑

217

evidence papers to both of you, and please raise any queries about the evidence to be clarified if any after you have read them.

B: How can we believe that the fax is original?

C: Well, your query seems to be reasonable, but you insisted that we didn't send you a fax. We have no way out.

A: OK. First, let's make it clear that the damage of the goods should be the insurance company's obligation to compensate, right?

C: Yes, we would claim the insurance company for this, but we did send you a fax.

B: No, and what about the losses caused by the delay?

A: I suggest you settle the problem by sharing the cost, for no one can prove whether the fax has been sent or not.

C: We refuse to accept the suggestion, for it's unfair to put the responsibility on us. But taking the future cooperation into consideration, we are willing to shoulder one fourth of the cost.

B: We also refuse to accept the suggestion, for it's not our obligation. We disagree.

A: All right. We'll meet again next Wednesday. You'd better give it a second thought.

问请提出并加以澄清。

B：我们怎么才能确认这份传真是原件？

C：你们的质问似乎有道理，但是你们坚持说我们没有发传真，我们也没有办法。

A：好了，我们先要弄清楚，货物的损坏应该由保险公司来赔偿，对吧？

C：是的。我们会向保险公司索赔的。但是我们确实发了传真。

B：你们没有发传真。延期导致的损失怎么办？

A：我建议你们共同承担损失，解决问题，因为没有一方能证明是否发送了这份传真。

C：我们拒绝接受这个建议，因为把责任推向我们是不公平的。但是考虑到将来的合作，我们愿意承担四分之一。

B：我们也拒绝接受这个建议，因为这不是我们的责任。我们不同意。

A：好吧，那我们下周第三继续讨论。双方再好好考虑一下。

口语秘笈

注意协商过程中双方的用语："We will not accept the suggestion."（我们不接受这个建议。）但是如果你方部分接受对方的建议，可以说：True, but...

例如：

A: Will you accept our suggestion?

B: True, but that will cost us too much.

A：贵方愿意接受我方的建议吗？

B：是的，但是我方的损失会大大增加。

2 应对及处理

第六章 法律诉讼

Unit 1　合同与协议　Contract and Agreement
Unit 2　破产与债务　Bankruptcy and Liability
Unit 3　消费者权益　Consumer Rights
Unit 4　知识产权　Intellectual Property

合同与协议
Contract and Agreement

词语宝典

consent	同意	obligation	义务
impose	施加、强加	terminate	终止、结束
lawsuit	诉讼	time-consuming	耗时的
non-performance	不履行	unilateral	单方面的

经典句型

- The parties to the contract have equal legal status, and neither party may impose its will on the other.
  合同当事人的法律地位平等，任何一方都不得将自己的意志强加给另一方。

- In case one party fails to carry out the contract, the other party is entitled to cancel the contract.
  如果一方不执行合同，另一方有权撤销该合同。

- Any failure by a party to carry out all or part of his obligations under the contract shall be considered as a substantial breach.
  一方当事人不履行本合同的全部或任何部分义务均应被视为是根本违约。

- You reasonably believe that there will be a fundamental non-performance of the contract by the other party.
  你们有理由认为对方当事人将会根本违约。

- In case of breach of any of the provisions of this agreement by one party, the other party shall have the right to terminate this agreement by giving notice in writing to its opposite party.
  如果一方违反本协议的任何一项条款，另一方有权以书面形式通知对方终止本协议。

- Any amendment of the contract shall come to force only after the written agreement is signed by both of us.
  合同的任何修改都应该经过我们双方书面同意以后方可生效。

时尚对白

合同与协议

A: Good morning! I am here to consult some legal issues about contract.

B: Good morning! I'll be very glad if I can help.

A: We signed a contract with ANC company in America in early March last year to supply 10,000 pieces of inertia rings to them per year, and we were informed yesterday that the company would stop receiving our product due to production reduction caused by financial crisis. But we have produced 5,000 pieces of inertia rings, and the shipment was just made last week. What should we do?

B: OK, I see. Did they propose to modify the contract to delay the delivery time?

A: No. There is no clear statement of that.

B: They cannot cancel the contract without first securing your agreement. Any party has no right to terminate the contract without another party's agreement. It is very likely that they may look the unilateral decision to cancel the contract, and you reasonably believe that there will be a fundamental non-performance of the contract by the other party.

A: Can we bring an accusation against them directly?

B: Of course, you can accuse them of breach of contract, but it will be rather complicated and time-consuming for the lawsuit in America under a different law system. Most importantly, you

---

A：早上好！我来这咨询一些合同的法律问题。

B：早上好！很高兴为你效劳。

A：我们去年三月份和美国 ANC 公司签订了一份合同，每年为其提供 10,000 件惯性环。昨天我们被告知该公司因经济危机导致的产量减少而拒收我们的产品。然而我们已经生产了 5,000 件惯性环并且已于昨天发货。我们该怎么办？

B：我明白了，他们有没有建议修改合同以延迟交付时间？

A：他们没有明确说明这一点。

B：如果没有事先征得你们同意，他们不能取消合同。未经另一方当事人同意，任何一方均无权终止合同。他们很可能会单方面决定撤销合同。你有理由认为对方当事人将会根本违约。

A：我们可以直接起诉他们吗？

B：当然，你们可以起诉他们违约，但是在不同的法律体系下在美国打官司既耗时又复杂。更重要的是，你们以前没有处理这种案件的经验。

don't have any experience to deal with this kind of issue before.

A: Yes, it will also be very costly to go to court in another country. Maybe they have already predicted that we may have this kind of problem to deal with these issues. Since the cost to return the goods is much higher than that of the products themselves, they may force us lower the price at last. They are so mean.

B: Anyway, it did happen. You can contact the China Export and Credit Insurance Corporation to help you settle the issue since they have rich experience in this field.

A: OK. Thank you. We'll try.

A：是的，在国外打官司费用太高了，可能他们已经预料到了我们在处理这个案件时可能会遇到此类的问题，因为退货的费用比货物本身还要高，最终可能会强迫我们降价。他们太卑鄙了。

B：不管怎么样，事情已经发生了。你们可以联系中国出口信用保险公司来帮助你们解决这个问题，他们有丰富的经验处理此类问题。

A：好的，谢谢，我们试试。

口语秘笈

法律用语的表述一般都比较正式，即使在口语表达中，也会经常使用一些术语，以确保表述的专业性和准确性。例如，在表述有关合同及协议的一些条款时，经常会使用一些正式的表达方式，如"terminate"、"impose"、"modify"，等等。同时，在表述合同条款时，经常会使用情态动词，不同的情态动词所表达的意义也有所差异："may"旨在约定当事人的权利（可以做什么）；"shall"约定当事人的义务（应当做什么）；"must"用于强制性义务（必须做什么）；"may not"（或"shall not"）用于禁止性义务（不得做什么）。

破产与债务
Bankruptcy and Liability

词语宝典

asset	资产	insolvent	无偿还能力
bankruptcy	破产	liquidate	清算
creditor	债权人	balance sheet	资产负债表
debtor	债务人	bankruptcy protection	破产保护
initiate	发起，提起	debt collection	讨债

经典句型

- The court appointed a receiver to administer and liquidate the assets of the insolvent corporation.
  法院指定了一个接管人以管理和清算破产公司的资产。

- Bankruptcy protection protects the debtor from debt collection by creditors.
  破产保护程序保护债务人免受债权人的讨债。

- The company was declared insolvent.
  公司被宣布无清偿能力。

- The creditors decided to initiate a bankruptcy proceeding.
  债权人决定提起破产的诉讼。

- If no payment of the debt is made, the party may be sued.
  如不偿债，该当事人可能会被起诉。

- The balance sheet shows the corporation's assets and liabilities.
  资产负债表说明了公司的资产和债务情况。

- The company collects debts for other companies for a commission.
  该公司为其他公司讨债以收取佣金。

时尚对白

破产与债务

A: Hi, how are you doing?

B: Not so good.

A: What happened?

B: Our company's biggest partner was declared bankrupt due to the financial crisis. The court has appointed a receiver to administer and liquidate its assets. They owe us a lot of money, and unfortunately the debt will be discharged in bankruptcy.

A: I'm so sorry to hear that. How about your company?

B: Our company is close to bankruptcy now for the huge debt.

A: Has your company filed for bankruptcy?

B: No yet. We have applied for bankruptcy protection, which can protect the debtor from debt collection by creditors.

A: I hope your company can pull through.

B: Hope so. Thank you.

A：最近怎么样？

B：不太好。

A：怎么了？

B：我们公司最大的合作方由于经济危机宣告破产了。法院指定了一个接管人以管理和清算破产公司的资产。他们欠我们很大一笔钱，在破产中债务将被解除。

A：听到这些我很遗憾。你的公司呢？

B：我们公司现在由于高额债务接近破产。

A：你们公司申请破产了吗？

B：还没有，我们已经申请了破产保护，破产保护程序保护债务人免受债权人的讨债。

A：我希望你们公司能够渡过难关。

B：希望如此，谢谢。

口语秘笈

本对话融入时尚元素，把当前所出现的金融危机话题引入其中，有很多新词可供学习者仔细研读，例如："financial crisis"（金融危机）；"receiver"（接管人）；"to administer and liquidate its assets"（管理和清算破产公司的资产）。

达人点拨

在商务沟通中，对于一些不好的消息，听到后通常用"I'm sorry to hear that."来开始谈话。在结束谈话时，通常说"I hope your company can pull through."（我希望你们公司能够渡过难关。），"pull through"的意思是"渡过难关"。

UNIT 3 消费者权益 Consumer Rights

词语宝典

cost-effective	划算的	down payment	首付款，预付定金
foreclosure	丧失抵押品赎回权	negative influence	负面影响
fraud	欺诈行为	take up a matter with	交涉
mortgage	抵押	unfair housing price decrease	不公平的房屋降价
Consumer Association	消费者协会		

经典句型

- I think that it is a fraud for the company.
  我认为该公司的行为属于欺诈。

- Can I bring charges against a seller for fraud according to Law of the People's Republic of China on Protection of Consumer?
  对销售者的欺诈行为我可以根据《中华人民共和国消费者权益保护法》提起诉讼吗？

- The law is formulated to protect the legitimate rights and interests of consumers.
  该法律是为保护消费者的合法权益而制定的。

- To determine whether it is a fraud, you need to have evidence to prove that the sales personnel did know the information of price decrease when selling the apartment to you.
  要证明是否属于欺诈行为，你必须有证据证明销售人员在向你销售公寓的时候确实已经知道了降价的信息。

- To stop effecting mortgage payment without good reasons will have very negative influence on your credit.
  无故拖欠偿还抵押货款会对你的个人信用造成非常大的负面影响。

- If you do want to stop the mortgage payment, you'd better apply for foreclosure to the bank.
  如果你真想停止偿还贷款，你最好向银行提出断供的申请。

- We have to bring an accusation against your company for breach of contract.
  我们不得不以违反合同起诉你们公司。

消费者权益

A: Shenzhen Consumer Association, can I help you?

B: I'm calling to complain about the unfair housing price decrease of NSC company.

A: Could you give me more details?

B: Yes. I bought an apartment in Tianhe Garden sold by NSC company in early July 2008, and the price at that time was 11,000 RMB per square meter. But just after one month when I paid down payment, the price was decreased to 7,900 RMB per square meter with free interior decoration. I think that it is sort of fraud for NSC company.

A: Have you taken up the matter with the NSC company about the issue?

B: Of course. I have discussed the issue with them many times to ask them to modify the contract with a lower price, but they insist that since the price decrease was after the signing of contract, the price cannot be changed. But only one month, and I think that the sales personnel should have known this situation when selling the house to me. Can I bring charges against a seller for fraud according to the Law of the People's Republic of China on Protection of Consumer?

A: Well, the law is formulated to protect the legitimate rights and interests of consumers, but there is no specific provision in the law to cover this issue. To determine whether it is fraud, you need to have evidence to prove that the sales

A：深圳消费者协会，有什么可以帮忙的吗？

B：我打电话是想投诉NSC公司销售房屋不合理降价的问题。

A：能说得再详细点儿吗？

B：好的。我于2008年7月初购买了NSC公司销售的天河花园的一套公寓。当时的价格是每平方米11,000人民币。但是在我刚刚付完首付后的1个月，房子的价格下降到每平方米7,900元人民币，而且送内部装修。我认为NSC公司的行为属于欺诈。

A：你和NSC公司就此问题进行过交涉吗？

B：当然了。我已经多次与NSC公司讨论此事，要求他们修改合同并降低价格。但是他们坚持降价发生在合同签订之后，因此不能更改，但是就1个月啊！我认为销售人员在卖给我房子时已经知道这种降价的情况。我可以根据《中华人民共和国消费者权益保护法》对这种欺诈行为提起诉讼吗？

A：嗯，该法律是为保护消费者的合法权益而制定的，但是其中并没有针对该问题的条款。要证明是否属于欺诈行为，你必须有证

personnel knew the information of the price decrease when selling the apartment to you.

B: I see, but it is really hard to find the evidence to prove that. I'd rather stop my monthly mortgage payment to the bank and buy another new apartment. It is much more cost-effective than now!

A: I don't think it is a good idea. To stop effecting mortgage payment without good reasons will have very negative influence on your credit. If you do want to stop the mortgage payment, you'd better apply for foreclosure to the bank.

B: OK. Thank you for your advice.

据证明销售人员在向你销售公寓的时候确实已经知道了降价的信息。

B：我明白，但是要找到证据是非常困难的。我宁愿不向银行还月供，再买一套新的公寓。这样也比现在划算啊！

A：我认为这不是一个好主意。无故拖欠还贷款会对你的信用造成非常大的负面影响。如果你真想停止偿还贷款，你最好向银行提出断供的申请。

B：好的。谢谢你的建议。

达人点拨

本对话是围绕保护消费者权益展开的，在对话中，作为需要维权的消费者应当对事实提供清晰的描述，正如本对话所示，因为是描述过去的事实，所以通常用过去时态。而提供咨询服务的一方，首先鼓励对方要详细描述事实，如："Could you give me more details？"然后，再询问对方与纠纷方的沟通结果"Have you taken up the matter with NSC company about the issue？"最后，根据相关的法律条文予以指导，如："The law is formulated to protect the legitimate rights and interests of consumers, but there is no specific provision in the law to cover this issue."（该法律是为保护消费者的合法权益而制定的，但是其中并没有针对该问题的条款）；同时，针对对方应该如何做提出建议"You need to have evidence to prove that..."

口语秘笈

起诉的表达方式很多，常见的短语包括"bring an accusation against，bring a charge against，go to court，proceed against"，常见的词汇包括"accuse，charge，sue，indict，implead，prosecute"等。

知识产权 Intellectual Property

词语宝典

deceive	欺诈	settlement	解决
dispute	争端	trademark	商标
copyright	版权	focal topic	焦点话题
exploit	开发	intangible assets	无形资产
patent	专利，专利权	intellectual property	知识产权
pirated	盗版的	legal backing	法律支持

经典句型

- A patent is governmental grant of an exclusive monopoly as an incentive and a reward for a new invention.
  专利权是政府对一项新发明授予的独占性权利，以给予该发明鼓励和奖励。

- Unauthorized use of the registered trademarks of others is illegal.
  未经授权使用他人注册商标是违法的。

- Goods that must bear a registered trademark may not be marketed unless an application therefore has been approved.
  规定必须使用注册商标的商品，未经核准注册的，不得在市场销售。

- It is illegal to take copies of a copyright work.
  复制受版权法保护的作品是违法的。

- Selling deliberately a commodity whose registered trademark is falsely used constitutes a crime.
  销售明知是假冒注册商标的商品可构成犯罪。

- The court granted the plaintiff an injunction restraining the defendant from breaching copyright.
  法院应原告申请签发禁令，制止被告侵犯版权。

- The sale of pirated discs has been banned.

禁止出售盗版光盘。

- To be patentable an invention must be novel, useful and non-obvious.
  要获得专利，发明必须具备新颖性、实用性和非显而易见性。

时尚对白

 知识产权

A: Some of the laws you mentioned are focal topics at present, for example, industrial property law.

B: Yes. In today's competitive business environment, with so many businesses exploiting innovative product, the intangible assets such as patents, trade marks and intellectual property are often the most valuable assets that a business owns.

A: Under such conditions, industrial property law provides the legal protection for business owners. In China, the industrial property law has two bodies: patent law and trademark law. A patent is a governmental grant of an exclusive monopoly as an incentive and a reward for a new invention. Unauthorized use of the registered trademarks of others is illegal.

B: I've learned a lot about industrial property law, but what's on my mind is why the law protects the consumer. As we know, it's a free market, and the consumer has the right not to choose.

A: It's because there always are a few dishonest or incompetent suppliers who deceive. Then, the laws for consumers provide the consumers with the legal backing, including the legal basis for settlement of disputes between the consumers and the sellers.

A：您提到的一些法律是当前的焦点话题，比如工业产权法。

B：是的。在今天的商业竞争环境中，许多企业开发出新的产品，因此像专利、商标、知识产权之类的无形资产已成为企业最有价值的资产。

A：在这样的情况下，工业产权法为企业所有者提供了法律保护。在中国，工业产权法包括专利法和商标法。专利权是政府对一项新发明授予的独占性权利，以给予该发明鼓励和奖励。未经授权使用他人的注册商标是违法的。

B：我学了不少工业产权法，但我不明白为什么法律保护消费者。大家都知道，现在是自由经济，消费者可以不去选择它嘛。

A：是因为总有少数不诚实或不合格的供货商进行各种欺诈。那么有关消费者的法律就给消费者提供了法律支持，包括解决消费者和卖方争端的法律基础。

口语秘笈

　　本对话中涉及许多专业术语，在谈判中需要提前了解掌握，如："patent, intellectual property , legal backing, legal basis" 等；在谈及法律条文时，语言的使用更正式，如 "under such conditions"（在这样的情况下）；在 "In China, industrial property law has two bodies: patent law and trade mark law."（在中国，工业产权法包括专利法和商标法。）这句话里，"body" 是一个法律术语，意思是主体部分。